The Words of Selves

atopia

PHILOSOPHY POLITICAL THEORY AESTHETICS

Judith Butler and Frederick M. Dolan

EDITORS

The Words of Selves

IDENTIFICATION, SOLIDARITY, IRONY

DENISE RILEY

STANFORD UNIVERSITY PRESS

STANFORD, CALIFORNIA 2000

Stanford University Press
Stanford, California

© 2000 by the Board of Trustees of the
Leland Stanford Junior University

Printed in the United States of America

Library of Congress Cataloging-in-Publication Data
Riley, Denise
   The words of selves : identification, solidarity, irony /
Denise Riley.
      p.   cm. — (Atopia)
   Includes bibliographical references and index.
   ISBN 0-8047-3672-3 (hardcover : alk. paper) —
ISBN 0-8047-3911-0 (pbk. : alk. paper)
      I. Psycholinguistics.   2. Self-perception.   I. Title.
II. Atopia (Stanford, Calif.)
P37.R55   2000
401'.9—dc21   00-022873

∞ This book is printed on acid-free, archival-quality paper.
Original printing 2000

Last figure below indicates the year of this printing:
09 08 07 06 05 04 03 02 01 00

Designed by Janet Wood
Typeset by James P. Brommer in 11/14 Garamond

Acknowledgements

Some of this was first aired at Bard College, the University of Pittsburgh, the London Consortium, the European University Institute, and the Pembroke Center at Brown University. I'm grateful for the observations, comments, and hospitality of all.

Many friends directly or obliquely provided assistance, even where they themselves might suspect the likely outcome. Colin MacCabe gave me more than one opportunity to test out these speculations. My chapters incorporate stories recounted by Liz Heron, Jerry Sokol, Francie Shaw, and Bob Perelman. I'm indebted in many different ways to those authors working now upon whose ideas these pages draw; and here I owe special thanks to Judith Butler, and also to Jean-Jacques Lecercle, whose writings have enabled me to start to think things together at last. Other friends have kindly commented on my drafts or suggested references, among them Phil Cohen, Douglas Oliver, Susan Pennybacker, Moustapha Safouan, Martin Thom, Elizabeth Weed, and Nigel Wheale. Joan Scott has again done all these things and more, having generously read through the entire manuscript. Following that theory of inescapable plagiarism it discusses, each of these people is to be held thoroughly responsible for my mistakes and misconceptions here.

Rose Riley's presence brightened everything.

I thank Lynne Tillman for permission to include an extract from her 'Madame Realism Faces It'. Earlier versions of some of this material first appeared in *Critical Quarterly* 39, no. 2 (1997) and *History Workshop Journal* 44 (1997), while the poems cited were published in *Metre* 1 (1997) and *Penguin Modern Poets*, vol. 10 (1996). My thanks to all their editors, particularly to Barbara Taylor.

D.R.

Contents

The Words of Selves

Introduction

> We like the world because we do.
>
> WALLACE STEVENS[1]

'Who do you think you are?', whether solicitous inquiry or derisive chant, is a familiar enough interrogation; but this essay is, in part, a defence of having nothing to say for oneself. It wonders why the requirement *to be* a something-or-other should be so hard to satisfy in a manner which is convincing to its subject; it decides that hesitations in inhabiting a category are neither psychological weaknesses nor failures of authenticity or solidarity. Instead, it suggests that as mutating identifications, sharpened by the syntactical peculiarities of self-description's passage to collectivity, decisively mark the historical workings of political language, a more helpful politics will recognise a useful provisionality in the categories of social being. The fairly recent appearance of a qualified sociological vocabulary such as that of 'hybridity' does admit the shortfalls, detected precisely by those they claimed to embrace, of the older bloc identities such as 'black', but it implies that refining those massive categories will allay the weaknesses of self-description. I suspect that they will remain recalcitrant. The following pages puzzle about why this should be so.

I

Naturally a great deal of self-presentation is asking, if somewhat hopelessly, 'Love me'. But first the identifications which go into my self-portrayal have exerted a kind of productive alienation, for I find my affinity with something outside me only by moving towards and accepting some externally given account of a self, which I then take home as mine. This can be a happy acquisition: Later I may burnish myself up a bit, until I can see the gleam of my own reflection in myself. But these ordinary acts of identification, as everyday structures of fantasy, also possess a characteristic syntactical shape. A brief scenario of identification, which could be imagined as a linguistic arc, curves outwards from the self. But its hopeful reach, and the ambitious smoothness of its trajectory, are jarred by perplexities which obstinately inhabit the language of self-description (a language which includes, but is wider than, the diction of identification alone). This essay will concentrate on these perplexities, incarnated as a felt unease. But it does not entertain any notions of language as a thing which guilefully leads astray the speakers caught in its toils. It will suggest that while this discomfort needs to be fully registered—and registered as both linguistic and affective—it needs also to be cheerfully tolerated. Self-description is undoubtedly an area of trouble, but its disquiet is vivid. It's greatly preferable to the costs incurred through any attempted anaesthesia against this doubt lodged in it. If the business of being called something, and being positioned by that calling— that is, interpellation—is often an unhappy affair, irony can offer some effective therapy. Self-presentation and irony, so readily pulled into intimacy, will be offered throughout the coming chapters as illustrations of a linguistic emotionality at work. Both being called, and actively taking on or discarding a name, encompass two conspicuous kinds of affect which are embedded in some ordinary fundamental workings of language; so while there's an inescapable failure to thoroughly *be*, involving a demurral, a discomfort, or a guilt which is linguistic, this failure may be relieved and brightened by an irony, which may well itself inflect a politics.

I may feel linguistic unease as I am necessarily and constantly displaced from my centrality to my own utterance. But I suffer something that I am tempted to call linguistic guilt when I am dethroned authorially by being spoken across by words (by the words' anarchic sound associations, by their echoing of others' speech, which I can never adequately acknowledge, within my own speech) and whenever I am understood to occupy a position societally, that of the originary writer, which I cannot occupy linguistically. Within some structures of language I am indeed a displaced person, yet my situation is not really so melancholic. It has released me into a democratic freedom to wander, although not without guides. Verbal irony—another affect of language—offers me its spontaneous running commentary on my situation as it observes and remarks, unabashed, on the great categories of being as they stiffen or sag. Illuminating the historicity as well as the arbitrariness of the categorical words that consolidate me, it affords me a way of analysing and accepting the inventively productive displacements I suffer with a measure of relief, and with good grace.

If this work of language also embraces its printed conventions and presentation, it's no news to anyone that a sentence's punctuation, layout, and typography carry some of its affect, and can be contrived to carry all of it. Just to glance at punctuation: the exclamation mark, a direct annotation of tone, is uninteresting because it is blatant, but other markers which are not such overt signals of emotion still quietly operate as such—the arch or the sarcastic apostrophes or 'scare quotes' to highlight a vexing word (and which, too liberally sprinkled, only vex its readers), the punchy or triumphant colon, the theatrical hesitancy of the dash, the demurring bracket which may hedge its bets, the self-important or nagging italicisation—while the very look of a semicolon is Nietzsche's walrus moustache in profile.[2] A typeface itself also speaks; there is a coolly democratic air to Gill sans serif, an elegance in Garamond. Here alone a whole school of rhetoric in miniature could be revived; while its long demise as an art is witnessed by the fact that all such prosaic considerations, as well as a great number of loftier ones, are now hived off to the territory of 'prosody' as the study of versification, yet are usually ignored as active elements within the everyday prose they animate.

But there are also less contingent and more deeply inherent aspects of language which do not refer and yet which themselves act; and this essay's tentative proposals stem from its conviction that the very architecture of language in itself carries some of the affect common to all speech. Syntax itself bears a formative as well as an informative impulse. At least some of the attributes of that famously vexed rubric of 'ideology' (which is not so much the label for a thing, as a gesture towards an open, always unfinished series of explications[3]) might be reascribed to this possibility that a language also works at the pervasive level of its musculature, quietly but powerfully, through its grammatical and syntactic joints. Syntax is also affective, and that ideology which positions its addressees *is*—to some extent—syntactic; this perhaps curious and counterintuitive assertion will be elaborated in the succeeding chapters, including through their test case of interpellation. I don't mean to imply that to be ungrammatical is to be merrily liberated from constraint—rather, that the very articulations and bonds of language themselves enact productive constraints, which include what we may call ideological effects. If the affect of language extends to its formal structures, then the intricacies of self-description, which is laced through with strange temporalities, can offer a critical testing ground for this intuition. I'm advancing it hesitantly, conscious that the proposal that there may sometimes be an inherent emotionality to grammar, that supposedly cool operator, may ring bizarrely. Certainly it's a quite different suggestion from that familiar suspicion that we are all prey to the 'seductions of grammar'.[4] Yet even that, if true, would be no matter for lament, since language 'seduces' only insofar as one needs to be seduced by life, in order to live.

Or is it simply that the arrangements of language are—undramatically and unsurprisingly—impure, since such a great machinery is likely to nurse a few small flaws? Or again, to translate that doubt into quite another diction, is Being bound to be fuller than its verbal representation? To counter such objections, these chapters won't exactly propose a monolith of language as an unbroken monument, but they will offer an alternative thought: that where a necessarily rigorous grammar and syntax is imbued with its own brand of affect, this affect may be strong enough to convey a disquiet which runs under what is being said. It might pursue, whisperingly, a perverse or an arteriosclerotic course. Yet this makes for a lively unease. A tangible emotionality is enacted at the very level of language itself, and in such a way as to make that old question of 'how do words convey or express feelings?' in part redundant. If words are accorded their own head, it's often hastily assumed that speakers must be rendered abject, as if any consideration of language's own affect must lead straight to human dejection. This false choice of loyalties—either to the word or else to the speaker—is encapsulated for easy swallowing. Fast thought has, like fast food, its uses—but, by a languorous fatalism, prêt-à-penser may slide prematurely into prêt-à-mourir. Yet if I'm sometimes tempted to linger over linguistic malaise, what might be said about linguistic happiness? And something of this may well up in unexpected quarters, since irony's hopefulness begins, not in innovation, but in the unmitigated monotony of reiteration.

Writing in and about only one language, I'm gloomily aware that my remarks must be parochial. Within this grave limit, it's clear that the whole tendentious affair of self-presentation—partly because of its extraordinary over-determination of linguistic with phenomenological peculiarities—is a site of strain. One could have no quarrel with it, if it did work satisfyingly and on the side of the angels. But it's readily observable that some self-naming induces little lasting satisfaction in its speaker—and that's unsurprising. Wordy manoeuvres, periodically driven in vain to span the inescapable gap between my political being and my social being, appear as the common unease with 'being a subject'. The resulting politics of identity are, by their nature, bound to fall short of their promised redemption, but this need not cause dismay. On the contrary: A lack of fit between my self-description as a social subject and my presence as a political subject is not disappointing but benevolent, insofar as the subject of political language actually requires a certain impersonality, or a nonidentity, to be able to circulate productively at all. In this sense, my awkward navigations to *become*, coupled with my constitutional failure to fully *be*, are what actually enable political thinking and language, rather than marking some lamentable shortcoming in my 'politicisation'. This makes briefly for an air of paradox: that some lack of politicisation (where that term is taken in its contemporary sense, to imply the keen embrace of some progressive identity) might be needed, in order for there to be mobility, and life, within political thought.

This string of mildly reassuring remarks can only reach so far, though. Two corollaries of hazard soon follow. If a category is, historically, poorly brought to voice (as it were), there's too much lack: an obliterating under-politicisation, productive of nothing but solitary misery. Conversely, plunging into a category and getting mired down in it, in an exaggerated *being* and an overpoliticisation, also mark out unhappier aspects of the political, yet usually will not completely swamp it—unless there is a one-to-one correspondence between the social subject which has undergone its politicisation, and the relatively impersonal subject moving as a figure in the sphere of politics, for instance under forms of fascism or in the politicisation of a supposed 'ethnic identity'. Then grave trouble ensues.

∽

Self-description is the broadest of churches while conspicuously prey to sectarianism. The self might find itself announcing its physical or temperamental individuations, its national genesis, its willed affiliations, its adoptions of some religious or political creed. So a long taxonomy of self-reference would be needed to distinguish between such very different incarnations; what, if anything, is there in common between 'I am white trash', 'In this household we are God-fearing people', 'I survived some years of being held in Dachau', and 'Vivaldi's "Stabat Mater" is sublime'—which are arguably all forms of self-presentation? These chapters do not attempt the necessary if inexhaustible classification of self-classifications. In practice, they touch largely on the more formal designations of the social person, such as 'being Han Chinese' or 'being a heterosexual man', but they must inevitably slide into the idiosyncratic traits that a self may ascribe to itself: 'I'm shy' or 'I am postsexual'. Each category of a self, too, owns its distinct evolutionary history. Sharply differing accounts of the settlement, the flourishing or the decay of such attributions as, let's say, 'I am Welsh Methodist', 'I'm in domestic service', or 'I am a depressive', would need to be drawn up. Some markers are relatively steady in their neutrality, such as 'I am five feet five' (although one can always dream up counterexamples: say, of voicing aloud that height in Lilliput).

Others, dragged in the wake of the great icebergs of larger shifts, are conspicuously volatile. 'I am Latvian' bears a weight greatly changed by whether it's uttered before, during, or after my country's fights for autonomy or its absorption within the former USSR. Yet other categories are haunted by a lingering semantic unsteadiness: 'I am a woman'. Each will also have some markedly altered standing in relation to whatever notion of a social whole it's declined against. (So to make much use of a newer term for the fusion of categorical wholes, such as 'hybridity', one would need the knack of prising apart its soldered elements to gauge their uneven thickness and the points of fatigue, as it were, at their joins.) The collectivity which appears sealed and fully rounded is the outcome of a struggle in which its articulation might have been no triumph of progressive thought but an accident, a compromise, something which has sprung up between casual cracks in the slabs of earlier monoliths, like a weed. Formed perhaps in antagonism or perhaps in self-defence, only once the fresh species has triumphed can its internal differences tear open again, in a struggle 'of egoisms turned against each other, each bursting in a splintering of forces and a general striving for the sun and for light'.[5]

Which self-description is to count as broadly societal, or which is to be assessed as a private quirk or an idiosyncratic characteristic, depends largely on the intensity of its potential 'politicisation' in play at any one moment—now taking that term, politicisation, to mean the rendering collective of some condition or affliction formerly understood as a merely personal and private contingency. If the voluntary telling of my life illustrates the intricacies of autobiography, its extracted and catalogued account highlights the riddles of sociology. Few attributes will appear for long as mechanically straightforward; we readily jib at the boxes we're instructed to tick for the purposes of census-taking, passports, or schooling because they so readily topple into contentious placings of the self. Am I to agree to be designated as 'Black British', or do I refuse this designation as in itself unwittingly racist because I am in fact 'English' and as English a citizen as everyone else, whatever my skin colour, and I don't want that racialised difference; do I settle for 'Afro-Caribbean' or for 'British, of African descent', or should I fight, tongue in cheek, to introduce 'Afro-Saxon', or had I better specify 'born in Holloway, London, of an Antiguan-born mother and a father from Jamaica'? Or do I give up, and tick, wryly, that final small square for all categorical residues which is marked 'Other?' A pick-'n'-mix gaiety here may also be sardonic—and wilful, in the face of the contingency of what counts as casually incidental, or what counts as critical for assessing my social being.[6] I am indeed minimally secured by the dates of my death and my birth, and usually I'll need to have confidence in the latter. Yet for many in the world, their exact date of birth can be questionable if they are born in shrouded circumstances into a society of weak record-keeping. Unless my remains are lost in some devastated war zone or in a massacre, or to a murder which has been successfully concealed, only the date of my death is certain. But that inscription on my tombstone is one form of interpellation whose certainty I shall, unhappily, not be there to enjoy. Meanwhile, my characterisation will often subside into my categorisation, and with uncertain results. It's rare for the self, in an untrammelled agony of exquisite choice, to invent its own names. The daily fact of societal description 'from the outside'—how I'm reported by others, what's expectantly in place, already chatting about me before I appear on stage—is integral to the dialectic of self-description. External imposition of a harsher sort—above all, the force of political change, which is always a linguistic violence—may wring from me some new self-description as well as utter its own hostile naming against me. In the early 1990s I might, under harassment from Serbian nationalism, have militantly discovered myself to be Albanian, whereas only a decade earlier, that characterisation, although certainly in play, wouldn't have been so peremptory.[7] Under duress, I may take on an 'ethnic' self-categorisation only as a counter-nationalism—not triumphantly, but wearily, reluctantly, cynically, and with a suspension of any real consent.

A historical phenomenology of self-naming would fill the world; the vulnerability or the impregnability of a category marks its history *as* the history of attempts to establish it and get it solidly installed, to politicise it, to dissolve it, to shred it. In the teeth of this, this solitary student quails, and only some narrow slivers of self-description's limited occurrences as self-identification are mentioned in this essay. Then wouldn't 'self-identification' or 'self-categorising' have been more precise terms for me to have used here, since with them comes a telling layer of linguistic compulsion, a forcible admission into the political sphere equipped with one's passport of identity? The noun 'identity' does stand at some semantic distance from the related noun 'identification'—itself a hot spot at which psychoanalytic and sociological arguments cluster thickly—yet I keep to the less precise but less fraught 'self-description'. I've stuck to this wider term largely on the grounds that its everyday hesitations are actually compounded and not relieved in the formal massifications of self-categorisation, even though the latter may aim benignly to serve some finer self-specification. For the same inadequacies commonly haunt each and any effort, systematic or personal, at describing the self. None of this, though, is to deny that real jubilation may colour its initial embrace. Yet even though some freshly named self might feel itself to be a family happily all alike within its discovered identification, if this should falter, an unnecessary wordless shame can seep back in.

What Adorno characterised as the authoritarian sympathies within 'the expression "as a . . . , I . . . ,"' have resounded of late.[8] Much energy has been expended on (to use the mildly pejorative term) identity politics. Was there some misplaced nostalgia for wholeness about this relatively recent turn to collectivised personal identities, succeeding as it did a different historical moment with its own broader understanding of solidarity? One precondition, though, for effective solidarity may well be that critique of an identity which rises from within it. 'Solidarity' as an ideal of a political altruism is rooted in some degree of identification, which it will also transcend. But its invocation is immensely delicate. For solidarity can veer between progressive warmth, pious constraint, narrowly tactical calculation, imaginative generosity, and unwarranted familiarity. Some less helpful versions of solidarity promote illusory centres, the seeming results of a consensus, yet where no one was ever consulted. Then solidarities inevitably fray into dispersal; now there can be no democratically settled agreement to, say, just what goes under the rubric of feminism, no agreed central affiliation. There are markedly differing periods in the solidarities of even apparently spontaneous visual perceptions, such as the recognition of another's physical appearance as also bodily damaged or also beautiful, or of the similarities of the skin's coloration. It depends on who is seeing whom and from where: so someone fairly light-skinned finds herself classified as 'red' in Kingston, her birthplace; yet once she arrives in Brixton in south London, she becomes for her non-Jamaican neighbours an undifferentiated 'black'. Then the question of how 'blackness' is understood, let alone 'whiteness', will take on a bitterly different taste for, say, the inhabitants of Jasper County, Texas, or of Eltham in Greenwich,[9] than for those placed to speak confidently of multiracial north London.

The impulse of the following pages is broadly anti-identificatory only as a counter to the hazards of zealous overinclusiveness. It doesn't promote a radical individualism to stand against all categorising (only a rabid ahistoricism might attempt that), and this isn't a manifesto of preferring the individual to the group. Instead, it tries to assert the influential daily ordinariness of that volatile disquiet which dwells in self-description. As that celebrated postmodernist, Hegel, observed in 1817, 'Everyone is a whole world of representations, which are buried in the night of the "I"'.[10] My claim here is that the hesitancy, the qualifications, the awkwardness, and the degrees of secret reserve which will often shadow a self-description aren't manifestations of an individual weakness, a failure of solidarity, but that such hesitancies really do lodge in self-categorisation's peculiarly fused linguistic-political nature. They need to be admitted. The virtue of those sociological categories of the person, enshrined as, say, antidiscrimination law, is not in the least diminished by considering the unspoken disappointments of trying exhaustively to live those categories from the inside. Meanwhile, some realistic dilemma as to how I should speak about myself will rarely get resolved for long by means of an 'identity'. So often conceived as a thing to be unearthed, my identity (if I am forced to locate such an object at all) may turn out to be not so much a matter of what it is, but of where it is; and some idea of an identity which is founded largely in dispersal—although without melancholy—is described in the last two chapters. These take tacit issue with the conviction that it's politically imperative to hang onto an asserted category, since any time spent reading in archives or through old newspapers (or simply living long enough) demonstrates that the collisions and shattering of identities have been as decisive for progress as their consolidations—while the latter have so frequently been disastrous that one could make a counterclaim for the historical necessity of the strongest identity to the most reactionary cause. It's hardly necessary to declare here that imperiously rigid categorising, in the name of group emancipation, may well reinvent the very unhappiness it has sought to assuage—that its newly bestowed categories of the self, in their purported embrace of communality, may lead, not to solidarity, but to a solitary dissatisfaction all the worse because it is what really dare not speak its name—indeed, has no name to speak.

If hailed or interpellated in the name of my destiny, I turn my head in an irrepressible hope. My horoscope in any newspaper column sings out to me, as does my fortune inside any Chinese cookie or the printed account of my character and fate which the elderly Parisian who signs himself as a deaf-mute drops at my café table to supplement his living. Their siren addresses to me are always somehow true, and they always work—quite irrespective of my very real and unshakable scepticism. On more serious occasions, to be described is to be located and singled out, which is rarely good news. A less philosophical way of considering how becoming a subject entails subjection is to reposition this slightly, now as a question of how identification is close neighbour to accusation. It's not only those lined up in the police station for an official identity parade who realise this. There's a proximity between 'being called' as a description and 'being called' as an aggression. Being 'called names' in the school playground means being called harsh names. Admittedly, being identified as a form of accusation is occasionally replaced by being interpellated as a form of sanctification; but this singularity is quite as risky as any other, for being inscribed in a good and noble category is apt to prove an unreliable bliss. Perhaps self-naming owes something of its com-

pulsive popularity to an understandable impression that if one is always going to be called a such-and-such from the outside, one might as well get in
first, to deflect the imposition by putting up one's own account of oneself
like an umbrella against a hard rain of attributes. That, though, would afford
a poor protection, since language does not possess that kind of an 'outside'.

This essay is not a lonely howl against 'identity politics' (although out
there the wolves have been gradually gathering). It does carry some implication of a need to recognise a complementary anti-identity politics. The
hope which animates asserted personal identities is evident: Instead of being
spoken for or glossed over, the misnamed, the forgotten, or the oppressed
would speak their own truths, would articulate their common situation,
would gain power through their own consolidation of their obliterated or
travestied needs and interests. Historically, such movements have had profoundly liberating outcomes (however periodically ambiguous; however
much, for example, those of us attached to earlier versions of feminism
might bemoan its recent incarnations). But if an emancipatory flow eventually becomes congealed through mechanical reiteration, its ostensible subjects, now subjected to categorical overkill, can't recognise themselves; then
its categories must take notice and move, or be washed up into a backwater
of obsolescence. Perhaps, though, it is enough to rely unperturbed on the
historical dialectics of description here, on the guaranteed mobilities of political language? Historical semantics totter—but their instability and where
they may fall can't be foretold. It may be hard to await, equably, the eventual
and merciful collapse of some current unhelpful massification. In the mean-
time, too readily formulated, too suffocatingly inclusive, or too piously exclusive categories will induce, not their intended comfort, but an increase in
private misery. That tidy self-categorisation now on offer may entail an actual descriptive impoverishment, concealed under the banner of a reforming
collectivity. If intricate and fine-grained accounts are thickened into a single
sanitised 'identification', then histories, under the kindly guise of being fa-
cilitated, are obliterated.

That even the most progressive self-description can make an ambiguous
kind of a weapon is not only historically clear but is anchored in its structure. Temporality and affect are also embodied as the syntactic musculature
of language itself, and together these support its forcefulness. But the meanings of the unquiet language of the self are liable to be corroded through re-

iteration, and in that lies its own undoing, as what should underline and re-inforce it may, gradually, eat away at it. Syntax's affect emerges through its very regularity and predictability, which also hold its potential for ironic de-flation; then the shape of the sentence becomes devalued and tarnished through its repetitions, and the old cadences begin to ring mechanically and without conviction, such as furious exchanges of 'Is! Isn't!' 'Will! Won't!', which carry on with no content other than a childish antagonism, at once both real and a parody of itself. If it is in the nature of 'the media' to repeat and repeat, it's also in the more dignified nature of the archive and of the hal-lowed litany of personal types, including the triptych of race, class, sex. Not that the structural affects of speech and writing usually have the strength to overwhelm semantic meaning—yet they do bring to bear a pressure, a tor-sion, sometimes a malaise. They can also engender a disquiet which is posi-tively useful, and may be lived with good humour. In this sense they form an element of 'the unconscious of language'; its tendency to undercut or to overreach itself, to crazily ramify, or to make itself unexpectedly heard within some other meaning.[11] The intuition of the following pages is that the often profoundly politicised affair of self-description offers a broad and vulnerable terrain which is open for such affects to exert themselves strongly. They cut both ways: in the uncomfortable fit of a benevolently meant category as well as in the harshness of an angry interpellation, so hard to shake off. These chapters won't try either to supplant or to embellish the standard psycholog-ical account of why a bad name sticks—that is, because it chimes with some internal and prior sentence, a damaging sentence that the self has already passed on itself—but they must trample across the familiar bounds of two pitched camps, the linguistic and the psychological.[12]

'The unconscious' is mentioned here neither through that analogy in La-can's aphorism, as structured *like a* language, nor, solely, as a mole busy be-neath the rational surface, heaving away, but implicitly and simply as the structure of language: *as* language. That's because all language in use (that which might be allocated by psychoanalysis to the domain of the uncon-scious, plus that which standardly wouldn't be) both is and isn't under the control of its speakers and writers. (One could speak, too, about 'an uncon-scious of the body', and bodies nurse and guard their own histories as mem-ories; but here it's words that are at stake.) If there is 'an unconscious' which is in part language, but if language itself can also be argued to have an unconscious of its very own and to possess a remainder, to be at the mercy of the invasive determinations of sound associations, of the wild and fruitful propagations of metaphor, and so on—then the speaker and the writer become even less the masters of their utterance.[13] For both the irrational and the reasoned elements in language escape from quarantine, to go running everywhere together.

My self-description may well be my self-fantasy. Perhaps each and every act of identification is fantastical—and not only such an evident candidate for the status of fantasy as that of a 'sexual difference' uninflected by history. Some apprehension that it constituted the Code Napoléon of the unconscious might vex an insistence on 'sexual difference' as fundamental. For fantasy *is* sustained metaphoricity. To be in fantasy is to live 'as if'. Some scene is being played out; and any act of identification necessarily entails a scenario. That celebrated script, 'a child is being beaten', suggests that if the structure of psychic identification invites a substitution (somewhere the hearer inserts him- or herself into the action, takes up a role in the scene), then such a substitution is so heavily engineered by syntax as to constitute a strong argument for the ordinarily fantastic nature of all identifications. Here each common act of imagination need not be characterised as in its nature either unconscious or as especially conscious. Perhaps, then, it's the very syntax of the sentence of identification which is enacting *me*. 'A child is being beaten'—but I could change the content of this sentence to avoid its sadomasochistic incitement yet still retain its syntax of passivity: 'A cake is being eaten'. But whether I am the devourer or the apfelstrüdel, I have some kind of positioned interest in the thing. Next, I could try to overcome this indolent construction by forcing some energetic meaning into the still-passive mood of the verb: 'Tonight the world heavyweight champion is being challenged'. But even this journalistic preamble still impatiently awaits the entry of its subject, waving aloft its gloves. Whether as boxer or as cake, there is ample room for me to find my true self in the architecture of these sentences.

As I project myself as being a such-and-such, I tacitly envisage myself participating in the wider social scene through some new identity category as I step, gingerly or proudly, across its threshold. Any act of identification is systematically askew, since I'm envisaging what I presume that I'm supposed, in the eyes of others, to really be. All is vicarious. By a consent which I could not anyway withhold, I become a voyeur of myself in the guise of a such-and-such, recognising that I'm looking at what I must look like, and through refracting lenses. Yet such identification fantasies—incarnate as they must be in language—are thereby very far from being ahistorical. They are heavily subject to time: to the historical mutations of words, to the altering production of social categories including classes, and to an altering expressivity of syntax as well as of semantics. History may, spasmodically, conspire with language to depict acts of fantastic identification as matter of fact and self-evident, but this air of sociological realism proves fleeting. That there is no timelessness ensures, mercifully, that no one can claim mastery. If affect is shot right through the forms of words, and if ideology is in part reiterated 'habits' of speech (to adopt Peirce's term[14]), then ideology, including the ideology of identifications, might be considered as an affective habit, yet a habit neither purely imposed nor purely obeyed—nor flouted. For what releases language from the suspicion that its overarching emotional architecture should be considered as a constraint is another of its inherent elements: its blessed capacity for self-reflection. Irony is one manifestation of speech which notices itself out loud. There are many other possible outcomes of this linguistic self-reflexiveness, ranging from comedy to boredom to irritation, but here irony will be ventured as the saving counterpart to another verbal phenomenon: linguistic shame. Despite its spasmodically poor reputation, irony does operate ethically, although necessarily without a manifesto. This is not irony as a deliberating parody or as the irritating knowingness which so easily tips into being arch—but irony as language presenting itself to itself.

The guilt of writing, discussed below, is only a facet, sharp enough, of a much broader linguistic unease. Given by what 'I' shall call itself and be called, this acts in the same moment through an emotional grammar and a linguistic psychology. Here again the integrity of the category of 'psychology' is disaggregated, and at least some of it is dispatched to 'language'—although this isn't at all to imply that the linguistic unconscious exhausts the entire domain of emotionality. And then while the Lacanian psychoanalytic subject is indeed constituted 'in division', what one might want to see admitted is a yet more ubiquitous division. Not only that formulaic division through language operating at the level of the unconscious, but division made convex, as it were, folded upwards and outwards to the surface, in a far more prolific but a stolid and quotidian scission, to be tolerantly grasped as everywhere in play.

This isn't to advance an aesthetic and perverse longing for fragmentation, but only a sanguine acknowledgement of how things do seem to be. Just how, or if, this sits with claimants to the vexed terrain of the unconscious is another question; and is this speculation merely a shaky spin of a Lacanian wheel? One certainly couldn't marshal any systematic opposition to this idea of divided unconscious from the side committed to analysing social forms of positioning selves, and Althusser himself sympathetically characterised Lacan's 'paradox, formally familiar to linguistics, of a double yet single discourse, unconscious yet verbal, having for its double field only a single field, with no beyond except in itself: the field of the "signifying chain"'.[15] Althusser went on to assert what he was willing to call 'the law of language'; the coming suggestions here will have more to do with the pragmatic but violently lawless materiality of words. Maybe there's more of an intimate link between 'language' and 'the unconscious' than that afforded by that customary analogy—and which, in the manner of most intimate links, blurs the character of both partners to the arrangement. In part, the unconscious *is* what the language does. Perhaps the unconscious hangs out there, between people, as the speech that they produce between them and are produced by. Might it be interesting to consider 'the unconscious' *as* language, through a grand act of compression, fusing some present concepts of the psychic unconscious with the idea of language-and-its-remainders, although without even the intervention of any scribe of the unconscious (to borrow Moustapha Safouan's metaphor[16]) to write down its idiosyncratic syntax as dreams? Indeed, Safouan has observed that 'today we can move on to the statement that the unconscious is nothing other than the language as it withdraws from, and overtakes, the intentions of the subject'[17]—yet this economical and engaging stance has already sidestepped those violent complications which erupt if we go on to scrutinise this vexed intentionality, including the impact of language's own unconscious, its inventive constraints, and its separability from its utterer's intentions.[18] This is a linguistic unconscious, not a psychic unconscious of a collectivity of speakers. I am not hinting at a gigantic and throbbing world-soul of languages. Nevertheless, that very invocation of language's own unconscious does start to erase the lines between these two, the psychic and the linguistic, and to recast their whole partition. Jean-Claude Milner almost, yet not quite, makes the elision between language and the unconscious when he glosses Lacan's *lalangue* as 'that by which, with one and the same stroke, there is language (or beings who can be qualified as speaking, which comes down to the same thing) and there is an unconscious' and again that 'Language is then what in practice the unconscious is, lending itself to all imaginable games, so that truth, under the sway of words, speaks'.[19] Lacan's own remarks stop, as they have to, at the verge of such an elision, for his conception of language as symbolic function is exterior and yet also internalised: 'This exteriority of the symbolic in relation to man is the very notion of the unconscious'.[20] Conversely, while it is the interior of the subject, it must be externally realised. The symbolic order of language may 'decentre' the subject, yet it does not drain from him this ambiguous interiority, even if that arrives from the outside.[21] This maintains a retrospective, mutually constitutive dialectic between inner and outer. Across all gymnastic contortions (and even allowing for the qualification that this 'subject' is simply not the same as the individual), a subject is still being constituted.[22] But the rather different conception that 'the unconscious' is language itself—or rather that *all* language is always haunted by a degree of 'unconsciousness' which is always externally given—would ditch this problem of the built-up subject, to step clear of its structuring geology of insides and outsides. Sometimes it seems attractive to be completely flat.

Nervously defensive or archly self-congratulating, the ambiguous question 'Who, me?' furnishes a motto for the earlier chapters below, which glance at what they treat as the linguistic psychology of taking on a description. Self-naming may function as a sort of communicative intent. What I have to say about myself is also a confession of feeling, which cannot help but sound as if, like a declaration of love, it's soliciting a responsive echo. The gestures of adopting a self-characterisation, or demurring from it, may well sink into inadvertent self-description. The contentious ideal of solidarity can't help here for long. Indeed, the long history of *amor fati* forces some reflections on the concept of bad faith. A furious will to be, as self-perpetuation, may be countered by a drive to an impossible authenticity or integrity, which, it's suggested, comes to a head over some unrealised ethics of authorship. The urge to instead dedramatise the described self may induce a longing for transparency, to be without qualities.

   At the mercy of an intricate anteriority, self-description also has an oddly projected topography: Just where out there are my self-categorisings felt to lean, to become animated, to circulate? There's also the oldest topographical metaphor, of that place where speech is formed: but the unconscious *as* the unconscious of language cannot be internal, deep and half-hidden, like some modern version of the soul. If it is linguistic, then it is external—yet this externality need not imply that it's either fully controlled *or* uncontrolled by its speakers. Instead of this opposition, a profound superficiality is ventured. (Only a superficial profundity may result here.) A history of some conceptions of 'being spoken' would embrace those convictions about the seductions of language, so strangely held in common by both Nietzsche and Wittgenstein, and these will be considered in the first chapter below as flowerings of a Venus fly-trap school of language.

The second chapter, 'Linguistic Unease', marshals a defence of that affect as naturally endemic to self-depiction: ordinary, defensible, and distinct from any reprehensible psychology of self-immolation. Unease lies on the verge of guilt, a condition elastic enough to encompass all too many definitions, of which one is that gnawing feeling of having failed according to rules that I did not make myself. Under this last heading (an altogether different affair from making grammatical mistakes), mightn't the very constraints of language-use induce this sensation that 'I' lies? I labour under what must be a common compulsion; that once I'm forced to speak about myself at all, I must through my own efforts make it sharply true—yet cannot. As if even the most subdued self-reference steered close to a demand for precision it must dangerously fail. In the same breath I fear and feel its fundamental lie. The very grammar of attribution enacts this uncertainty. Defensive lie and defensive truth are both couched in the same syntax of denial, 'I'm not an *x*', while both the well-meant identification and the harsh accusation share the common syntax of bad naming, 'You are an *x*'. The thing which is invoked only to be denied still hovers around ominously, by virtue of being voiced at all. Grammar, then, carries its weight of affect. But is it morbidly exaggerated—a linguistic hypochondria, or else an overblown synaesthesia—to speculate that one can feel grammar? If this were exaggerated into a 'linguistic–ontological' guilt—'I speak, therefore I am culpable of falling into the traps of grammatical quirks and syntactical snags'—and taken solemnly, overliterally, it would follow that any speaker is always already guilty, dogged by unease with no cure until death stops her mouth. Avoiding that florid generalisation, I cannot avoid the fact that there's a difference between the diffused disquiet which shadows lived language (for which I can't be held to account) and the 'real guilt' of my private conviction of failure. Certainly I must ask whether a linguistic malaise is merely fancied, or is actually, although undercharacterised, solidly felt. At sensitive historical moments of linguistic–political change, it is (I think) felt, and acutely so.

The strains of describing the self are also acute within those literary genres reliant on a covert self-presentation; hence it is a liar who writes, and a liar who tries lyric. Wishing not to take credit where credit isn't due, the aptly worried poet finds that the working conviction of 'being written' demands an oblique or a transverse account, in which neither the text nor the author wins outright. The absence of any ethic of alluding gives rise to yet another rendering of 'Who, me?' It's suggested here that another incarnation of guilt's strange temporality arises through interpellation, in the sense of being described forcefully from the outside. That accounts for some of the unease endemic to that self-description which is a grudging assent to interpellation, while any confiding 'let me tell you about myself' must herald a blatant lie.

Robert Frost, asked what one of his poems had meant, is said to have replied, 'You want me to say it *worse?*' In a possible reversal of this ratio, some lines which directly argue these questions of nationalistic, literary, and 'narcissistic' self-description are wheeled out in my third chapter, since they chew over some preoccupations (rehearsed throughout other chapters in prose) with Echo, with anteriority, and with the limits of notions of self-knowledge, all in the light of the follies of aesthetic self-presentation. The polemical aim here is to cut a so-called creative writing's diplomatic immunity to critique and to render its claims less distinct from those granted to any language. Poetry often reduces to a decorative feature those elements which prose has suppressed within itself. If poetry's stance—what it's actually proposing about the world—is rarely examined, conversely the consideration of prose's affect is instead redirected towards poetry. There's an inexplicable reverence for the narcotic adjective 'poetic', whose arrival on the scene heralds the death of thought; any dealer in the diazepam of the poetic not only slips by but is allowed free passage instead of being shot on sight. Perhaps this is because of poetry's status as prose's alibi, so that poetry can function as the unexplored but sanctified repository for whatever irrational elements prose may suspect it harbours within its own confines, and may wish to evacuate. An intention in these pages is to render the domain of poetry less artificially protected. Such a status rather resembles that protection once granted to certain classes of women: a respectful contempt.

Lucretius' vivid maxim 'the wounded fall in the direction of their wound' furnishes the motto for my fourth chapter, which moves from linguistic wounding and the forms of its horrified contemplation to the possibilities of linguistic healing. Here the fixity of what I am, in the notion of my self-ascribed 'character', hovers strongly. Yet Aristotle, tough-minded, would have cut clean through such niceties by insisting that character *is* habitual action—so that to be a good information technologist consists in computing data well (although what it is to be a good husband may resist such briskness). By their fruits ye shall know them, for the question of acting well is determined retrospectively, on results, and not by any appeal to the nature of the doer. Reiteration's impact makes an appearance here, in the effects, not of any character's 'obscure hurt' of the sort which troubled Henry James, but of determinedly inhabiting some injury to found a whole identity. The last chapter introduces irony's possible work, not as a satirist, but as a powerfully productive contributor to the political. It suggests that verbal irony (not that of a situation or a temperament) is, far from being a mark of disengagement, vital—this, despite its historically doubtful reputation, and irrespective of its endless possibilities as costume. Since there are likely to be perpetually irritated 'identities' and only ambiguous gains in fresh categories of the self, there is political advantage in irony. It offers an antidote to lonely disappointment, while it both mimes and enunciates a hope of change for the better. If an apt rejoinder to some aggressive interpellation might be, 'But what interest do you yourself have in consigning me to that harsh category; why do you want me to be that bad thing?', such a turning of my attention towards my accuser's frame of mind would demand an extraordinary and competent detachment of me. But irony, which emerges in the oddness of some reiterated name as it rears up for scrutiny, might offer a less fortuitous route to emancipation.[23]

Language, luckily, cannot bear to stand on its own dignity for long. No sooner have I fumbled my way towards *The Words of Selves* as my somewhat ponderous title for this volume than, of its own accord, it has happily somersaulted into *The Swords of Elves*—apt enough for the puny defences afforded to us through brandishing personal identities. My sole justification for so portentous a title is this criss-crossing of its letters, a felicitous accident which enacts a theme of the essay by becoming apparent to me only in retrospect and not as a result of any authorial ingenuity, but of the sheer ingenuity of the language. Or, apart from the ever-present chance of such spontaneous verbal corruption, even the inflection allowed to a single word will change the sense of the whole sentence; bored children must still mentally run through a sentence to alter its meaning by heavily emphasising each of its words one by one. But what, in practice, does the reiteration of the word itself bring about? We talk and listen at a time of identificatory rage and of confessional directives, even if this gratifies no one for very long. What may cause this will to be to falter, if it overhears itself enough? The categories of the self, repeated a thousandfold, pass through early consolidation and settlement, and gradually fan out towards disintegration, via folly. Rehearsed enough, any identification may come to sound increasingly bizarre and strangely thinglike, much in the way that any common word printed too many times on one page will leap out, absurd, its sense suddenly drained out of it. But this effect of absurdity, which may helpfully puncture a bloated category, will only come about within the particular historical circumstances enfolding it. Then a politics of irony makes itself felt, if namelessly. Irony, as the rhetorical form of self-reflexiveness, is also turned outwards to the world. The sheer iterability of names, including typologies of people, may generate an ironic recoil in their ostensible subjects. Not always; remorseless hammerblows of aggressive speech, or the corrosive slow dripping of venomous naming, may wear down their targets but not themselves. Irony's failure may, at times, be marked as racism. Yet—although, to reiterate the mantra, only under particular historical and therefore linguistic conditions—Echo herself may generate the ironic. This is another of those enticing moments at which a tangible materiality of language floods into its referents. For irony, as a possible outcome of the excessively repeated word, does not rise through this sonorousness alone but through a critical crossover point at which the sheer noise of the word's reiterated sound clashes with both the established memory and the anticipation of its semantic sense. This irony embodies the recognition, driven by Echo, that something is going wrong once the word's reoccurrences come to erode its former meaning. Echo is my figure of transformative reiteration. This phenomenon is not only of aesthetic interest; it is as evident in the history of the degeneration and crumbling of political categories as it is in their present. Nothing can be guaranteed about the time of such ruination. Sluggishness and torpor may long hold sway. Yet even within them, an abruptly effective work for the ironised subject may be to counter some false politicisation of the immediately 'ethnicised' subject.

It is within the ears of its own speakers that reiteration will first start to ring hollow and perhaps to hint at the uses of its own corruption or senescence. Adequate exemplification here would be endless. An earlier attempt played out one long illustration—of the category of 'women' as both an inescapably ambiguous irritant to, yet the ground for, feminist politics and the corresponding need to tolerate and exploit this ambiguity through a tactical agility and foxiness.[24] Here I can only hint at a few more possibilities, if scattered over a broader ground. The reader is also asked to tolerate some fluctuations in the 'I' used in the following pages. Usually this is the impersonal or generic first person, but sometimes it will seep into the personal form, and where I've noticed that it's done so, I've exaggerated the slippage, in order to make it undefended. A blurred indeterminate *I* runs counter to a common tendency to erect a strong partition between those academic and psychoanalytic theories that interrogate the concept of identity, and the tacit supposition that sustained doubt about the conceptual integrity of my personal *I* is merely neurotic. A curiously schizoid division of labour has arisen, in which the theoretical *I* has to be cross-examined in the name of intellectual vigour at the very same moment that the personal *I* has to be affirmed in the name of emotional health. These pages propose, instead, that the personal *I* will suffer its endemic misgivings and instabilities, but for the soundest historical–linguistic reasons (there is a continuum between these two), while the theoretically conceived self, if it stays indifferent to the impact of this everyday linguistic fact, must remain ahistorical and limply inadequate to the task it has set itself. But this 'subject' of theory might be animated by historicising the first person: admitting both its semantic and its syntactical quirks, its anxieties of identification, and its fertile constraints.

ONE

'Who, me?' Self-description's linguistic affect

the scene of my selves, the occasion of these ruses

FRANK O'HARA[1]

Fussing

What am I up to, when I depict myself? There's a fairly innocuous school of self-description: me as my enthusiasms. 'I love just walking around cities for hours on end' or 'I was a great fan of Antonioni's early movies'—this sort of thing fetchingly colours in the self and has some potential as a seduction technique: 'You're sympathetic to my tastes? Then do be sympathetic to me, too, since, quite clearly, you already are'. I circulate my confession, turning my cards face upwards, exposing my devices, flashing them around. All this accompanies a tacit invitation to my listener to offer a fair exchange, to give as good as he or she's just got. But my instrumental truth-telling need not be considered cynical, even if I do work to a recipe. Many formulaically cheerful admissions are sprinkled over everyday conversations: 'Well, I suppose I'm one of those fogies they call technologically illiterate' or 'I have to admit that I'm probably just an unreconstructed old chauvinist here, but. . . .' These speakers are congratulating themselves, yet hoping that some charm of their confession might work for their audience. Sometimes I inscribe myself whimsically and passive-aggressively inside a category I don't much care for, can't altogether avoid, and won't take straight: 'Naturally, I'm just another abandoned mistress'. Or 'Me, I'm trailer trash'. Or someone remarks, with lugubrious satisfaction, 'Oh, I'm middle-class, middle-aged, and middle-brow'. Any serious self-deprecation would flee that formula. Yet something is being intimated: a staged satisfaction, which has also realised and wants to convey that it is ill at ease. The masterpiece of aggressive-defensive presentation is that short rejoinder 'I'm only human'. Its self-aggrandising quality is well deflated in an anecdote from one of Lynne Tillman's essays:

> Madame Realism liked it when aggrieved people insisted: I'm only human. It was impossible to understand what that meant, since, on its face, it was simultaneously obvious, grandiose, and self-effacing. Hearing it said reminded her of Sammy 'The Bull' Gravanno, who'd ratted on Mafia don John Gotti. Gravanno was once interviewed on Diane Sawyer's TV show. Sawyer leant forward, brow furrowed to mark her sincerity and perplexity, to ask him, one human being to another: How could you kill your wife's brother? Didn't you ask yourself, What kind of person am I? Didn't you ask yourself, who am I? Like Atlas, Gravanno shrugged, nonplussed by doubts about his humanity, and answered: I'm a gangster.[2]

This particular Mafioso, a good Aristotelian who was faithful to his job rather than to his essence, managed to duck his interviewer's rhetorical expectations. A more indirect, yet forcefully directing, rhetoric is that communicative intent which hovers behind a statement's overt wording, and yet is integral to the weight of the whole: like a pointed sigh of 'Someone had better make that telephone call'. Or 'My back isn't half aching!' uttered by someone standing, arms akimbo, next to her heavy shopping bags; a perhaps aimless plaint, but more likely a half-rehearsed appeal to someone else in her company to carry them. Announcing what I am may similarly labour under its burden of communicative intent, for my self-definition can be a determined appeal for recognition. Proffering its calling card, it's also an RSVP to invite its recipient to display his own, in a ritual exchange. In this sense it may well be a performative, like a first declaration of love. Its effect on its hearer may have the force of an injunction.[3] Any initial 'I love you' is barely possible to enunciate without its implicit—however unwilled—claim for reciprocation. I can utter it for the first time in the most clear-hearted man-

ner, as if the sentence rose unbidden to my lips, driven by a huge and innocent force of feeling. And yet, to my mortification, this declaration, which I
would so want to bring into the world freely and without its price, must at
once circulate as coinage within the relentless economy of utterance as exchange. Declaring itself, it's also a violent plea for a response in kind, and
the addressee who truly can't reciprocate may feel guilty of, at the very least,
linguistic bad manners. (The rhetorical 'I love you; what business is that of
yours?' is its parasitical inversion—and which, even as a mannered display,
doesn't remotely convince.)—But isn't this an absurd example of mine, because the embarrassment of failing to echo the 'I love you', or the joy of being able to do so, are not linguistic but emotional reactions? Yet in a first announcement of love, aren't we hesitating on an engaging threshold between
the linguistic and the psychological, where each is resolving itself into the
other? This declarative instant, in its capacity to outrun the intentions of its
speaker, is what we might christen 'the emotional performative'. (There's arguably another characterisation of the 'I love you': as an act of interpellation,
but this thought opens a can of worms, which must writhe quietly inside it
until the next chapter.)

And if this 'I love you' spontaneously solicits its returning echo, then
doesn't my self-description often operate likewise, as an automatic provocation to its audience? It's not necessarily a provocation to be complicit. For in
declaring myself a such-and-such, I may tacitly separate myself from the
communality you had expected to inhabit with me; or I may embarrass you
with my proud unbreachable difference; or I may make you, now suddenly
debarred from my club, feel your solitude sharply; or I may indicate that ir-
reparable lapses of time have buried me in my idiosyncrasy; or I may challenge you not to be swayed by my quirks; or I may claim the superiority of
having been discriminated against, in a way you've been protected from; or
I may proffer the unrivalled exoticism of my upbringing. In brief, 'I am an
x' may function to exclude: 'and so you are not an x'. Or, like the sentence
of love, it can indeed be an appeal to not leave me needlessly alone with my
x-ness, to realise that my x-ness is the happiest of states, to crouch inside the
generous bracket which could shelter us both.

For Hegel, a useful estrangement of the self from itself 'takes place solely
in language' and it is, he continues, exactly as the spoken word that it possesses its authority. At this point, he is in fine Austinian vein: 'It is the power

of speech, as that which performs what has to be performed'.[4] Self-portrayal's affect embraces a prominent performance genre of staged admissions: that of confessing. The ritual of confession in the Anglican church declaims aloud, 'We have followed too much the devices and desires of our own hearts. . . . And there is no health in us'. This surely cannot be felt exactly as it's phrased, unless by those who relish the rolling cadences of self-abasement. Such knowingly abject enunciation resembles the technique of method actors, who will a suspension of their disbelief for just long enough to put on a show which is thoroughly convincing to them, too. Then can there ever be a true confession, not extracted under torture? Must it usually have the structure of lying, with its bowed head? For self-indictment readily slides into a theatrical self-blame, becomes portentous, and perpetuates some grandiose guilt. Once self-revelation becomes militant, it can swing towards self-flagellation. And there's an everyday self-accusation which, although not in the least insincere, constitutes an instruction to its hearer to repudiate it eagerly: 'No, you are not a loveless monster—no, believe me, really you're not!' Here the penitent's loud self-reproaches have become a perverse performative—still a communicative intent, but where its intention is to be heard as the inverse of what its literal words say.[5] Yet certainly he is not being ironic.

'For myself, I am neither "jealous", nor "inquisitive", nor "hunchbacked", nor "a civil servant"'.[6] Then why, anyway, all this fuss about self-description; why should it be especially worrying? In fact, need the business of characterising the self be espoused at all? Perhaps it's only a narrowly academic neurosis that hovers obsessively and plaintively about self-description, while the rapid and casual takeaways of spoken utterance haven't the time to fuss, so must just get on with it. Have I anything much to say about myself? Not really. Having made myself into a descriptive standard component, I can just slot myself in. I could issue a date and place of birth, just enough biographical data for its bureaucratic occasion. There is only one 'identity' that I need, and it's thoroughly pragmatic: whatever identifying markers are required to let me count as a citizen and traverse national boundaries. Beyond this, settling in to some description might be cosy, like joining a club after a flurry of resolve and an evening's nervous introductions, easing back into a leather armchair, attempting to feel quite at home, like an older member. Isn't characterising myself often this sort of inert affair? For there's little pain, except to my vanity, in supplying a checklist of my identifying weight and hair colour. Yet the task of stepping into some fraught social category entails a quite different order of sheepishness. Still, it would be fruitless to draw up tables of innocent versus perilous classes of self-categorising, since the thing is always deployed to some end or other. People regularly sway between their mildly parodic sociological self-labelling and private reservations: 'I suppose you'd have to call me an Old Labour voter', or 'I'd have to admit I'm a bit New Age-y when it comes to iridology'; the intersection between my solitary misgivings and my public designation can be lumpishly handled as I fumble to place myself out loud. Phil Cohen has written of his London childhood, 'To grow up a mitchsling, a Jew to gentiles, and a goy to Jews, whilst perched precariously between threat of descent into the ranks of the local working class and entrée into the charmed circles of a national élite, might seem in retrospect to be a good apprenticeship for a subsequent career as a social re-searcher'.[7] And today's television and radio and newspaper chat, with its sharpened assessments of everyone's identity categories, has forcibly turned all of us into habitual amateur sociologists. Social research of this kind has replaced an earlier century's gentlemanly pottering about with natural history. We are all sociologists now.

My only practicable emancipation from the insatiable question of how to speak the truth about myself might be, perhaps, to lose the slightest interest in striving to answer it. To walk well away from it. My self might be considered, tautly, as consisting of nothing more than what it does. No transcendent 'character' need swell like a miasma over and above its actions; as Aristotle was convinced, it's in my performance that my truth is to be found.[8] From this brisk perspective, any quest for a precise self-characterisation becomes a sustained error. On the contrary; to resolutely dedramatise myself is often the precondition for some clarity of behaviour. Then sheer boredom, too, can truncate lengthy self-scrutiny. The self can readily—and merci-fully—become deeply uninteresting in its own eyes. It cannot gossip with much enthusiasm to itself, about itself, for very long (although one can think of exceptions). The outside world and other people draw me on, 'out of myself', until some equable self-balance is restored. And my relieved turning away from some finally outgrown account of myself is like giving up alcohol, or love; there's little grasp of the actual moment of crossing that threshold of resignation, but only a nervous impression that the untraceable instant of disengagement is far more deeply mysterious than was my initial engagement. Preparation for relinquishing some constricting self-narrative may be hard and slow; I might disentangle myself only by laboriously picking away at its great coils with my fingernails. Yet in an insistent climate of cultural and therapeutic expectation that 'telling oneself' must be taken with deep seriousness, one can't do other than react somehow or other to this incessant question of what one truly is. The next couple of sections will reflect on some of its commonly invited responses.

Self-advertisement, self-annihilation

'The self' as mode lies photographed and bound in a stout portfolio of types. Journalism reels them off: the solitary existentialist's self is no longer modish, and romantic loneliness has stalked away into the dark with the hero of the late 1950s and early 1960s, his coat collar turned up against the damp as he strikes his match under the lamplight, drawing ruefully on his cigarette. He can be consigned to a nervously inventive parade of effigies which might also star the new woman of the 1890s and her reincarnation as flapper in the 1920s, the teddy boy of the late 1950s, the mod of the 1960s, the yuppie of the 1980s, the smug urban marrieds and all their proliferating acronyms of the mid-1990s. There are infinite fashions in selves. Sometimes their rotations are rapid. Within my own lifetime, I might even find myself coming round again. As Frank O'Hara sighed,

> Now I am quietly waiting for
> the catastrophe of my personality
> to seem beautiful again
> and interesting, and modern[9]

—and with any luck, time's rotations may be kinder to me than I am to myself.

Such easy vignettes aside, the extensive history of conceptions of the self is too elaborate to accord it more than a respectful nod here. Historicisations of 'the individual' include the capacity of altering relations of production to produce those who dwell in them too, as Marx suggested;[10] and those altering religious consciences within their apt economies, laid bare by Weber.[11] Some social psychologies also proffer a self which is historically formed, such as Mead's account of the ego as something to be grasped only in its collectivity.[12] Mauss's evolutionist pursuit of the self starts with something first embodied in the ancient roles and masks studied by anthropology that then works its way onward, through a slow drift of interiorisation, to that ethicised psychology which makes up the modern person. Aiming to trace what he called 'the social history of the categories of the human mind'[13] through the self's incarnations, to this end Mauss drew an anthropological sketch of the self as a role-player.[14] In his exposition, classical history emphasised the great mutability of what was taken to constitute a self at all.[15] A Stoic ethic came to enrich the Roman idea of 'a man clad in a condition'[16] and led in the direction of the Christian responsible individual, who himself suffered a further sea change; 'It remained to make of this rational, individual substance what it is today, a consciousness and a category'.[17] During this long march of the self, the seventeenth and eighteenth centuries' religious movements intensified considerations of personal liberty and conscience.[18] According to Mauss's tirelessly evolutionist account, this very development paved the way for Kant's speculation as to whether the self was actually a primordial category.[19] And it would follow that philosophies of a fundamental self, such as Fichte's idea of the Ego as the unknowable ground of everything apprehended, own an analogous ancestry, however subdued.[20] What would they have made of the possibilities of an emergent collective subject of cyberspace? It would be an enticing if unending task to flesh out the conviction that the concept of 'what a self is' does, strikingly, metamorphose.

Less ambitiously, we need only glance around us to sense that the least venture into any confessional—whether as deliberate autobiography or indirectly as poetry or history—produces obstinate knots of self-presentation. Any writer will inadvertently historicise herself in her work, however non-self-referential it aims to be. Describing myself, I set out the stall of my self, however reluctantly, as advertising. And if this is so, can speaking the self ever be managed without flattery or abnegation? Scrutinising my desire to present my better profile to that autodescriptive camera lens which is constantly snapping away, I sense how much becomes coloured by the longing for a little glamour, however small the stakes. If I caught myself insisting that I don't fish up my Scots ancestry to sidestep the blankness of being solidly English, I'd not believe myself, and 'I came from a working-class background' would be hard for me to utter without that hint of virtuous self-aggrandisement, 'and proud of it'. Transparently self-interested, it would cast a dubious glory on its speaker and be automatically deployed to distinguish her from her present bookishly protected environment. The drab truth is that I'm unlikely to reach for less flattering descriptions of my present condition—that I am a middle-aged homeowner—with the same enthusiasm. Outlining the most elegant silhouette of the self proceeds, too, under the guise of more sober reasons. 'The sugar side of the dead', the better aspect of the face of the fresh corpse, was photographed for posterity.[21] Sugaring my living self, my failure to set it in the astringent history of the present, may be equalled, for dullness, by the opposite risk: an overdone self-historicising. The investigating self as its own historian, modest yet vainglorious, tacit heroine of its researches, poses an obstinate problem for the history it writes. 'But that's enough about you, let's talk about me'—the historiography which made the progress of the self an object for politicisation also suffered the risks of being charming to itself, within this sometimes admirable reflexivity. Earlier formations of feminist history exemplified this. To come to see oneself as a little burnished bead, strung out, tiny and firm, among millions of others along an intricate chain of socialist women—all that significant presence of the self in its own self-telling, even the self shot through and through with history—embodied a fascination which in itself requires scrutiny. Then the axioms of the women's liberation movement, became, at least in part, ammunition for determining why, in one's own situation, things were as they intractably were. Despairing cries of 'my life, my beautiful life!' were understood to be echoes of a distressed society. Did this matter? From one aspect, no. It would be a chilly and antihistorical, indeed an amnesiac, severity, which denounced in retrospect all these attempts to write a dynamic history of 'the personal as political'. There's also a broad argument for writing the histories of far more selves, for having as many accounts of as many genres of being as possible, for producing a dream of a social collectivity so swamped with characterisations that any self can find itself in there, since a myriad aspects ultimately boil down to a pure water which must reflect whatever peers into it. Let them all have names! As many as they want! Still, the charm of being a piece of live history to oneself cannot retain its sheen. Not that it's regrettable that being caught up in a political movement so often entails a surge to historicise the self and its dramatic scenarios, to fish up and to refurbish half-lost histories and identifications and loyalties—in any event, to not be so damned alone. Just that, once you have realised that some inescapable leaven of self-fascination is busily at work under the banner of reinterpreting oneself as a sliver of the history of the present, then you are forced to speculate about exactly what it's up to there. How someone will speak about herself is deeply and immediately historical. To overhear one's self, though, is to witness it singing an aria, the evaluation of which demands the hardest criticism and a knowledge of every rhetorical trick in the book.

Impatience, in the teeth of all this, readily kicks in. I could paper myself with a dozen attributions, some blandly subdued, others vibrant with uncertainty. Scrutinising several, I'd handle some at arm's length, picking them up cautiously. Suddenly sick of this timidity, a happy recklessness might rush in with its ideal democratic solution: to open up all identities to all claimants, and then today's cultural obsession is at once relaxed. Everyone to be everything! And being everything at once may boil down to the same thing as being nothing at all. In many ways I would like to float 'Glad to be nothing' as a slogan—but then I'd immediately need to back off from the consequent ascription of indeed being something: a nihilist. Certainly to be described, against my will, by others is far worse—and sometimes murderous, if I'm assigned to some grouping earmarked for hatred. Then, in the face of such visibly grave consequences of others' hostile characterisations, perhaps the flimsy study of self-characterisation ought properly to be consigned to the bonfire of the vanities? This sceptical train of thought (which also relies on maintaining an unrealistically strong separation between what I'll call myself and what I get called) could lead to very different conclusions. My self-description might limit itself to a constant defensive negation: 'No, I'm not that bad thing you call me'. I might try to steer clear of assenting to any category, because all naming, as interpellation, does have the structure of a latent accusation. Or I might fear some slippage, a strong drift from my own readiness to place myself towards my willingness to adopt categories in which to deposit others. If I am so clearly one of this lot here, might a mechanical antagonism to that lot over there develop in me? In reaction, I might elect to fight against owning attributes at all, becoming an emptied-out space, drained of all defining characteristics. Would it be ideal to be, like the hero of Robert Musil's novel, a 'man without qualities'[22]? To be like glass, translucent to others? Divested of every self-interested attribute, out of my glassily clear state I could perhaps dream a politics founded instead on a broad altruistic conception of the needs of others. Or I could develop a quirky pride in my versatility, like Charles Dickens's Miss Mowcher, who 'made herself useful to a variety of people in a variety of ways' and was given to crying, 'Ain't I volatile?'[23] Then my most conscientious self-effacement may act, infuriatingly, as an inadvertent self-promotion. The only result of some theatrically self-cancelling refusal to describe myself may be to adver- tise myself:

> No single word of this
> is any more than decoration of an old self-magnifying wish
> to throw the self away so violently and widely that interrogation
> has to pause, since its chief suspect's sloped off to be cloud, to be
> wavery colour bands.[24]

The dream of transparency may end in a passion for blankness. Then to shun any concentration on my characteristics might lead me, instead of obliterating them, to give them away all over the place. I could, risking a reputation for wilful psychosis, try to make my single self vanish by that hugely exhilarating tactic of becoming many. As Whitman repeatedly cries, 'I embrace myself, I contain multitudes', 'I am several of me', 'I am many'— though his was no Emersonian transcendence, since his invoked collectivity is affectionately itemised again, in fine grain. Through joyous multiplica- tion, I might manage to become so singularly large in my own eyes that I disappear to myself. Certainly self-magnification, although in a dejected mode, is perpetuated by some professional lives. One could become a mon- ument to oneself. My self-monumentalisation would rest on suppressing any faint trace of ironical curiosity about what had led me to my lofty posi- tion, what sustains me on its heights. I might, fatally, come to feel that I am my rank and status. There are, of course, somewhat more palatable ways of being it. I may be convinced that in the solemnity of my fresh identity, a truth is enacted; its inevitability may dawn on me from the vantage point of its far side, just as if I'd undergone a spiritual conversion. I could fall gladly into some category of being, and inhabit it like 'the sob in which pain re- laxes'.[25] In a burst of éclat, I might sense myself always to have been what I'm brightly illuminated as being. In a dislocating leap of faith, a twist in mid air across descriptive modes, I pass from my separateness to inscribe myself anew. There's a peculiar timing to this acceleration towards fresh self-designation. Along the lines of the hymn 'Amazing Grace', that I was blind, who now can see, the truly converted might testify: 'I hovered on the brink of an admission, of a decisive act of signing myself up; but only now that I've arrived securely on its far shores do I realise how committed in advance I'd been to my plunge. Perhaps I was really already up to the neck in my own resignification. Perhaps I always was what, gladly, I now realise I am'. A similar gratified hindsight marked what the women's liberation movement, by analogy with the Maoist confessionals of 'speaking bitterness' and briefly blind to their orchestration, once termed 'consciousness raising'. Such reassuring arrivals at the new place may never quite convince, shepherded along as they are by the powerful relief that 'so I wasn't really lost then after all; I just hadn't recognised myself in the new terrain I'd reached'.

Yet anxiety needn't always shadow self-depiction. Prosaically enough, a speaker may want, not a dedication after long heart-searching, but only a simple ease of self-reference—or to be casually fashionable. Identification may not stem from a postulant's conviction in a faith, eagerly assuming its truth. I can come out instead as a knowing debutante before the linguistic court, presenting myself pragmatically, strategically—or resignedly, provisionally—or else sardonically, instrumentally. Or money may flow to a tribe, figuratively or literally: A reformulated ethnicity may become a candidate for governmental funding, and I might find it expedient to discover my credentials and to polish up my roots a bit, yet perhaps also take it on solemnly, in full assent to whatever anthropology it's part of. Or I might be reassured by the strongly vicarious element in self-categorisation—that once I adopt a designation, it ensures my restricted but undeniable circulation under its banner: Without any further exertion on my part, it is all being done for me, out there.

Smoothed and polished up, my announcement of myself may be designed as a conversation stopper. A self-presentation of any interesting awkwardness may, in its thick verbal skin, defend against a felt linguistic threat. It slams my cards on the table; it presents me, in a way which invites no response. Like a piece of militant body art, a tattooed slogan, it may be intended as a declaration rather than a conversation—in your face rather than to your face. Yet it's a declaration which knows that its audience knows that it's staging itself. If my worldly classification involves a degree of masquerading, nevertheless any masquerade demands to be taken half-seriously, although both spectators and performers realise perfectly well that theirs is a frail armoury of veils, lorgnettes, and feather boas. All recognise a ritual: Here you are not only 'supposed to be' but are supposed to be seen to be supposing to be it. Like a stage actor, I must be an ardent borrower from a repertoire, an absorbed learner of my set script with its attitudinising. Nevertheless, to cross over into a new social being does imply that something truly novel is at stake for me, something beyond play-acting. If there's a self-consciousness and mild theatricality in proudly stepping out, there's also a serious tension, which is at once grammatical and affective, between the self and its future collectivity. Taking a deep breath, the person must walk into the room of the subject.

Linguistic emotion

Silence in grass and solace in blank verdure
Summon the frightful glare of nouns and verbs.
The gentle foal linguistically wounded
Squeals like a car's brakes,
Like our twisted words.[26]

Then how does someone move from contemplating a category, to deciding to cross its threshold and to speak from inside it? Do I come in with my hands up and join all the rest? But it's not as if I slip alone into a description, as if I'd hesitated in a doorway before making my plunge into a crowded party. 'I' start out as an accidental linguistic perspective—yet my contingency is not exactly lonely, for within it lies the realisation that I'm no Crusoe, isolated on a desert island.[27] I hardly stand apart in a virgin clearing within language, gazing down from a height through the branches on the swarming throng of babblers below. My very self-description, even if it looks like my own confessional intimacy, has been sent to me by invitation. My entry merely delivers me to where I have been assigned. Indeed some new description may have seeped into me from the outside, by the time I've agreed with myself to register it as mine. I'm steeped in the world's words already, am well marinated. If there's an expectation that only my 'interiority' can bestow integrity on my self-portrayal, then in practice, this someone I painstakingly describe as me may resemble rather more of a Not-Me. My proffered self is always something of a dislocated 'I'—recalling the protagonist of Beckett's monologue who speaks in stage blackness, her face reduced to a mouthing pair of shrouded lips, her name simply 'Mouth'.[28] The notion of the self's displacement nurses the metaphor of the empty centre, resonant with blankness.[29] But actually this 'blankness' need not be so unhappily characterised, and it's not facile to talk lightly of the fact that 'there is no centre'.

Nevertheless there's still some flicker of my consent when I admit myself into some societal category. For the definition of my kind must somehow be made to resonate as my own as I pass from my truth in private to my truth in the world—all the while awkwardly aware that this very 'me' itself springs from the most acceptably conventional diction. Taking on some rendering of myself through the diction of emancipatory identifications is not some venerable matter of how I tell my truth through introspection but instead of how I can properly come to inhabit a categorical truth which precedes me— in short, of how I become a subject. I venture into a looming account of my self, walking as an ostensibly private thing right up to and into its cavernous mouth. This way of writing the pronoun as two words, 'my self', was common until the eighteenth century, after which the term tended to become fused into a single word. To separate these two syllables once more makes prominent the temporal riddle of its division and its wholeness. It's as if I constituted myself in advance of myself because something out there had chimed with me. A flashing recall rises here of Freud's 'Wo Es war, soll Ich werden'—where it, the id, was, there shall I, the ego, be. But what exactly is it that utters that delphic line? Some wilful yet tentative I, poised in an embryonic present tense, while anticipating its gestation and birth as a fully hatched capital I? In the ruthless logic of the excluded middle, the declaration of where it was, there I shall be, is an impossible prophecy—for either there's a self to speak, or there isn't. Yet in this strange retrospective and anticipatory modal logic, the voice which speaks from strictly no place to announce that 'where I was as something undefined, there instead I shall establish my name', is itself the vexed grammar of self-description.

Here is one instance of the strange temporality of language as a kind of anteriority—the anterior future perfect tense of interpellation where you become what, hearing yourself called, you acknowledge yourself to be[30] (as the second chapter discusses). (But if language does incorporate this anteriority, by no means does that constitute its 'inner' secret. It's hard to fight with a homophone. But 'anteriority', despite the seduction of the paired sounds here, is not at all the same as 'interiority'. On the contrary, anteriority comes closer to characterising what one might think of as language's externality, for instance, in its tendency to constantly glance over its shoulder and in its rearview mirror.) This convoluted temporality can't be peeled off from its imminent linguistic embodiment. 'Some casual shout that broke the silent air, / Or the unimaginable touch of Time'[31]—but these two possibilities are actually not alternatives. It's the sheer accident of that casual cry which constitutes in itself the impress of passing time. In the flash of interpellative recognition, a second's indeterminacy bangs closed. It's like that briefly open temporality of rhyme, where a shadow is cast backwards on the ear by the anticipated rhyme which falls somewhere between the uttered word and the approaching word yet to be articulated. The whole affair runs only by means of a settling retrospect in which the machinery of the achieved rhyme—like the syntactical devices of interpellation—will usually close down that suspended instant, which had to have been momentarily held ajar.

By now, it's sounding as if some fully impersonal mechanism must drive self-description. Then has all my earlier speculative chat about the personal psychology of adopting a designation been witness only to a lamentable fastidiousness with sources in darker areas than it has understood? But in the course of these pages, I'll try to disengage that question from its implication that to 'make a fuss' about describing the self is merely an extralinguistic bother. I want to float an effort at rescuing all this from a truncated idea of psychology—that is, from 'psychology' understood as somehow in opposition to the category of 'language'. Some 'truly psychological' element cannot be cleanly isolated and extracted from the language, syntax, and grammar of self-description. I've emphasised this affect involved in adopting a self-portrayal, not as some psychological frill pinned onto some sterner stuff of linguistic subjectification, but because these emotions, these sentiments, do inhere in it. They are not extralinguistic. They are profoundly implicated in the ungainly affair of writing and talking oneself into or out of a social category. They are, indeed, rhetorical—but, exactly as such, they are very far from trivial or residual.

Language is radically historical, and not as any secondary or superstructural effect—but immediately so. Might not this robust historicity of language also dwell in its emotionality, which lives in it, and which again is not something secondary or expressive of an inner thought sunk well below the linguistic skin? For language does not so much 'express' feeling, but (to use American English) in itself it 'does' feeling. (It does not follow that greater verbal fluency implies a larger affective range because no claim is made for language as emotion's sole enactment. Nevertheless, to possess wider possibilities of verbal description can, as my concluding chapters propose, offer some effective first aid against verbal violence.) That commonest of phrases, 'to express a feeling', does presuppose a near-perfect transcription of what's in the speaker's heart, an enunciation flowing from inner to outer, where nothing extraneous is added through its actual articulation. 'To put it into words' is one of those ordinary sayings possessed of an extraordinary and temporally impossible syntax, which forces it into a doubled implication: that the 'it' is already formed before it is rendered verbal, yet it comes into shape through its own utterance. But this observation doesn't assume that there's no such thing as interior speech; and anyone who's ever had a slight aneurysm may recall being disturbingly aware of sudden failure to get a word out, of sentences literally becoming unutterable, while running in one's head. The struggle 'to find the words to say it' is another daily version of the old conundrum of how the preverbal can be recognised in its wordy incarnation. It's neither that affect may be 'conveyed in' words nor that in a coldly reductive manner it is 'really only' words—but that in a full and exuberant sense, sensibility *is* words. Not that there aren't a myriad emotions never verbally shaped, stubbornly resistant to being voiced, or comical if translated; not that the most vehement don't surge upwards wordlessly. To think of the unconscious as incarnate in language stakes no territorial claim to exclusivity and by no means obliterates the affect which is not in language, or is in 'the body'. But feeling, articulated, *is* words and is also *in* the words. To distinguish here between language as carrier of emotion and language as emotion is impossible, and pointless. Uttering convincingly affecting speech, one may of course lie. Still, taking the hearer as key here, he's deceived because he is at the mercy of what the words themselves are doing. But affect is not only conveyed 'by means of' the word as a vehicle; to some extent, the forms of language immediately enact it in themselves. They can also enact on autopilot. There's a remorseless scaffolding to a sentence of oafish pornography, with the upshot that its shape of 'he x'd her y' is so de rigueur that it will infect, say, 'he parked his car in her garage'. Other well-worn syntactical forms may shoulder their burden laboriously; so the rhetorical grammar of laying to rest the virtuous dead makes the radio newscaster intone, 'They buried her at noon today', that anonymous third person plural, used for no other end, immediately ushering in its worthy occasion.

Ambiguities of sex can't be carried in the certainties of pronouns, and this arresting sentence, again phrased in American English, emerged in a spoken tale of someone born with a physically indeterminate sex, assigned as male, and brought up as a boy until his adolescence: 'And then he got his period'. As the sentence tracks the young man-woman's shock, its strangeness hits the listener's ear. But is it any easier to assign this jarring to 'the grammar' or to 'the meaning' of the sentence? Its status is ambiguous. But 'ambiguity' frequently suffers as a word from its closeness to 'ambivalence'; even its most principled espousal may get interpreted as vacillation, an inability to make a proper commitment to one side or the other. Yet ambiguity is not a personally subterranean affair. Nor is it even simply perspectival. Instead, it inheres; the lettering goes all the way through. In the same way, the linguistic aspect of affect is not detachable. Not only is there a grammar of the emotions, but there's also an emotional grammar. Or in shorthand, which will be transcribed here later: there really is an accusative case.[32]

The linguistic can be productively distinguished from the psychological only by fleshing out that cool and watery image of 'language' in the popularised, supposedly post-Saussurean legacy, to replace it with something older, more sonorous with history, and stouter altogether. 'The flesh of words'[33] is better suited to a material touch. To assert that language is itself 'material' might cause dismay, if this claim is taken to mean that a noisily wild and booming depth, all howls, whoops, echolalic gabble and babble, are what you must espouse.[34] Its antithesis, equally exaggerated, is an ostensible post-Saussureanism (which has rather little to do with Saussure's own work) glossing language as the realm of mastery and cool deliberation, a perfected, refined instrument. Its floating veil is nonetheless credited with mesmeric powers; an ectoplasm, yet tough and rubbery enough to determine being. So unsatisfying a notion invites the counterassertion about language's materiality, which soon gets distractingly yoked to its presumed irrationality. Next a

resulting heavily hypostatised Language gradually becomes hot, a smoulder-
ing or sweaty thing, a mass dried out in patches, oozing in others; granite in
some places, swamp elsewhere, fed by bubbling rivulets or else sluggish with
sedimented toxic waste. Or Language may undergo a sadistic personification
and is given the whip hand, to speak its speaker. Yet if we elect to run with
that supposition, it should not be restricted to describing only hysterical
speech, infantile ululations, sobs, and gibberish. For automated speech will
more commonly be issued from uniforms than from those mad as the racked
sea in crowns of cuckoo-flowers and nettles.[35] The most seemingly controlled
and tightly structured of languages—the knee-jerk response, the rigidly formulaic diction, the legalistic or mechanical utterance, may run strictly on
autocontrol—so mastering he who pronounces it. Both ritualised call and
answer can be played out within one speaker. Then modes of verbal constraint proliferate; the bafflement of inarticulacy, the eliding smoothness of
formulaic diction, the disabling ease of cliché, the bullying dictations of
rhyme, the seething ramifications of metaphor, and a million others. But that
notion of language as a vast unwieldy obstruction forgets its kinder powers to
resolve some painful inarticulacy—for instance, for a child exhausted by her
lack of mastery over words, who then gradually becomes able to allay her
own passionate incoherence through her speech. This is a sober aspect of the
'materiality' of language (its untidy vivaciousness is not best served by that
worthy word) which could be revamped by steering well clear of that familiar opposition of deeply glowing feelings versus the tepid superficiality of
words.[36] Instead of that deceptively neat arrangement of cool language with
its hot underbelly, if we were to conduct some of the heat away into syntax
and grammar, that might helpfully disarray the thing. For language does not
cruise at an altitude well above what it then stoops to conquer: the rough
warm realm of emotion. Yet there's a lingering conviction that it must, due
to the belief that language is 'superstructural', the spatial metaphor again un-
derlining the imagined apparatus of surface and depth. And this seems to
outlive the impact of all supposedly poststructuralist thinking.

Musing about the entrenched peculiarities of self-description, I've found
myself referring to something distinctive there, which I've wanted to think
of as its linguistic affect. But doesn't this intuitive formulation unhelpfully
bestow an agency of its own upon some exaggeratedly hypostatised entity of
'language'? The notion that there is a stealthy language which gets up to

things behind the backs of its speakers, distorting their intentions, has clear drawbacks; although a venerable body of thought does suppose just this. I'll mention some nineteenth- and twentieth-century variants on this old theme of language as a wily seducer, prefacing this with a note of a different and ancient means of attending to the effectivity of words. Here the known assembly of Greek and Latin writers on rhetoric, a thoroughly mixed bag, would nevertheless have agreed for a while on the broad supposition that even though the modes of civic rhetoric were vehemently disputed, it was a vital exercise in speech and writing as decent arts. Their question was not whether the emotionality of language was a reprehensible thing, but how far one could develop a useful psychopragmatics to grasp it and work it purposefully to make it vivid. But this commitment was no matter of cunning. The rhetorician Quintillian, although from his account of it profoundly saddened by the death of his remaining young son, sets about explaining about how such feeling might persuasively be imitated by an orating speaker—by means of an identification with the passions of loss, in a studied yet by no means insincere process of what he calls 'making terrible'.[37] The performer should come to deeply feel that which he is, in fact, imitating. Such heartfelt mimicry might be anchored in technique. So Demetrius[38] explains in his firmly prescriptive manual *On Style*: 'To show that asyndeton suits an actor's delivery, let this be an example; "I conceived, I gave birth, I nurse, my dear." In this disjointed form the words will force anyone to be dramatic, however reluctantly—and the cause is the asyndeton. If you link it together to say "I conceived and I gave birth and I nurse" you will, by using the connectives, substantially lower the emotional level, and anything unemotional is always undramatic'.[39] And Longinus argues, 'We must begin now by raising the question whether there is an art or sublimity of emotion, for some think those are wholly at fault who try to bring such matters under systematic rules. [. . .] For my part I hold that the opposite may be proved'.[40] His treatise on rhetoric also traces the detailed workings of style, including how to render affect by manipulating syntax: 'For just as you deprive runners of their speed if you bind them up, emotion equally resents being hampered by connecting particles and other appendages. It loses its freedom of motion and the sense of being, as it were, catapulted out'.[41] That language, so patently affecting, could therefore stand accused of irretrievably distorting thought, would not have been an engaging conception for the ancient rhetoricians. But their robust scrutiny of how words worked comes to falter, and the decline of rhetoric ultimately mutates into an inversion: to the suspicion of the autonomous wiles of words and a corresponding nervous interest in stalking them. An elaborate history is still to be furnished of this conviction that language in itself 'seduces' to impose its dictates onto our thinking. (That there is an erotics of writing and of reading, and of utterance, is a quite different story.) And indeed the idea of thought itself conceived as a kind of painted imagery also undergoes its own slow devaluation. So for Longinus and the Stoics, a fantasy, *fantasia*, was a usefully innocent thing, a visualisation needed to kick-start contemplative thought into acting;[42] but Augustine famously came to suspect images as seductions to undercut one's moral and intellectual guard. Even in the late nineteenth and twentieth centuries, there are reincarnations of a not unrelated apprehension.

A Venus fly-trap school of language

It may be a novel prospect to consider Wittgenstein as a Nietzschean. Yet slipped into his theories of what he considers as the traps laid by language are ideas with a strong resemblance to Nietzsche's idea of 'grammatical seduction'.[43] That look of seduction, its characteristic air of 'as if', also colours Wittgenstein's understanding of the logic of language.[44] Here grammar dazzles, entraps the fly in the fly bottle, offers the glitter of 'false appearances', and leads the enchanted thinker astray through a philosophy which is the terrain of error. 'Philosophy is a bewitchment of our intelligence by means of language'[45]—yet, sternly revamped, it may become his broom for clearing away confusion, indeed as harmless as a witch's broomstick in the cool light of day. When Wittgenstein anxiously cross-questions what he sees as linguistic solipsism, his chosen metaphor closely resembles the careful preparations so critical for seduction. He talks often of grammar readying itself: 'When one says "He gave a name to his sensations" one forgets that a great deal of stage-setting in the language is presupposed if the mere act of naming is to make sense. And when we speak of someone's having given a name to pain, what is presupposed is the existence of the grammar of the word "pain"; it shews the post where the new word is stationed'.[46]

Are these seductions of language almost visual—including the very look of grammar, in its misleading spatiality? This seems to be what Wittgenstein's predecessor in this affair, Nietzsche, is implying about the effect of 'it looks as if'. Readiness slips into entrapment. Where there is bewitchment and mazy error, then there are, as if mechanically wheeled on, female bodies. To speak of the flesh of words captures both their stoutness and their vulnerability; but this fleshiness is rendered curiously girlish by Nietzsche. Although he considers most speech to be reprehensibly blunt, for 'language cannot get over its coarseness'[47] and lacks finesse, its enticements remained formidable. Unpicking those philosophical claims which he saw as themselves overblown captives of the 'seductions'[48] of language, he didn't have to comb the verbal wilds to find the sources of intellectual entrapment. It is 'the common philosophy of grammar'[49] which dictated its own psychological attitudes to thought. For grammar shares mastery with the emotions. It behaves as what Nietzsche terms an 'unconscious' tyrant over the speaker and writer: 'Language belongs in its origin to the age of the most rudimentary form of psychology. . . . It is *this* which sees everywhere deed and doer . . . which believes in the "ego", in the ego as being . . . Being is everywhere thought in, *foisted on*, as cause . . . I fear we are not getting rid of God because we still believe in grammar'.[50] Primitive tyrannies, whether of theology or the schoolroom, still hang on to reinforce this primary linguistic credulousness: 'Are we not permitted to be a little ironical now about the subject as we are about the predicate and the object? Ought the philosopher not to rise above the belief in grammar? All due respect to governesses: but is it not time that philosophy renounced the beliefs of governesses?'[51] False syntactic causality erects an imaginary subject behind an action which has, in reality, no agent:

> Even as the people will separate the lightning from its flash and take the latter for its doing, the effect of a subject called lightning, so popular morality will sever strength from the manifestations of strength, as if behind the strong man there existed an indifferent substratum which is free to manifest strength or not. But there is no such substratum; there is no 'being' behind doing, acting, becoming. 'The doer' is merely a fictitious addition to the doing; the 'doing' is all. People in reality double the doing when they make the lightning flash. That is doing-doing; the same happening being once posited as the cause and again as the effect of the cause. Natural philosophers do not much better when they say that power moves, power causes, and the like. All our science, despite all its coolness,

its freedom from emotion, still labours under the seduction of language and has not yet got rid of the changelings which were foisted in, the 'subjects' (the atom is one of those changelings, also the Kantian 'thing in itself').[52]

Again pointing to the dictates of grammar, Nietzsche objects to the assumption sanctified in the Cartesian *cogito*, that a subject must lie behind what is thought; 'The inference here is in accordance with the habit of grammar; "thinking is an activity, to every activity pertains one who acts, consequently"'.[53]

There's an ambiguous aspect, though, to all his confidence here, for the subject is thought as a side effect of a grammar which is askew in itself yet is also responding to human confusion. This ambiguity facilitates Nietzsche's exoneration: that there's no holding a force of nature accountable, that the strong man could not have acted otherwise, any more than could the lightning or the lion. All are sheer thoroughbred action on legs. There are, then, no culpable subjects behind natural aggression to resent. Yet 'the people' are systematically misled by syntax and, in search of something to blame, will set about inventing a detachable subject, a subject which could have behaved otherwise. A puzzle arises at this point: Who is the accuser delivering the judgement which sentences the subject into being through the accusative mode? Nietzsche replies: It is 'the weak' themselves, those who have suffered from nature's force. That compensatory authority to invent, and then to christen, the imaginary subject as bad accrues to its victims. If identification may work through a wound,[54] then in *A Genealogy of Morals* it works, curiously enough, through someone else's wounds. In an odd retroversion, those who are wounded hit back at their purely fictional agent of damage, and they name 'it' as such. This faint retaliation, though, would easily run off the back of the Nietzschean subject, which, like lightning, simply doesn't exist in a state to be fingered.

Interjecting tersely that 'we really ought to get free from the seduction of words!'[55] Nietzsche nevertheless leaves little space for such a liberation to come about. No doubt his concept of linguistic seduction takes its colouring, and its intractability, from his famously lurid depictions of Woman.[56] In any event, it leaves us with a decision: Given that we can't choose to speak outside grammar without lapsing into psychosis, how should we best accommodate ourselves to this inescapable deceiver? One answer's amiably cynical: to enjoy it, while perfectly registering what's going on, and periodically inquiring of our seducing language just what it thinks it's getting up to. But first we might pursue the logic of this metaphor that Nietzsche uses so frequently, both crossly and lovingly. His 'seductions of language' are a strange amalgam, poised with tantalising ambiguity, indeed like sexual seduction itself, between being active and being passive. But doesn't seduction really incline rather more towards one of these alternatives? The intuitive response is that it's active; yet a considered answer becomes less decisive. For seduction entices whatever is latent to make itself overt, and it does so by means of a careful attentiveness. It sets the stage; it expels distractions. It may consist in itself of an ostentatious display of preparation, of a barrage of signs, their meaning humming to be deciphered.[57] Seduction, above all, readies itself. It will have foreseen and cancelled all possible social distractions, switched incoming telephone calls to the answering machine, arranged fresh flowers, decided on the dinner, uncorked the wine, polished the table, put fresh sheets on the bed, and after all of this it can sit back to wait confidently for whatever may transpire. Its confidence resides not in securing the outcome it hopes for, but in its own readiness. Well before any overt gesture determines the ensuing scenario as actively seductive, thorough housework has already prepared the ground. An energetic passivity sits and waits. Then, to push on with this analogy, how does language itself manage to make ready the scenes of its own triumphs? Nietzsche's answer (for he nurses a cheerless view of seduction) is that it lays traps through grammar: 'a thought comes when "it" wants, not when "I" want: so that it is a *falsification* of the facts to say: the subject "I" is the condition of the predicate "think". *It* thinks; but that this "it" is precisely that famous old "I" is, to put it mildly, only an assumption, an assertion, above all not an "immediate certainty." For even with this "it thinks", one has already gone too far: this "it" already contains an *interpretation* of the event and does not belong to the event itself'.[58]

Yet, to extend Nietzsche's own reasoning, this same stricture could properly apply to language as well, once it too is treated as an agent. There *is* no isolable Language, in that it's no actor and has no power to seduce anyone. For there is no 'it' lurking behind ascribed linguistic agency, itself a retrospectively conjured-up and fanciful tale about what words in their natural life just do; words really without guile, in themselves plot-free as Nietzsche's lightning gleams. Then to invoke the 'seductions of language' is, it appears, an unhelpful way of speaking—although it is as an inspiring irritant. But need we still retain some notion that there are pitfalls in language? I want to maintain that the very features of syntax *do something*—so I need to find a way to assert this without having implicit recourse to a faintly diabolical machinery of Language the Deceiver and its cozened human speakers. Again, self-description is my test case here. Can I really talk, as I began to do, about the affect of grammar, without merely repeating all those florid difficulties about the seducing of reason by language?—Only, perhaps, by remarking on the telling *presence* of grammatical and syntactical affect, while strenuously refusing to construe this active presence as a distortion. Instead it might play a part akin to what Merleau-Ponty has called an unsuspected 'thought in speech'.[59] But I'll leave this in suspense for the moment, to turn to an instance of what would, for a hard-line Nietzschean (and far harder than the man himself), demonstrate a working seduction.

Self-naming's topography: where is it felt to happen?

> Nothing determines me from outside, not because nothing acts upon me, but on the contrary because I am, from the start, outside myself and open to the world.
>
> M. MERLEAU-PONTY[60]

'Outside from the start': This characteristically helpful formulation of Merleau-Ponty's short-circuits my convictions of my innerness. A misleading air of intimacy marks what is in fact already external: the out-there nature of language. Thought is active in speech, not in some silent mental preamble to utterance: 'Thought is no "internal" thing and does not exist independently of the world or of words'.[61] This mistaken 'interiority' of thinking, which really becomes alive to itself through the spoken word, is echoed in the awkward indeterminacy of self-categorising, which demands an animating will it can't acquire either as a completely external rhetorical act nor can draw solely from its private resources.

Entering into a self-description suffers badly from topographical metaphor. Is this, then, one flourishing subspecies of the 'seduction of language'— this metaphorical spatiality, so entrenched in thought? If so, self-describing could stake its own specialised claim to being an encampment of linguistic seduction, since there does appear to be some link between such spatial and consequently temporal figures of speech, and the strains inherent in self-naming (although to establish this one would need to find somewhere in the world an unlikely language devoid of spatial metaphor). How can I take on an identity? There's a flash of consent where I let myself into a category of social being, or there's a jarring reluctance when I demur; but what's the shape of these instants of will? Is there some hiatus which requires a dislocating leap, a balletic twist in mid air, in order to move from my separateness to installing myself in a collective being? This sketched transition is spatial; it's impossible to move clear away from this all this imagined topography, its gaps and its arches, its inwardness and its breadth, and from there its deeps and shallows. This metaphoricity so saturates thought that it's not matter of isolating it but of plumbing its presence. A quick tour of depth metaphor could run something like this:

It is a curious convention that physical depth should be the measure for 'profundity' in its sense of sagacity and that a literal 'superficiality', that belonging to the surface, should be synonymous with shallowness of feeling or judgement. This convention fascinates, since it's the vanishing point of what is to count as metaphor; there is an enticing blur where the metaphorical slips, almost indistinguishably, into the literal, seeming to dissolve any distinction between them. Examples swarm. Some figurative term referring to the passage from inner to outer is often used to characterise self-identification. Or, if I don't want to be taken 'at face value', one implication of that metaphor is that my truth crouches under my skin. Veracity's putative innerness has its many local histories. So under his sardonic banner of 'Skin and Intestines',[62] Wyndham Lewis attacks those fashions succeeding the 1914 World War, and which, parasitic on popular science, try to burrow into the innards of being:

> A preoccupation with the vitals of things is related to *vitalist* enthusiasms. 'Life' (of the Up Life! Down Art! cry) means invariably the smoking-hot inside of things, in contrast to the hard, cold, formal skull or carapace. The *emotional* of the bergsonian drama is the heat, moisture, shapelessness, and tremor of the vitals of life. The *intellectual* is the ectodermic case, the ideality of the animal machine *with its skin on*. Finally, the bergsonian (jamesesque, psycho-analytic, wagnerian Venusberg) philosophy of the hot

vitals—of the blood-stream, of vast cosmic emotion, gush and flow—is that of a *blind* organism. There are no Eyes in that philosophy.[63]

Once started, this kind of speculation about depth metaphor is indeed hard to restrain. It obsesses Michel Tournier's fictional narrator Robinson, who on his desert island describes in his notebook that awful literalness which jumps out at him from the most everyday language; in solitude, he scrutinises the pervasive idea of depth, in phrases such as 'a deep love'.[64] This reminds him of the reverence accorded to interiority at the expense of exteriority, as in the idea that people conceal inner treasures and that the further you excavate, the more you bring to light their riches. Yet what, Robinson muses, if there is no treasure within? Perhaps, then, only the curtain of the skin itself is truly significant, as it demarcates the outer from the inner.[65] The solipsist's sky is credited with a depth it does not really have, while everywhere a greater valuation is arbitrarily accorded to what is deep at the expense of what is extensive. 'It is a strange prejudice which sets a higher value on depth than on breadth, and which accepts "superficial" as meaning not of wide extent but "of little depth", whereas "deep", on the other hand, signifies "of great depth" and not "of small surface." Yet it seems to me that a feeling such as love is better measured, if it can be better measured at all, by the extent of its surface than by its degree of depth'.[66] In reaction to these hypnotic figures of speech, the longing for a purer language, scrubbed bare of spatial metaphors, can become fiercely stubborn; and Wittgenstein, too, was greatly exercised by language's topographies. 'The problems arising through a misinterpretation of our forms of language have the character of *depth*. They are deep disquietudes: their roots are as deep in us as the forms of our language and their significance is as great as the importance of our language.—Let us ask ourselves: why do we feel a grammatical place to be *deep*? (And that is what the depth of philosophy is.)'[67]

Preoccupied again with the directions ascribed to thought, Nietzsche's animated sketch traces the growth of human interiority as an idea. It is blown up, like a child's party balloon; 'All instincts which do not discharge themselves outwards will *receive an inward direction*—this is what I call *the internalisation of man*. It is only by this process that that grows up to man which later on is called his "soul." The entire inner world of man, being originally thin, as if it were stretched between two hides, has become expanded and extended, has received breadth, depth and height, in the same measure as man's outward discharge has been *checked*.[68] There is an immeasurable history to this spatialisation of thought. Hegel touches on it when he quotes Goethe's verse to support his own refusal of any immutable distinction between internality and externality, holding instead 'what is outer is, first of all, the same content as what is inner':[69]

Nature has no core or crust,
Here everything comes at once[70]

We could indeed come to the conclusion that epistemology itself is the product of a particular conceptual geography, and a geography which it has long since indifferently forgotten. Here, in a resolute attempt to grasp instead its habitual directionality of ideas, Deleuze has mapped the topography which shapes philosophies of truth: 'As we ask "what is it to be oriented in thought?" it appears that thought itself presupposes axes and orientations according to which it develops, that it has a geography before having a history, and that it traces dimensions before constructing systems'. Thus, he continues, the pre-Socratics 'placed thought inside the caverns and life, in the deep. They sought the secret of water and fire', whereas Platonism, with height as its Orient, looked to ascend. Post-Platonic philosophy has tended to exclude the ex-centric in the name of the essential, or of 'a meaning of history',[71] but the Cynics and Stoics had operated instead 'where there is no longer depth or height', neither contingency nor necessity, nor essences nor appearances; but instead, a myriad unstratified causes. Hercules, the Stoical hero, would drag his captures back from the heights or the depths and into the benevolent flatness of day. Everything takes place, and is said at, and must eventually return to this plain—even that great Idea of Platonism itself, its claims to epistemological and spiritual supremacy dethroned; as Socrates had archly inquired, was there also an Idea of hair, dirt, mud? Then the philosopher must creep attentively, for he is 'no longer the being of the caves, not Plato's soul or bird, but rather the creature on a level with the surface—a tick or louse'.[72] In this same deflationary and scrupulous spirit, Deleuze does not 'deny' depth and heights; instead he redraws the spread of surfaces, truly unexplored continents where whatever happens, happens. This isn't systematically opposed to elevation; it's simply what there is, for there is nowhere underneath or further back to go. The best place to hide is always at the surface. What is most deep is the skin.[73] Such intensely and literally down-to-earth thinking follows that of Lucretius, for whom Nature remained tirelessly diversified, never to be swept up into a single great body. A vitalism of seeds, or a pantheism of mothers, resulted.[74] That is Deleuze's rendition; and an anti-Platonism also marks Foucault's lack of concern with dredging up buried structures of belief, with acts of retrieval understood only as recovery, or as unearthing some Idea running below the outcropping of history. Instead the historicity which carries us is bellicose, restless, abraded by old battles; and just as there is no destiny or glorious teleology but instead accident, so temporalities are not quiescent. Economic, political, psychological; the discursive gears may be out of sync, shift roughly, or crash. Faced with this disarray, a benevolent positivism can only labour to delineate what lies irretrievably scattered, beyond reinstatement in some soothing established order; to accord it its idiosyncratic gravity, rather in the spirit of William Blake's insistence that 'a line is a line in its minutest subdivisions, strait or crooked it is itself and not intermeasurable with or by any thing else'.[75]

Then, insofar as self-description possesses its little streak of Platonism, we might conclude that it's a hopelessly flawed endeavour; and one induced by an anxious culture (if we can really like that terminology). Naturally undeterred by such speculative misgivings, our selves will continue to nurse their secret envelopes. Or perhaps clear plastic folders of imagined inner selves, which can then be flipped outward:

> My quietness has a man in it, he is transparent,
> and he carries me quietly, like a gondola through the streets[76]

Reprovingly ticking off metaphor is no good, and anyway metaphor will win. This seemingly universal spatial and temporal metaphoricity means that one wants at least to track its obstinate ubiquity, to incorporate these metaphors as natural features, and to not consider them as misleading defects, distortions, or seductions. To 'rehabilitate the surface' does make an encouraging slogan, and it starts up a useful polemic. But it would be idle indeed to proscribe the intuition which is compelled to think, for instance, that 'despite my composed and calm exterior, inside I am a morass of agitated feeling', or that wants to declare that it really is the heart, that the heart does hurt, and that's no metaphor. It does; but it is and it isn't. Undecidable for thought, in practice the figurative speech of interior depth remains solidly as it is. It is—to stage another of those captivating vanishing points between metaphorical and nonfigurative speech—profoundly embedded in language.

But one still cannot subside at this point of prudent compromise. I want rhetorically to defend the superficiality which entails interrogating that concept of interiority, pitched as body talk, which resurfaces as the 'integrity' demanded by any self-accounting which aims to be truthful. As to what the inside of my body might be, other than live meat of the kind made reassuringly familiar by recent art and by televised surgery, I have little conviction. Today's innermost self lurks subcutaneously, like the soul it gradually replaced. But in reality I live my life superficially, broadly, and sideways, out of the corner of my eye. I see out, not in. My eyes swivel outwards, to where all that is familiar to me lies. To be flat doesn't, though, mean that I see everything, plainly and dully in my panopticon's view. Espousing externality does not mean boredom, and what is one-dimensional retains its mysteries. If my unconscious is on the surface of my skin, fished up from the depths of a supposed interiority, nevertheless my skin wraps me all around and well out of my own field of vision. I can't see how it looks between my shoulder blades. A description of my unconscious is always given to me from elsewhere, is analysed in me by an onlooker. Perhaps emotionality, too, has its own external quality. It can arrive from the outside. This speculation repeats, oddly, the drift of astrology, where affect is beamed down, though the influencing machine of language is less starry, and noisier. But this vision soon falters; if at times feeling may palpably hang in a charged ether, seeming to belong to no one in particular, nonetheless one claimant or another will recapture a part of the affective field:

The day is nervous buff—the shakiness, is it inside the day or me?
Perhaps the passions that we feel don't quite belong to anyone
but hang outside us in the light like hoverflies, aping wasps and swivelling
and lashing up one storm of stripes. In tiny cones of air.
Yet you enact that feeling, as you usually *bzzzzzzzzzzzz* get to do it, while I,
I do this.[77]

'Gimme shelter' is a demand that easily coexists with that other familiar street cry, 'give me my space'. The travelogue of the self-describer is the passage through the self's narrow aperture into the broader reaches of communitarian being, walking out into a large bowl of the sheltering sky, an encircling social hoop. A self-locating speaker moves through possible categories spread over a vast field. The imperative to be *something* in this expansive world is a hard directive to familiarise myself in an exposed terrain. 'I, a stranger and afraid, / In a world I never made'. How, then, to make it mine? That act of identification which seems most inwardly found must rely on borrowed diction; its personal speech cannot be other than the most public, yet an illusion of shelter still shadows it. Zygmunt Baumann's remarks about the dream of home could readily be applied to the dream of the house of social being: 'Real, familiar houses hover awkwardly half-way between homes and prisons: the "home" of "home-sickness" is one house with a money-back guarantee in case it veers uncomfortably towards the prison end. Such a home is a dream of permanent abode; but permanence is the nightmare part of the dream. The "home" of "homesickness" keeps its seductive powers as long as it keeps its portability'.[78] And nothing appears more portable, more malleable than the promises of self-depiction; there's a place for us, somewhere, sometime, somehow. Everything can be custom-built to suit, the offer implies: Its realisation fails. As Heidegger has it, Man dwells in the house of language.[79] Man may, though, feel less comfortably at home in a prefab. And it is prefabrication which marks the societal identities available for purchase.

Still, sometimes a topography of my self located only uncertainly 'somewhere out there' may have its mild attraction. That fin de siècle sentiment of aesthetic withdrawal, which twitches away its skirts from the everyday—'Living? The servants will do that for us'[80]—can, ironically, find its faint echo in today's collectivities which allow my official engagement to mask my personal absence. Here I may substitute my designation for my presence. To join some church of identity, whether religious or secular, may permit my faith to be enacted for me, 'out there' in the world. Self-named, I'm already more than halfway out of my dully private skin. I am being lived. Through the illusory agency of my membership, my subscription, I can function vicariously, while I am reassuringly enrolled in the collectivity to which my solitariness could never attain.

The will to be, and truly being it

> Stout as a horse, affectionate, haughty, electrical,
> I and this mystery here we stand.
>
> WALT WHITMAN[81]

'Me and my attributes': The romantic hope that unsparing introspection may plumb the self's depths to dredge up its truth is deflated by self-labelling's reliance on hand-me-down phrases. Its rough and secondhand dealings may nevertheless stagger along under a crushing longing for authenticity. I want to show myself truly, and to make it relentlessly certain that I have been properly read. Struggling for this, I may try to short-circuit all obstacles by becoming declarative. One common enough proclamation begins, 'I'm the sort of person who . . .' and is followed by some cameo of myself as right-thinking, 'who under duress will remain faithful to my ideals' or 'who cannot live a life which entails deceit'. This speaker understands himself as ethical. Yet he has inadvertently set out his own advertisement, and of a flattering kind. Under that rubric of self-depiction, 'I'm someone who will always . . .', the most principled may convey only a reverent egotism. Such an immobilising self-characterisation can erode any practical ethics, and compound the difficulty which demands a pragmatic attack. But the inveterate self-describer will only understand the abandoning of self-description here as an act of cynicism, a coolly instrumental abjuration of moral guidance. Nonetheless, just such a 'cynicism' may be the prerequisite for a genuine altruism, free to work without proclaimed qualities and untrammelled by the prior and deathly attribution of 'That's the kind of person I am'. Yet some versions of ethics do incite unhelpful self-profiles, if they propose a concentration on the type of person I should be. If this kind of choosing a soul-type seems doomed, would a better approach stick at becoming something, rather than being it?[82] But even this aspect of 'becoming' still aims to credit its bearer, eventually, with characteristics. There seems to be something fatal in the aim to possess any attribute. But this reservation must also include setting out to have that attribute of having no attributes. Even the will to not be anything at all is still overwhelmed by its own project to not be. Dull enough as an observation, this fact still has repercussions for the deliberations involved in adopting an identity.

Are there any limits to performing? Aristotle, convinced that virtue was, like the proof of the pudding, best assessed by its results, sets out a conception of goodness which is resolutely practical, to do with achieved effects. This train of thought could be extended to conclude that only the performance signifies. Hegel inclines firmly to the Gospel's view that by their fruits ye shall know them, since 'the essential unity of inward and outer generally holds good; and hence it must be said that a person *is* what he *does*', leaving no scope for consolation to what he calls 'the mendacious vanity that warms itself with the consciousness of inner excellence' where its results are poor.[83] For my life's history offers final and eloquent testimony to what I am, irrespective of my self-conceptions: 'although a man may certainly dissemble and hide a good deal in single instances, still he cannot hide his inner self altogether; it reveals itself infallibly in the *decursus vitae* (the course of life) so that even in this connection, it must be said that a man is nothing but the series of his acts'. Yet to the author of the behaviour himself, more seems to be demanded of him than his flawless enacting of roles. He cannot emulate the case of that successful impostor, the ardent medical amateur who gains entry to a hospital with forged testimonials to enjoy a career of happily competent surgery. Take the case of a man gnawed by a secret feeling of inauthenticity, which dogs him despite his scrupulous observance of his responsibilities. On a strongly performative model, we could, with only subdued cynicism, argue as follows: If he's functioning as a devoted parent, a conscientious teacher, and a faithful husband, and if these are all effective as acts, what is there beyond such successful impersonations? What is there to be revealed behind his front of appearances? For perhaps there's even less than that melodramatic thing, 'a void', perhaps there's simply nothing at all, not even a blank space; nothing to worry about. Indeed, it can be pleasurable to deliberately play into the positional clichés that family life holds out—to talk the talk of an amiable parent to the point of self-parody. Or we could appeal to mathematics to try to reassure our 'inauthentic' man. Like a Venn diagram, the sector of being married partly overlaps the sector of being a state employee, which partly overlaps the sector of being a father, which partly overlaps that of being an adult son. The most heavily cross-hatched area of the diagram denotes their densest overlay; and just that shaded and irregular shape is what the ensemble of 'the self' is.[84] Isn't the truth of any life only the working conjunction of all such impersonations? If this character is so skilfully managing to button down this elaborate social upholstery, then why (asks the sceptical onlooker) should he rip all the stuffing out of it, in the name of some lack of inward conviction? Then this inner conviction that he seeks might prove even more intangible, for though he has the impression of inhabiting his own centre, his sensed concentricity could be considered instead as an overlay of many unrelated slivers of other people's lives.[85] The self is a bundle of results, a cluster of effects and outcomes. Or as Nietzsche paraphrases this realisation, 'L'effet, c'est moi'.[86]

Next, our successful impersonator of roles, not yet reassured, could attempt to console his guilt-ridden core by imagining its dispersal: 'Where the soul pretends unification or the self fabricates a coherent identity, the genealogist sets out to study the beginning—numberless beginnings, whose faint traces and hints of colour are readily seen by a historical eye. The analysis of descent permits the dissociation of the self, its recognition and displacement as an empty synthesis, in liberating a profusion of lost events'.[87] But I may preserve my own necessity by secretly anchoring myself to my solid social being and to my visibly written lines, a conviction readily maintained despite all such theories of the constructed self. Then the shadow of my inauthenticity remains free to rise. There is a well-worn ethics of authenticity,[88] but there is also an ethics which does not rely on wholeness, making on the contrary a virtue out of fragmentation. This is really more of an aesthetics of fragmentation, an imitative decentring, crudely mimetic; 'everything's broken up and alienated in contemporary life, so art, like life, should be fragmented, to be authentic'. An imitation of life is indeed what our conscientious actor of social roles lives; but this philosophy would be a miserable gruel to offer one who still longs for something to ring true 'underneath', solidly sustaining his skilful performances. For him this is a deeply unsatisfactory and chilly theoretical solution to his mortification at so successfully appearing to be that which, in his heart of hearts, he is not. (That was exactly Althusser's distress, to be touched on in the coming chapter.) Displaced from the warm centre of his own agency, his conscience cannot be assuaged. This conscience is not altruistic, since in fact he is doing excellently by others. Insistent that he should fully inhabit his acts, it's in his own eyes that his conscience has lessened his standing.

Perhaps that shadow, cast by a strong version of performance, is the secret retention of a notion of authenticity. Behind the brisk insistence that im-

personation is everything, there lingers a romanticism of 'the subject', lurking behind the façade. Swish aside its formal grey curtain, and there is not
the expected void after all, but instead the presence hovering triumphantly
in its writhing ectoplasm of effects. What a relief! Suddenly the thin world
of appearances is comfortably fleshed out. But what could really cheer up
our troubled role player is not this demonstration of spiritualism's secret revealed or any coolly theoretical defence of impersonation. He would need
some reconciliation of the truth of that necessary impersonality in performing a social part, with some better idea of how his own consent to perform
could enter into it, without undue cynicism.

This he might unearth through contemplating the nature of consent to a
common process which one does not exactly choose, yet within which one
may hope to find oneself—an act of self-description. Giving myself away to
find myself, I might even feel perversely and mysteriously generous. For
stepping into the public is sometimes presented as, in itself, an act of common virtue. There's frequently a promise of hope in societal identities, as
they offer new communalities in which loneliness might be assuaged and
some wide sea of optimism joined. Then that very gesture of joining may be
a mark of my own generosity towards the future. In practice, this gratifying
thought is harder to sustain. There is another version of giving myself away,
which results in my losing myself. Hegel's portrayal of self-awareness struggling to see itself in another, and 'another self-consciousness as itself', as its
very mode of entering societal life, soon becomes an account of a self happily wrecked as such by its purposiveness; 'In carrying out this law of its
heart, however, it learns that the individual, in doing so, cannot preserve
himself, but rather that the good can only be accomplished through the sacrifice of the individual; and self-consciousness becomes *virtue*'.[89] Extended,
I become turned inside out, like a glove; 'Speech and work are outer expressions in which the individual no longer keeps and possesses himself within
himself, but lets the inner get completely outside of him, leaving it to the
mercy of something other than himself'.[90] This inner, though, was always
constitutively shaky, for either too much inwardness was retained in what
had become officially the outer, or else too little. Fichte had also, if differently, held that you could only come into being as creative ego through the
state, outside yourself. Others among those now bundled together as 'German idealists' entertained some idea of a necessary self-objectification, a

readiness 'to be seen as'. For Schelling, 'Individuals are only phantoms, like the spectrum', and their true embodiment, again, was to be enacted in the state. How, though, could a phantom drift across into a societal corporeality? If, classically enough, knowing lay in my own recognition of my insufficiency, this very awareness was in itself a desire to change. Schelling's conception of absence was determinedly optimistic, marking that first vital movement of nothing out towards something, through a twist of inhibition; 'Whatever wants to grow, must first curtail itself'.[91] To become, I must move out of myself, and I start from my zero, the precursor to my mobility. My own cancellation is what kick-starts me.

But if this idealist tradition takes the business of entering social being to be demandingly fraught, although it is the ethical impulse's necessary path, the offer of contemporary identities is more straightforward: self-reconstruction, to achieve a self. In this respect, identity politics lies closer to a sacrificial religion than to a civic ethics. An act of giving the self away, like a bride, may be almost devotional. Or fervently sloughing off my old self, I may conduct my stripped being into a new dispensation, like a postulant nun stepping through the shrouded archway of a convent's closed order. But (to anticipate the coming chapter) if once in there I try to sign my will as a speaker entirely away to some Mother Superior of Language, then my zeal has overreached itself, having mistaken for pure virtue its own ardent embrace of the passivity of 'being spoken'.

Linguistic unease

> The I of each is to
>   the I of each
>   a kind of fretful speech
>   which sets a limit on itself;

MARIANNE MOORE[1]

A confession. I've long been nursing a shapeless suspicion that there's a particular guilt, associated both with writing and with taking on an identification, which is itself *partly* generated and fed by the workings of language. Might not language itself arouse an anxiety which it must also try, through its other circuits, to assuage? These remarks, though, will have little to do with the psychology of guilt, although I'm aware that psychoanalytic theory would want to know to what extent the proximity of 'language' to 'the unconscious' is being either assumed or ignored here. Perhaps to try to speak about a guilt carried at the level of language can only feebly parrot that familiar Lacanian account of the unconscious structured like a language.[2] And 'guilt' itself is a vague, catch-all, and easy word, one of the mildly negative emotions freely admitted to, as if it's perfectly innocuous. That in itself is suspicious. Some imagined maxim along the lines of 'The greater the guilt, the more swollen the ego that it masks' comes snaking to mind. Nevertheless, there may still be something rather different at work, if also quite modest—a surface emotionality *of* language itself which is carried, simply and broadly, on that level, and that this is somehow acutely in play when it comes to writing; that there's a lyrical guilt as well as a linguistic unease, the two knotted into each other through the curious temporal effects common to both. Perhaps there's not only a grammar of guilt but a shamefaced sociology of authorship. Unwilled plagiarism is one facet of this. Still, Fran Lebowitz can offer a brisk half-consolation here: 'Original thought is like original sin: both happened before you were born to people you could not possibly have met'.[3]

My suggestions remain tentative; and any generalisations about poetry need to be taken with the proper pinch of salt, since they're partial. I'm speculating in a hinterland between psychology and linguistics. Neither entirely of the *psyche* nor entirely of the *logos*, this 'linguistic unease' fishes up the drowned etymology of psychology. And then this interrogation must painfully bite its own tail. For while I cross-question the first person, I also deploy it heavily, if most often in its conveniently impersonal form.

'I' lies

The feeling of inauthenticity under certain linguistic circumstances, of not being able to tell the truth, however strenuously one struggles to reach it—isn't this feeling commoner than is usually acknowledged? But self-description's familiar doubts and torments aren't exclusively the writhings of some personal pathology. If I say 'I am an *x*'—or deny it—then I'm confident only that now I am something of a liar. As an article of blind faith, I'm compelled to suppose that this feeling is not purely idiosyncratic; this chapter will offer suggestions as to why it is not purely psychological.

An obvious first way in: The very grammar of the language of self-reference seems to demand, indeed to guarantee, an authenticity closely tied to originality. Yet simultaneously it cancels this possibility. Any *I* seems to speak for and from herself; her utterance comes from her own mouth in the first person pronoun which is hers, if only for just so long as she pronounces it. Yet as a human speaker, she knows that it's also everyone's, and that this grammatical offer of uniqueness is untrue, always snatched away. The *I* which speaks out from only one place is simultaneously everyone's everywhere; it's the linguistic marker of rarity but is always also aggressively democratic. To appropriate Hegel here: 'When I say *I*, I mean myself as this singular, quite determinate person. But when I say *I* I do not in fact express anything particular about myself. Anyone else is also *I* and although in calling myself *I*, I certainly mean me, this single person, what I say is still something completely universal'.[4] My *I* never does exist, except (and critically) as a momentary spasmodic site of space–time individuation, and its mocking promise of linguistic originality must be, and always is, thwarted in order for language to exist in its proper communality.[5]

All this is old hat. Wittgenstein floated the idea of a private language only to capsize it as oxymoronic; such interiority was impossible because it guaranteed unintelligibility. Derrida has described the emptiness of a linguistic ownership which is always appropriated: 'The structure of theft already lodges (itself in) the relation of speech to language' and 'The speaking subject discusses his irreducible secondarity, his origin that is always already eluded; [. . .] a place that is always missing'.[6] My autobiography always arrives from somewhere outside me; my narrating *I* is really anybody's, promiscuously. Never mind the coming story of my life; simply to enunciate that initial 'I' makes me slow down in confusion.

But maybe the 'structure of theft' is still closer again to home than 'in the relation of speech to language'; perhaps it's lurking in the language itself and, a bold burglar, had put its feet up there long before the unsuspecting speaker strolls into it. To be stripped bare of ownership isn't the only kind of linguistic dispossession, for this can also come about through plenitude. Sheer proliferation bewilders. Artaud writes desperately of forgetting how to think, of interruptions and 'fissures' which thwart his articulation and can never be mended, often because he is rushed down diversions which branch out unstoppably; 'There is therefore one single thing which destroys my ideas [. . .]. Something furtive which robs me of the words *I have found*, which reduces my terseness of mind, progressively destroying the bulk of my ideas within its own matter'.[7] He insists that such broken thought is 'terribly abnormal', radically destructive, and not merely what happens to everyone:

> In a way, we might consider the impossibility of formulating and
> prolonging thought on the same level as the stammering which overcomes
> my external utterances just about every time I want to speak. Then it is as if

my thought shrinks every time it wants to manifest itself and this is the contradiction which slaps my inner thought down inwardly, compresses it like a spasm. The thought, the expression stops because the flow is too powerful, the brain wants to say too many things, it thinks all at once, ten thoughts instead of one rush towards the exit, the brain sees thought as a unit in full detail and it also sees all the multiple points of view with which it could ally itself and the forms with which it could endow them. A vast conceptual juxtaposition, all seemingly more essential and also more dubious than the next and which all the syntactic brackets in the world would never be able to express and explain.[8]

His readers, if filled with an empathy of recognition, may want to challenge his assertion of the abnormality of this experience. He voices a familiar enough chaos which cannot be tidied away by the concept of the I's shortcomings. That false feeling of an I-pronouncement can't be to do simply with its air of claiming to originate, despite that common sensation that one is first being spoken by language, that 'I' is a pretender to an impossible throne. In this vein Heidegger describes language as an invocation to which man, although its ostensible speaker, must resonate. Or as The Platters less gloriously had it, Oh yes, *I'm* the great pretender. Yet it would be absurd to attach so much blame to the grammar of 'I' which is, after all, necessarily everyone's for language to be possible—as if secretly you longed for a marker, such as that private language which Wittgenstein mocked, all of your own. That idea of the I's linguistic 'alienation' can only get so much done, and an unhappy mess soon overwhelms its efforts at taking on all the housework. Despite Wittgenstein's hygienist notion of philosophy as a broom and its task as sweeping up language's detritus, we're stuck with a recalcitrant heaped-up untidiness, the awkwardness stubbornly attached to using the first person.

A liar writes

When I—for I can't speak for anyone else, and yet probably this emotion is widespread—when I write *I* and follow up the pronoun with a self-description, feelings of fraud grip me. Not always: I can easily say, 'I'm worn out; I've just got the shopping bags home on the bus', but certainly can't say, for instance, 'I'm a writer'. Then only under the most baroque circumstances would I have to utter, 'I'm a woman'. Steering clear of the great sociological–sexual categories of identity, which are almost easier to grasp in their historical discomfiture, just what is the awkwardness of the particular self-attribution 'I'm a writer?' Is it the halo of self-regarding leisure alone— or dread of the demand to prove it by coming up with the goods? Is it the incongruence of the stamp of a supposed authorial originality with the cultural capital, always derived and borrowed, on which my writing *I* draws? Is it that the real novelty of anyone's *I* resides not in its pronouncements but in its accidents—its style, unwilled and incriminating as a fingerprint, its lingering cadences, its flavour, or its smell, almost? The writer may, even to her own revulsion, hit on a tone arbitrary and inimitable as a signature. These aspects are completely beyond my management, a fact which may or may not be worrying. But it does force a gap between notions of 'originality' and of 'control'. There's a hum of language at my ear; I swat it away, it rises up to resettle in thick clouds. It's outside me, I do not make it up, and yet it doesn't quite make me up. I go on trying inside this doubled failure of origination. I learnt my English out of books, which perhaps increased my sense of learning it as a foreign language, as a borrowed or a stolen thing, but this impression of displacement isn't solely due to any such biographical accident. So my guess is that while indeed there's an embarrassing sociology of 'being a writer' (let alone a parodic element of being an unworthy candidate for ordination, called to a vocation), there's also something more intimately to do with the imperatives of writing, something which is an intensification of a common enough guilt.

To claim to be a writer is like making a special claim to be a breather. It's easy enough if you have the minimal materials, and the activity can be carried out secretively. A student confesses 'I don't want to admit to my friends that I write. I won't come out to them'. But everyone does it, I want to reassure her; it's quite natural, really nothing to be ashamed of; my phrases are unconvincing emollients which would only sharpen anxiety. Then her next worry would come hard on its heels: 'And exactly because everyone does it, what right do I have to make public my own concerns? Why should my life's ordinary preoccupations be of the least interest to anyone else?' One hears this concern a hundred times. It's a serious question, and it can't be properly addressed as merely evidence of a quite frequently female psychology of low self-confidence. Many who've survived creative writing classes must also feel silent doubt when exhorted to just describe what they've experienced. (In place of the amiable pedagogies of 'creative writing', one longs to substitute a new practice of 'destructive writing'. Then we'd arrive in time at a happy synthesis of sheer Writing, where all zones are democratically and mundanely 'creative', yet none is protected from that fearsome risk of being taken seriously.) It is a further benign cruelty to encourage such students of creative writing to 'find their own voices', especially when, under the same institutional roof, a pedagogy of criticism may be drilling them in the intertextuality of literature, where everything's quotation. This hopeless drive for originality resembles the problem of writing an original love letter (or, rather, a convincing letter, since any emotional originality here is impossible: the truer the love, the more unapologetically ordinary its language)—a letter that could convince its author of its constancy and of hers, when inevitably she finds herself echoing the same expressions used to others before. It is a linguistic humiliation when the apparent rarity and singularity of feeling announces itself as, after all, condemned to verbal repetition, yet it seems cheapskate to reiterate the phrases written in all sincerity over the decades. *Così fan tutte* is from this angle a hideously upsetting opera (to sidestep the question of its truth) since in its cruel and backwards logic, what generates love is playing the part of a lover. But if there's no originality in emotion, there's none in language. This reflection is hardly consoling. (Perhaps, then, the real inquiry to put to the impenetrable object of one's affections is not the standard 'Do you love me?'—always fatal, since any positive answer to it, irrespective of its accuracy, must always be structured as a lie—but a twist on this: A 'Do I love you?', not as introspection but asked aloud of the object, is more likely to get an informative response.)

While I can't believe in a selfhood which is any other than generated by language over time, I can still lack conviction if I speak of myself in the necessarily settled language of a sociologised subject. This self-describing 'I' produces an unease which can't be mollified by any theory of its constructed nature. The falseness of my persona telling its tale resounds in my own ears despite my best attempt at accuracy, and however plausible it may sound to its audience. What purports to be 'I' speaks back to me, and I can't quite believe what I hear it say. My uncertainty isn't so much with lying to others, which I think I'd know about, as it is with lying to myself, which I wouldn't. Polonius's strictures in *Hamlet*, 'to thine own self be true, / And it must follow, as the night the day, / Thou canst not then be false to any man' offer me not an instance of tautology but of hopelessness. No solace can be found in the usual evasions—for example, that what you write is simply floated out with no destination, in no expectation that it should be read. Or that writing is one prolonged act of instructive repudiation—getting rid of it, in order to find out just what it is that you think. For then the rational gesture would be—to delete the work. Then there's the figure of the writer costumed as a tease, the jack-in-the-box who'll elaborately hide himself only to bob up again. Underlying such familiar equivocating, what persists is a recognition of being as derived as I am derivative. What's a style? A veneer, irresistibly imposed, yet by no identifiable agency. As with my physical appearance, it's not what I'd have chosen, given a free hand, but it's what I'm stuck with and have to live with. Tracing a writing style in others, I can't refashion mine. Easy enough to parody myself, but impossible to work up a truly fresh style, not even by theft.

But in the case of poetry, it's often seemed a relief *not* to possess that old desideratum, 'a voice', and not to resemble oneself. In Foucault's incantation: 'I am no doubt not the only one who writes in order to have no face. Do not ask me who I am and do not ask me to remain the same'.[9] Like many others, I imagine, I can only leave a poem alone once it no longer resembles any product of mine, even if it may still get read later as 'characteristic' of its writer. Here the strange convention of the poetry reading ushers in a theatrical self with a vengeance, the performing *I* bringing her accidents of voice and costume and mannerisms to flesh out her starved text, married and reconstituted with it in fullness before all eyes, like wartime powdered egg soaked in water. Inside this show and working against it, the borderline inauthenticity of the lyric 'I' gets relieved only inside the performed I's speaking, where everyone, you hope, finally sees the truth of the matter— that it isn't you. Yet there are more plausible and simpler ways of defamiliarising oneself. Does the writer nonetheless repeat the dubious *I* with an agnostic's wager of making, against all odds, a successful appeal, or repeat in a trusting dream of telepathy? Despite such doubts, one still circulates something on paper; and sometimes people speak as if only the act of publishing could fix any trace of this half-repudiated *I* onto the world's surface. If self-description remains a dangerous fiction, there's the anchorage of a signed piece of work; so Marguerite Yourcenar has spoken of an uncertain and floating sense of self, pinned down only by the work she happened to have written.[10]

Is this discrepancy between the glue of the printed byline and the hesitancy of the lying writer the reason for that sharp embarrassment at the sight of something of mine in print? Posting a typescript to its publisher, I've thrown away that work. I haven't exactly disavowed its contents, but it must take its chances. I don't know how I'd defend it if asked to, and certainly don't ever want to see it again. However serious its effort, once it's written and sent off, then it's also written off. Somewhere in her diaries, Virginia Woolf mentions the embarrassment of noticing a letter she'd sent lying around in the house of the friend who'd received it. What familiar shame, though, is this? It arouses faint thoughts of the sequel to the end of the affair, when you'd far rather not clap eyes again on the lost person who once aroused such devastating emotion. It's unseemly for me to see my letter, once sent. It's no longer for my eyes. Is glimpsing it disconcerting because it's relentlessly out in the world, taken over, no longer mine to recall and revise? 'The word in language is half someone else's. [. . .] Language is not a neutral medium that passes freely and easily into the private property of the speaker's intentions; it is populated—overpopulated—with the intentions of others. Expropriating it, forcing it to submit to one's own intentions and accents, is a difficult and complicated process', wrote Bakhtin.[11] But suppose you suspect that language itself also possesses its own designs and that your word is already not 'half' but is wholly 'someone else's'—is already *everyone* else's—and can only be copied, or stolen back again?

Then suppose that things are worse again than this. Perhaps some of this discomfiture is that, while I quietly believe that I cannot be seen, any letter in my handwriting gives the lie to this conviction of mine; it's evidence before all else for the ontological prosecution. It looks as if I must be visible to others after all since I leave, and choose to leave, these papery trails everywhere behind me. Yet no one should be taken in by them. Emily Dickinson describes a disembodiedness here, but she revels in it: 'A letter always feels to me like immortality because it is the mind alone without corporeal friend. Indebted in our talk to attitude and accent, there seems a spectral power in thought that walks alone'.[12] Less spiritual, I can only feel that to catch sight of myself as if dead, to become a revenant, is—to feel sheepish. Yet I'd rather go with phenomenology's truth to accept that I do live outside myself, am

clean of all depths, am no darkly glowing cavity stuffed with dreaming se-
crets. So a first inspection in an art gallery of Damien Hirst's *Mother and
Child Divided* came as a relief—neither the dead cow nor the dead calf's
skull offered the least vacant space for the soul or the unconscious, for all
was crammed full of pallid organs, right up to the edge of the skin. Pronouncements, once published, also come to lack interiority. Enunciation
comes from the outside. Its most magisterial forms make this all too clear.
The weekly winning lottery numbers, once announced, take on a blinding
self-evidence. Of course it's 2, 16, 39, 44, et cetera—how come I hadn't remembered their proper sequence at the time I filled out my ticket? These are
numbers always known, yet somehow stupidly forgotten, incorrectly transcribed. Broadcast, they have all the gravitas of an Ian Hamilton Finlay
maxim handsomely lettered on stone, noble, inevitable. They're given from
elsewhere, like Moses' tablets borne down from the mountain—alas, such
retrospective knowledge always arrives too late. I should consistently espouse
this being 'outside from the start' in its lived intelligibility[13]—yet it must
have its limits for me, since the surprise of glimpsing my letter propped up
at its destination still remains a near-death experience, as if it's a sliver of
what it's violently improper for me to see: my own death. My letter, though,
is living on very nicely without me. It flourishes better alone, since it's one
witness to my past that I can no longer argue with. There's enough evidence
of autobiography as thanatology: 'Everything that we inscribe in the living
present of our relation to others already carries, always, the signature of
memoirs-from-beyond-the-grave', Derrida writes.[14] 'All talk of "my life" is
talking about death', concludes Parret.[15] And even the modern fable of 'the
death of the author' lapses where it condemns a still-living writer to return,
unhappily, to haunt her own productions; it's not gratifying to be the *Un-
heimlich* who hasn't quite expired, so who can't be in any position to make a
comeback.

   If my letter is something that survives me even during my lifetime, how
absolutely am I dispossessed by my graphic traces? Am I, in practice, written? Sometimes it sounds more desirable that I *should* be written. In an
ironic twist to the much-needed, if largely unwritten, history of modern
rhetoric, it's Heidegger who has proposed a benevolent account of linguistic
passivity. His is a blocking-in of ideas, its propositions tied, arched in together, like dry-stone walling. Any summary must be tentative—but in brief:

His positive conception of invocation renders calls as summons into being, like God's and Adam's joint exercises in naming species before the Fall, and not as accusations. An active silence calls forth a naming which is far from any self-generated descriptiveness: 'Man acts as though he were the shaper and master of language, while in fact language remains the master of man. When this relation of dominance gets inverted, man hits upon strange manoeuvres. Language becomes the means of expression. As expression, language can decay into a mere medium for the printed word'.[16] In place of such debased expressivity, there's an ideal power of stillness to which speaking is a response. Stillness is a fullness, and its 'peal' is bidding or invocation. To hear becomes dynamic, a concentrated attentiveness. Then 'Language speaks'. It's in charge, but its rule is not repressive—on the contrary, it's markedly inventive. 'Does it merely deck out things with words of a language? No. This naming does not hand out titles, it does not apply terms, but it calls into the word. The naming calls'.[17] So, for Heidegger, to name is not the same as to bestow an identification, and it does not work through a wound. Originary naming is without threat. That's unlike other accounts of categorising, such as Althusser's interpellative tableau in which naming brings into being by issuing an aggressive charge against its addressee. Heidegger's calling does have its own energetic tension, and invocation also guarantees a lively distance. To answer his own questions of 'What is it to speak? What is this naming?', Heidegger goes straight to the praxis of poetry. 'Language speaks' in the poem, and marks a productive nonidentification. 'Language speaks in that the command of dif-ference calls world and things into the simple onefold of their intimacy', but in the same breath, 'Language goes on as the taking place or occurring of the dif-ference for world and things'.[18] Here is a high conception of poetic function which lifts language above 'man' and towers above any local concerns with the guilt of authorship. I'll resume a beetle's-eye view.

A liar tries lyric

Poetry in its composing is an inrush of others' voices, and in this respect it is no more than a licensed intensification of the very same property in prose. So 'finding one's own voice' must be an always frustrated search, fishing around in a strange fry-up or a bouillabaisse in which half-forgotten spiky or slimy things bubble up to the surface. Words crowd in uninvited, regardless of sense, flocking not through the brain but through the ear, like the Byzantine iconography of Christ's conception. This is well established. Jakobson writes mildly, 'paronomasia, a semantic confrontation of phonemically similar words irrespective of any etymological connection, plays a considerable role in the life of language'.[19] In poetry you may succeed in exploiting its tacit permission to put sound in command over semantic meaning. Sound runs on alone, well ahead of the writer's tactics. The aural laws of rhyme both precede and dictate its incarnation—and this is only one element of an enforced passivity within the very genre where that annoying term 'creativity' supposedly holds court most forcefully. Style in its idiosyncratic rarity is often recognisable without its author's written signature. This tone isn't produced by my deliberation, any more than I can alter my stature by taking thought. This fact can be an irritant. It's all well beyond control. I may suffer not from galloping consumption but from galloping metaphor. Yet the lyric 'I' also advertises its simulacrum of control under the guise of form. It's a profound artifice, and the writer and reader both know it. There's a semblance here of craft, but craft of a strange sort, since it can only be exercised retrospectively. Held by form, I work backwards, chipping away at words, until maybe something gets uncovered which I can acknowledge as what I might have had to say.

Yet there are venerable alternatives to this notion of thought being made in the ear. Again it's Heidegger who proposes a high and a genial account of poetry as dictation. It utters and is heard as a calm and clear call: 'For, strictly, it is language that speaks. Man first speaks when and only when he responds to language by listening to its appeal. [. . .] The responding in which man authentically listens to the appeal of language is that which speaks in the element of poetry'.[20] Heidegger proffers his own brand of knowing through an attentive waiting, held in a listening reserve to hear the commanding peal of stillness. What's important is 'learning to live in the speaking of language', and this needs a capacity to respond through listening, 'anticipating in reserve'. A dynamic hearing, then, is needed. Poetry marks a resonant absence, and Heidegger, elucidating one of Georg Trakl's lyrics, demonstrates what he means by this notion of listening to its calling. But aren't things always more agitated from the point of view of the writer, even one who seems serene once beached on the page?

You see what you've said only as you look at what's cropped up on your page. Here again, some tentative concept of 'retrospective knowledge' is endlessly enticing, breathes a doubtful charm, and may hold wide sway, for how often in life do you discover what you meant via some backwards route? But it's an odd idea: What can it mean to only *come to know backwards*? And what curious kind of credit might anyone ever take for such an over-the-shoulder knowing, to see what you 'meant to say' only in the course of, or just after, the act of writing down? How should I speak for something that has enacted itself ahead of me? As Tristan Tzara remarked, with dazzling accuracy, 'Thought is made in the mouth'[21]—but it reverberates also in the ear, a more passive orifice. And there is a puzzle of that necessary fertile passivity involved in finishing a piece of writing, which literary criticism might then overgenerously hail as exemplifying 'control' —that it's in practice a febrile 'being written' which seems to turn half-mechanically on the very stuff, the active materiality, of words. This isn't the contingency of the relation of sound to sense, which Mallarmé worried over when he explained that both the words 'la nuit' and 'le jour' sounded wrong to him for what they denoted because the sound of 'nuit' had a light timbre (as it does in the English 'night'), yet the sound of 'jour' had a dark timbre.[22] But it is something differently contingent; this process, labelled as a knowing craft, is actually given to its writer through the words' material. Any rationality gets exercised largely in retrospect, through self-editing. Writing, you can feel like a blindfolded sculptor slapped around the head by damp lumps of clay which you must try to seize and throw back at the haphazardly forming art object before it stiffens itself into some shape you never quite intended. This sense had embarrassed me, not only because this being 'written through' by the energetic materiality of words seemed to go largely unacknowledged, but also because I didn't want to have to espouse unconvincing theories of 'irrationality' to cope with it. 'When the mind is like a hall in which thought is a voice speaking, the voice is always that of someone else',[23] describes one impression of being spoken through. But there's also a less straightforward directionality, one which is not 'through' the writer as conduit and not quite despite the writer—but *across*. The common experience of the retrospective knowledge that rears up from the page can be alarming, not because of its possibly worrying content, but because the inherent force of the linguistic process is revealed in a disquietingly oblique way, and the way it has spoken is somehow transverse, is *across* the writer.

The headache of this adverb 'across' is how to figure its directionality. A spatial metaphor of direction from down to up, or the reverse, would be easier, espousing either one's abasement before, or one's control of, language. And yet. We know about 'the death of the author'—still, in the morgue, toes can itch to twitch. Heidegger writes that speakers inhabit the house of language. Yes—but when the landlord calls round to collect the rent, isn't there likely to be some backchat? Agreed, the sensation that one's being made, like a nervous secretary, to 'take a letter' by the old-fashioned boss, Poetic Language, must be common enough. Still I'd rather revive some notion of the dialectic as a quite modest mutuality between the great dictator Language and the writer, even if the boss inevitably retains the upper hand. If kneaded by language, then needed by language. Reaching for a fragment of mastery always falls short. But you do try. Otherwise there are two standard ways of considering the problem. You could make an aesthetic out of varnishing your fingernails, reclining under the autonomous power of language in a blissfully resigned surrender to the process of being written—or else you could set your jaw at a stern angle and beat the language trollop into behaving herself while you shape her up nicely in verse. Neither aesthetic seems enticing or accurate. To write is both a duller and yet a more disconcerting matter than either one of this pair of unattractive metaphors implies. And it's arguable that a slogan of 'allowing the free play of the signifier' or 'conceding control to the signifier' secretly elevates an older notion of authorial power, since the writer is then, by special appointment, the vatic mouthpiece through which the language frolics. Its opposite, an unwavering control over the signifier in the name of 'craft', is coldly unrealistic.

In practice, a hurried pruning and snipping away at the thickets of verbal foliage luxuriating everywhere across the page can turn the poet into a determined topiarist, one hell-bent on shaping a peacock where a wilful bushiness is running riot. Embarrassment lies partly in finding out, too late again, that one has, despite all one's vigilance, been once more done over by language. Sound-determinations and puns have surreptitiously issued their usual forceful dictations, so that I have written both above and beneath what I 'really meant'. Then comes a confession of near helplessness, such as W. S. Graham's:

What is the language using us for?
I don't know. Have the words ever
Made anything of you, near a kind
Of truth you thought you were? Me
Neither.[24]

So a shamefaced 'That is not it, that is not what I meant at all' may arise in response to some amiable critic whose congratulations to the poet on her 'choice of language' are commendations she can't accept with a clear conscience, since she senses that language has arbitrarily lighted upon her, and that really she had intended to imply far *less* than the critic has so conscientiously unearthed from her text. The impact of sheer contingency may get a hearing, but often only as a defence against the accusation that an obscure reference is 'elitist'. The writer may retort, 'No, it's not elitist, it's aleatory—it's chance, I wanted to incorporate accident into my work to suggest randomness, a lack of solemnity, and so let the air in a little'. But if you don't happen to buy that line, then the domination of accident will go unmentioned. The missing question here can't be put as a problem of authorial volition or a failure of linguistic accounting, such as Jean-Claude Milner on the linguist's domain as slipped under a sardonic banner of 'proud to be boring'.[25] It won't be, What does the author or the linguist want? but, What does the language want? A question with something of Graham's:

What is the language using us for?
It uses us all and in its dark
Of dark actions selections differ.[26]

The linguist Roman Jakobson dwells on the writer's lack of control, prefacing his remarks with a qualification from Saussure on its indifference as to whether the critic on the one hand, and the poet on the other, might like it or not. Sheer accident could not, Jakobson thinks, possibly determine the poetic complexities he digs up through his own linguistic analyses; such a rich design must be accorded to the poet, since 'any significant poetic composition, whether it is an improvisation or the fruit of long and painstaking labour, implies a goal-oriented choice of verbal material'.[27] But the poet is not always, continues Jakobson, the deliberating chooser: 'There remains, however, an open question: whether in certain cases intuitive verbal latency does not precede and underlie even such a conscious consideration. The rational account (prise de conscience) of the very framework may arise in the author ex post facto or never at all'.[28] This is delicate and compelling ground, rarely discussed, although Jakobson has retrieved some historical precedents. So Schiller, corresponding with Goethe, held that the poet starts off 'merely with the unconscious'—but Goethe replied that he himself wanted to go further, to assert that true poetic creation happened unconsciously, while everything done after careful reasoning happened only casually. And the early twentieth-century Russian formalist poet Khlebnikov, continues Jakobson, 'joined all those poets who acknowledged that a complex verbal design may be inherent in their work irrespective of their apprehension and volition (*que . . . le versificateur . . . le veuille ou non*) or—to use William Blake's testimony—"without Premeditation and even against my Will."'[29] Jakobson scrutinises Khlebnikov's analysis of his 'Grasshopper' to establish that even the poet's retrospective analyses of its sound patterns—which occurred, as Khlebnikov says, 'without the wish of the one who wrote this nonsense'— fell well short of being exhaustive. Linguist easily outstrips poet in his exegesis of the phonemes' patterning: 'The chain of quintets which dominate the phonological structuration of this passage can be neither fortuitous nor poetically indifferent. Not only the poet himself, originally unaware of the underlying contrivance, but also his responsive readers spontaneously perceive the astonishing integrity of the cited lines without unearthing their foundations'.[30] Jakobson, however, ploughs on to reveal a formal ingenuity of which its author is innocent: 'The poet's metalanguage may lag far behind his poetic language and Khlebnikov proves it . . . by the substantial gaps in his observations'.[31] Then who, or rather what, has done this sophisticated poetic choosing? Jakobson's tentative phrase is 'intuitive verbal latency'. This seems close in its implications to a concept of 'the remainder of language', especially if one pushes this thought onward a little further, to reach 'the unconscious of language'.

But suppose one just rejigged the idea of 'poet' to mean—anyone who submits to words for the time being, but with the clear plan of fighting back, through self-editing, later on? Or is this just what's tacitly understood and accepted by most people anyway, and is it labouring an unremarkable point quietly taken for granted to dwell on this backwards aspect to writing? Quite probably. Still, there's an obstinate temporal problem here—a more imme-diate puzzle about time than is given by the conception of the writer consti-tuted by habitual self-checking. There's a strange *time* of rhyme. (The felici-tous rhyming of these two words in English makes one long to throw in 'mime' as well, like a latter-day follower of Jean-Pierre Brisset, the linguist who entertained an idiosyncratic etymology founded on sound-associations.) You anticipate the rhyme's arrival, but you can hear it in retrospect; aurally, it works forwards and backwards, although on the page you can see it com-ing. Though conventions such as the couplet or terza rima establish their own aural regularities, for a less rigorously shaped writing, only an aural hope can be entertained by the ear. Then it works by a gratified anticipation, or else through jarring and denial. Jakobson talks of a 'regressive action' in lan-guage, illustrating this with a slip by a radio announcer whose actual script, 'the convention was in session', he broadcast instead as 'the confession was in session'; so Jakobson's 'regressive assimilative influence' had been exerted by 'session' upon 'convention'.[32] It's the sort of example which Sebastiano Tim-panaro would seize upon later in his *The Freudian Slip*[33]—while an orthodox Freudian reading would gladly have made more of that substituted word 'confession'. It's also a case of reading-into-speech, in which the radio an-nouncer's eye has run ahead on his page and his eye has instructed his tongue. But writing is a different case, for sound-anticipation runs in the ear well before the eye gets to track and to pull back what's typed. Instead, the ear instructs the eye, while reason must intervene later. This eccentric tem-porality, this time of rhyme in its strange undecidability, is an instance of ret-rospective knowledge.

Jean-Jacques Lecercle's electrifying *The Violence of Language* (1990) may have laid the foundations for that desirable third path between a sheer hege-mony of Language on the one hand and the controlling Writer on the other. Although he politely concedes to the authority of the poet, this is a conces-sion that the implications of his own work undercut—most usefully so, for they relieve the poet's private awkwardness at being written, and at scrab-bling for belated self-editing. It gives a nonpsychologised account of this process, in part through a description of how metaphors work: through ramification. It elaborates the odd potential of that 'multiple analysis' of lan-guage espoused by Brisset, whose 'etymology gone mad' took itself to be the truth not about words but about the world, in that 'all the ideas expressed with similar sounds have the same origin and all refer, initially, to the same subject'.[34] Here's an abbreviated example:

> Les dents, la bouche (The teeth, the mouth)
> Les dents la bouchent (Teeth block it)
> L'aidant la bouche (The mouth helps it [the blocking process])
> L'aide en la bouche (Help in the mouth)
> Laides en la bouche ([Teeth are] Ugly in the mouth)
> Lait dans la bouche (Milk in the mouth)
> Les dents-là bouche! (Block [hide] those teeth!)

One of many engaging questions raised by Lecercle is: How far does language actually behave, against the wisdom of modern linguistic opinion, just as Brisset suggests? My own footnote to this surmise would ask if this isn't a phenomenon which dogs the act of writing poetry. Not the familiar critical idea of an 'ambiguity of meaning', which suggests finely poised alternatives among richly suggestive interpretations under the control of the skilful poet; but a far less malleable affair, a continuous white noise, an anarchic whirring-away, unstoppable, relentless, sinking sometimes into the background, sometimes dominant in full cry. So homophony affords just one fertile menace among many others here—words which deploy the same sounds for different semantic ends, such as 'rough' and 'ruff', so congenitally at risk from the interference of their double or triple meanings. Once you hear them in a room which demands close listening or you scrutinise them laid out on the page, those suppressed other meanings cannot but spring forward. And what reading a poem entails is facing it down, staring at it until you're at risk of dissolving it into a plurality of possible meanings, or are a little further on towards nonsense. Or it reduces you to helpless wanderings down its byways, down thin goat-paths of association. You put it at your mercy, but you are put at its mercy. You're never sure which of you has got the upper hand, or of quite what to make of this half-acknowledged struggle.

These concerns are familiar enough from nonpoetic contexts, and the idea that there's method in linguistic madness is venerable. Freud differently exploits it in his many analyses of dreams and jokes. *The Interpretation of Dreams* offers 'condensation' as one subclass of those overdeterminations which characterise the content of dreams, as he unpacks a chain of jammed-together meanings out of the 'nonsense' words or strange neologisms which the dreamer utters or reads.[35] A vast scholarly literature now annotates or interrogates this work. Among those who are mildly sceptical, Timpanaro's discussion of parapraxes deploys philology, the effects of banalisation, and printers' errors to cross-question Freud's *The Psychopathology of Everyday Life*, inquiring to what extent all linguistic slips may be attributed to a 'Freudian' motive. Timpanaro also asks whether instead of 'the polyglot unconscious', a more prosaic explanation in terms of a 'superficial psychology' such as a haplography (the shortening of a sound duplicated in a word) may be found.[36] He doesn't, he explains, want to follow Freud's belief that neurophysiological and other mechanical sources are, while real enough in themselves, significant largely as occasions to let a psychically driven slip flourish. Instead he ventures a revised version of the unconscious; could there be 'a much more mechanical–instinctual unconscious, and thus one less connected with the individual history of the person who committed the "slip"?'[37] How close in their ultimate effects, although not remotely in method, Timpanaro's suggestions are to Lecercle's conception of 'the remainder' of language is debatable, for both seem to propose an underbelly of language, vast enough to overwhelm any speaker. Less demanding is the antipsychiatrist R. D. Laing's liking for examples of the misattributed insanity that follows if you fail to decipher condensed speech. So when a young schizophrenic patient declares of herself that she 'was born under a black sun. She's the occidental sun', Laing delightedly comments that she really was 'the accidental black son'—unwanted, scorched by family hatred.[38]

Poetry, you could say, is systematically 'mad language', although not at all because of its authors' psychic tendencies, but merely because that half-latent unreason endemic to all ordinary language is professionally exploited by poetry. That—not something more ethereally glorious—is what poetry does, what it is. The writer is then in the delicate position of giving her limited assent to this craziness in its infinite ramification of sound-associations and puns and affective cadence. How grudgingly or how readily that assent will be given depends partly on the fluctuations of taste and fashion. In short, it's a matter of history, of the solid history of words in the world. Wallace Stevens suggests that 'a language, considered semantically, evolves through a series of conflicts between the denotative and the connotative forces in words; between an asceticism tending to kill language by stripping words of all association, and a hedonism tending to kill language by dissipating their sense in a multiplicity of associations. These conflicts are nothing more than changes in the relation between the imagination and reality'.[39] Or, you might prefer to say, changes in intellectual fashion.

Taking credit where credit isn't due

It's a peculiar business to work today as a writer of lyric who suspects something about her own death, yet who still fears her own disinterment. I'll sketch what must be a common experience. When reviewers interpret a poem, they may confidently misconstrue an allusion. Often they'll think up the most ingeniously elaborate sources for something in the text that had a plainer association, a far less baroque connection, behind it. This habit marks, not the genre of reviews which imagine character profiles or amateur psychoanalyses of the author (all too common) or attempt technical commentaries (all too rare), but reviews which base their evaluation on detailed textual interpretations. Sometimes these arrive before they're published, sent to the author by the critic. As both of these characters know that the writer, as such, has virtually had it, she has to perform an awkward trick of propping herself up on her deathbed on one elbow before collapsing artistically prostrate again (as in the painting of another famous impostor, Thomas Chatterton) to say, 'I'm grateful for your careful interpretations and all your attention to this text, but as it happens, all that I was referring to by "x" was y, but naturally I don't want to set myself up as privileged author or claim any special weight for the allusions I actually intended in my text here'. The reviewers habitually ignore the author's politely spectral murmurs. They go right ahead and publish their original copy as if they hadn't ever been impelled to make their detour to the monument of the moribund author. It's as if they'd embarked on a pilgrimage, but one undertaken after the knowing loss of their faith—like marxists who'd despite themselves really wanted to set out for the shrine of Marx in Highgate Cemetery, but, disappointedly, had discovered only withered carnations from the North Korean embassy there. Then, since the writer doesn't respond to published reviews—if she follows the etiquette—that's the end of it.

Or secretly, it isn't, quite. Her near-death experiences leave her floating above her body on the ceiling of the operating theatre, in some dismay. It's odd to be left gasping *sotto voce*, 'But I . . .', when one doesn't believe in a sacral *I* of the writer. Maybe there is a moment, just before death via publication, when the organic connection between the author and her text isn't quite severed—or in the old metaphor, when the umbilical cord hasn't yet been cut, so that the work hasn't quite come to birth as a text which will trot off on its own. But as soon as something has been posted off, printed, and distributed, one loses all attachment to it and is drawn on to the next project or swears to give the whole business up. This underwrites the temporal disjunction between the writing person and her later entombment as author who's stiffened into that being only by the act of undergoing publication. Maybe such hair-splitting is mildly useful because it suggests that 'the author', once published, really was always already dead. That moment just before the writer is interred, through the process of publication, into the catacomb category of 'the author', is the moment of protest: to sit up suddenly in the bath like the she-villain at the end of the movies *Les Diaboliques* and *Fatal Attraction*, and roll her eyes.

There are other difficulties concerned with 'taking responsibility' for that which has at least half-written its writer. The problems of what results when you allude go largely undiscussed, a curious absence, or else they are obscured within an uninteresting and merely scrapbook conception of 'intertextuality'. To allude brings up the risks of impenetrably private reference. Footnoting might cover this, although it lays you open to charges of being pedantic. But the case of misattributed allusions will perplex anyone who can get haunted by sound-echoes, aural ghosts of lines from, say, Wordsworth or Auden. Periodically this writer has to give in to their persistence, put her hands in the air and settle to use them in some lyric, hoping that they'll be recognised as borrowings by the reader. A critic, however, reviews the thing according to his own reading, overlooking the origin of lines whose cadences she has stolen, against her will, senselessly and under compulsion. He credits her with inventing them. Then, mortified, she wants to say, 'No, I'm sorry, I was stupidly making an allusion I couldn't help; do forgive this tendency of mine. One can't always use footnotes, not for this kind of insignificant sound allusion'. Moribund, she can't. There are no channels for communications for the dead. The only answer to this dilemma would be to excise all such traces from the work; to her horror, they're always liable to creep out of the text again, just when she'd thought them all safely cleaned up. There seems to be little which *isn't* driven by sound-association, maybe in the form of puns, maybe in the form of cadence, maybe in the form of half-realised borrowings. I don't mind not being 'original'; indeed, there's no possibility of true originality. But I do mind being credited with something I didn't invent. Perhaps some complicating retrospective knowledge operates intensely at the site of these guilts which, I think, are related— an unease of writing, and an unease of refusing to be or not be named. Called a writer on the site where I know that I'm actually least inventive, I can't be convinced of my attributed status. I have my own suspicions about what the language, working across me, gets up to. Like Althusser, I feel guilty under that interpellation. But at present there is no outlet through which I can debate my guilt as poethics, or even as poetiquette.

There's a curiously different treatment here of the academic text and of the 'creative' text. If my spectral demurrals, under the unattractive flowery hat of poet, about some 'misreading' of my text aren't granted the power to sway a critic, nor should an academic's objections to any 'misreading' of a slice of his theory enjoy that power. The literary author's intentions aren't pertinent; nor are the critical author's. What's sauce for the literary goose should be sauce for the theoretical gander. But the critic doesn't usually behave in such an egalitarian fashion. He argues in print, he refutes misinterpretations, he writes yet another book to disarm his critics, and he engages in fully armed defensive warfare. Its severity is limited only by his ethical convictions, his modesty, or his susceptibility to the letters page of the *New York Review of Books*. He wriggles to reinsert himself, a Houdini reversed, into his book; and he wriggles posthumously, for he won't be gracefully killed off by the act of its publication; he fights for control of its destiny long afterwards. He uses his lungs to argue his case, which he is confident is simultaneously his book's case. Academic and journalistic conventions encourage him to do this. His text is more open to intellectual attack, but it has more channels for its protection under the alibis of 'a stimulating exchange' or 'a scholarly debate'. The poetic text is more open to biographical speculation, against which its author, given her moribund state, has no comeback. The critical author lives on to dissect the always already pickled literary author. It is an occasion for her character to be interrogated, her sexual history guessed at, her unconscious readily analysed, her 'influences' inferred or invented. But, as literary author, she has—and quite rightly—no redress.

That there's little by way of a critical history of literary criticism itself only serves to isolate that supposedly originary integrity of the 'creative' work. If the poem is tough enough, that doesn't matter. As Heidegger, quoting from Trakl, commented, 'Who the author is remains unimportant here, as with every other masterful poem. The mastery consists precisely in this, that the poem can deny the poet's person and nature'.[40] The less tough poem, however, gets criticised in that name of its author, which it can't disavow. But *I* as writer can always disavow *it*. I did not quite write that poem, which almost wrote me, but didn't quite.—By now, all this is beginning to sound suspiciously like something else, something rather different but which also significantly depends on a defensive guilty disavowal, twisted through time, of agency—and which is an instance of linguistic unease.

The timing of guilt

In remoter Cornwall, sacred wells and chapels may still flourish; an alder tree overhanging the spot will be draped with white rags tied on as votive offerings by modern pagans. Encouraged by these festoons, the secular onlooker hangs her own torn-up paper handkerchief on its branches. 'Interpellation' is another shrine which still compels revisiting, attracting fresh comment layered upon older commentaries. Althusser's scenario was built in a few paragraphs,[41] but it retains the lure of a grotto in the woods to which the faithful or the curious are repeatedly drawn. I traipse well behind two recent visitors to this shrine.[42]

For a native French speaker, the resonances of *une interpellation* are to do with calling someone to account, but it makes an awkward word in English. It remains a gallicism. The *Oxford English Dictionary* gives the word 'interpellate' a sixteenth-century currency but holds that it was reimported from French in the nineteenth century to signify 'The action of interrupting the order of the day (in a foreign legislative Chamber) by asking from a minister an explanation of some matter belonging to his department, 1837'. The dictionary also pleasantly cites Carlyle's 'incessant fire of questions, interpellations, objurgations', which comes close to its etymological sense of interrupting, thrusting, or cutting across another's speech. 'Interpellation', then, wasn't so much an originary act of authoritative naming but more of an aggressive interrogation to disrupt normal business by breaking in on some existent status. But it's the former sense which has overshadowed this key word, once it's carried into English, just as it is this sense which marks Althusser's French.

First, faithful to Althusser's injunction to decipher an original text, let's return to his decisive essay. He's painstakingly cautious to lay out his scenario. Ideology, he explains, functions to turn individuals into 'subjects' through interpellation,

> which can be imagined along the lines of the most commonplace everyday police (or other) hailing: 'Hey, you there!' [. . .] Assuming that the theoretical scene I have imagined takes place in the street, the hailed individual will turn round. By this mere one-hundred-and-eighty degree physical conversion, he becomes a *subject*. [. . .] Experience shows that the practical telecommunication of hailings is such that they hardly ever miss their man: verbal call or whistle, the one hailed always recognises that it is really him who is being hailed. And yet it is a strange phenomenon, and one which cannot be explained solely by 'guilt feelings' despite the large numbers who 'have something on their consciences'.

But he footnotes this passage in a sentence studded with scarequotes: 'Hailing as an everyday practice subject to a precise ritual takes a quite "special" form in the policeman's practice of "hailing" which concerns the hailing of "suspects"'.[43] That is, Althusser carefully denies that guilt is the sole motor of interpellation. He then announces that interpellation, irrespective of this puppet show in the street, issues a call which always gets it right. Yet he's sketched in a powerfully distracting vignette. What he himself terms his 'little theoretical theatre' is a prop which he sets up to undercut by rapidly rewriting it without its temporal sequence, so that it's to be understood as 'always already' in play. For, he explains, interpellation and subjection both happen in one and the same blow. Actually there is no balletic spinning round, and no outdoors either; 'But in reality these things happen without any succession. The existence of ideology and the hailing or interpellation of individuals as subjects are one and the same thing. I might add: what thus seems to take place outside ideology (to be precise, in the street) in reality

takes place in ideology'. And ideology, he continues, always works, as subjects 'work all by themselves'.[44]

Let's concentrate on what seems, at first sight, to be the sheer perversity
of this scenario of Althusser's, its tendency to undermine the conception
that it was ostensibly devised to illuminate. The timing of the turn is deliberately wiped out by its creator's insistence that really all this happens simultaneously. It looks as if his model is quietly corrosive of his thesis, since
it starts to eat into his own theory of subjects who are always, as such, in
place. (It also gives rise to some glaring misgivings as to why the call always
gets it right, if it does; and its bothersome details must have vexed practically
minded readers for years, since any half-competent villain would refuse the
temptation to glance round but would carry on purposefully walking or leap
insouciantly onto a bus; while most passers-by would, if the shout was forceful, crane round themselves.) Yet interpellation's fascination as a model obstinately outlives such commonsensical complaint. How? A provisional answer may come from a detour around the strange timing of guilt. And this
might offer a more convincing way of accounting for the theory's durability.

Why should interpellation so often entail guilt? Partly this is because not
all but most interpellations (such as Althusser's tableau of the shout on the
street) *are* verbal attacks. 'You angel!' is a cry I don't often get to hear. But
isn't there a circularity here when the Althusserian subject, whom interpellation calls into place, is produced as guilty of being himself? And if a ready
guilt lies dormant in wait for its own incarnation, longing to be fleshed out
by interpellation's accusatory grammar of 'You *x*!', then there must also be a
half-hidden psychology latent in Althusser's story, oddly like one of Rudyard
Kipling's Just-So stories, of How the Subject Comes to Be. Some readers
may turn contentedly to his autobiography, *The Future Lasts a Long Time*, as
clinching evidence for this point—as if the guilt, latent in the essay on interpellation, has finally become manifest in this final self-examination of the
elderly killer.[45]

It's not at all clear, though, that the psychology of confessional guilt
which undoubtedly courses through the autobiography is *the same sort* of
guilt which shadows the scenario of interpellation. I begin to think that
these two operas have different phantoms. To dwell first on the former: In
any life's story, a sense of being an impostor may well follow mechanically
from its architecture of the 'I' plus the past tense, in an inescapable deceit

exacerbated by failed memory and the blurred reconstructions of lost events. But, well beyond this ordinary unremarkable hesitancy, Althusser's autobiography lays bare several sharp worries about imposture. What's patent is his discomfort with his assigned childhood and adult roles, and with his mortification, but also with his readiness to take them on, even if he did so resentfully or histrionically. He also feels horror at succeeding in these roles; this horror of being taken at face value seems crucial to his account of what it is to play a social part.

There is also a guilt in a rarer kind of being interpellated: as loved. If we administer a strong dose of saccharine to Hegel's scenarios of recognition and so end up with the implication that desire is the desire to be recognised,[46] then this resulting formulation, now flawlessly public-spirited, ushers us straight back towards the territory of interpellation. The word 'recognition' can hover between its meanings of being known accurately and of being acknowledged respectfully. If it's accorded a far more tender-hearted and anodyne coloration than it ever possessed within Hegel's portrayed struggle for supremacy, then what is it to feel oneself 'recognised', if not to respond to what becomes, here, a benign and successful interpellation to which I can gladly assent, not because I am admired (which is always insupportable) but because I am correctly seen? That rare and relieved acknowledgement of 'Yes, that's me; I can tolerate being seen since I feel myself to be known', marks, if fleetingly, the sense of feeling loved—not beyond interpellation, but *in* interpellation. And here bad interpellation offers me only a systematic misrecognition, or a falsely benign because premature recognition, whether I refuse it angrily or whether I succumb, as I am heavily induced to do, I fall into a trouble that I can scarcely name. This inappositely loving interpellation, which so torments Althusser, carries its own possibilities of a counterinterpellation, which, like any other, need not take the shape of a direct refusal of love. It could, for example, love back; but it might do so angrily, or satirically, or theatrically. For this reason, *The Future Lasts a Long Time* is shadowed by a slide from *appel* to appeal. What Althusser claims he fears from others is being seduced by them. And he describes himself as becoming, accordingly, rather good at initiating such enticements himself, while he despises himself for his own acting skills. His feeling of being an impostor is intensified by shame, not so much at any achieved act of cheating but at being so broadly fluent in deceitful seduction. His whole childhood, secured by metaphorically seducing his mother through appearing to be what she wanted him to be, depended solely on pretence, he writes. To save himself from his pressing sense of shame at this deception, he had to strive to devote himself, quite inauthentically, to his mother. Lamenting the awful intimacy between a sentiment's semblance and its achievement, he describes how, since the artifice of his seduction was so bound up in deception, he had not truly won her heart. Incidents of quietly paranoiacal guilt pack his story as responses to real or imagined accusations; so the couple of random shots fired among a noisy crowd at a sports stadium, into which he and his father had slipped without paying for their tickets, were, he half-imagined, actually meant for him.[47]

His mother had misnamed him. The 'who, me?' of interpellation was always, from one perspective, wrong in Althusser's life, for as he narrates it, it was one vastly prolonged case of misidentification. Yet even a misidentification as an interpellation is always inevitably right too, since it works, it does secure the subject that it wants for itself. He feels that he has no existence since even his name isn't his; his mother loved not him but an original Louis, and his 'Louis' was always really meant for another, the name of that man, *lui*, his mother had truly wanted but who had died. The son was a successful impostor although planted in place by someone else:

> Deep down, unconsciously (and my unconscious desires endlessly found expression in reasoned arguments), I wanted at all costs to destroy myself because I had never existed. And what better proof of my non-existence could there be than to draw from it the conclusion that I should destroy myself, having destroyed those closest to me, all those on whom I could rely for help and support? It was then that I began to think that my life consisted of nothing but endless artifice and deceit, that it was totally inauthentic, with nothing true or real about it.[48]

Althusser's guilt at being prepared to be the seductive impostor he describes does resemble the underpinning of his theory of interpellation—but at the critical level of its temporality, not its psychology. If everyone spins round when interpellated, that's because each is so well primed in advance that each feels always already guilty. There is an affective syntax, in that there is linguistic guilt here. And this guilt is effective, for it secures the allegiance of those it has fattened like geese for this end, with a contrived inevitability reminiscent of John Milton's doctrine of divine 'right reason'—'And reason He made right'.

Lecercle announces his own work on the ubiquity of theoretical imposture as an act of filial piety towards Althusser after his death, of dragging the corpse away from the vultures and safely back inside the city walls. To counter a rash of triumphantly psychologistic and reductive readings of the autobiography, and against its author's own confessions as analysand, he studies it 'against the grain of the text, as an instance of irony. I wish to take imposture not as a confession of guilt or psychoanalytic symptom, but as a philosophical concept, even if the narrator himself appears to insist on a psychoanalytic reading'.[49] He then tries to deflect these 'psychologistic' readings by offering an ingenious and persuasive philosophical–linguistic one, turning, roughly, on the inescapable mutual parasitism of text and theory. Though emotional guilt as a unifying device does in the autobiography return with a vengeance, its deployment is, as Lecercle remarks, almost 'too pat'. Certainly when you read through *The Future Lasts a Long Time* you get a vivid impression of someone who's telling himself like a case history. Lecercle holds that Althusser was, in effect, displaying the possibilities of irony as a trope. I think myself that 'irony' isn't the word, because the sense in the autobiography of a pupil repeating a lesson is too strong—and Lecercle's account of the ubiquity of imposture, though in itself compelling, does leave the schoolboy and the adult Althusser still alone and devoured by the guilt which had always haunted him.

Maybe the figure of the helpless impostor comes close to the figure of Echo, the nymph unloved by Narcissus. I've retrieved her in the next chapter as an emblem of lyric's troubled nature, in that both are condemned to hapless repetition. Echo's copying was involuntary. But the capable impostor is also burdened by a weight additional to anyone's vulnerability and derivative helplessness in the jaws of language; he's an intentional as well as an accidental thief. Then if, like Althusser, he's conscientious, he will feel shame. That is, Lecercle's idea of an inevitable linguistic–theoretical imposture, that we are all impostors now, is not necessarily contaminated by a psychologism if we attach to it an idea of guilt—albeit guilt of a distinctive kind. For you can't entirely replace the individual shame in cheating with a concept of an innocent collective cheating, blamelessly endemic to every writing and reading life. So perhaps there's a position halfway between understanding the genesis of imposture as purely archival and linguistic, and the emotion of guilt as purely privately psychological—in which that very real feeling of being an impostor, which remains so obdurately intact at the end of Althusser's story, could be recognised as not so rare or pathological at all, but as itself immanently generated *as* feeling by the everyday machinations of interpellative language. That's a paraphrase of my speculation that, in shorthand, *some* guilt is linguistic.

A strange temporality

Time taken up in pleats is quietly critical for Althusser's idea of how subjects come to be themselves—not least because they do so 'in no time at all'. Sequence is obliterated in his idea of the simultaneity of the subject's interpellation with its recognition of its place. This, under the logic of grammar, seems implausible. Yet Althusser, knowing all about the temporal strangeness embedded in his theory, had deliberately made it integral to his polemic. Sticking to this oddity of the interpellation vignette's timing, I wonder if it can be clarified in just so far as its temporal logic is shared with guilt.

Perhaps Althusser's famous adverbial adjective, his 'always already' with its strange-but-true temporality, in itself possesses a shading of guilt. It does have an elective affinity to guilt, as the emotion that runs in advance of the deed and is always primed to be activated. Guilt's temporal structure is bizarre. Unlike shame, it can precede some wrongdoing which may never be enacted; it can often be an anticipating emotion. The whole scenario of aggressive interpellation can only work through its silent understanding that the temporality of guilt does indeed run backwards. Then first before any crime comes the subject, ripe to be instantly turned into himself by means of an accusation. Not forgetting the harsh truth of Madame Althusser's death, the autobiography *The Future Lasts a Long Time* is also crammed with remembered guilt for what its author had never done or which he's relieved not to have yet done. This is all too like a textbook illustration of a popular psychology, the guilt which invents the misdeed. Police time is regularly wasted by habitual confessors, inept innocents for whom feeling guilty of something is to have committed the crime, if only in the hope of achieving wickedness. That florid thirster after the happiness of the knife, Nietzsche's 'pale criminal', lay at the ready for his accusers through the mouthpiece of

Zarathustra: 'Listen, ye judges! There is, besides, another madness, it is before the deed'. (And indeed there's an immediate intimacy between the verbs 'to do' and 'to be culpable', emerging in the theatrical cliché of 'he did the deed', the dark act.) This pale criminal's 'highest moment was when he judged himself': only afterwards did he contrive a crime to match his anticipated punishment; 'But one thing is thought, another is deed, another is the picture of the deed. The wheel of reason rolleth not between them. A picture made this man pale'.[50] And Freud's own 'criminals from a sense of guilt' are close cousins to the others among his vexed character types, 'those wrecked by success'. They star in some of his most celebrated case histories.[51] Less dramatically, one of his patients might well contrive to do some wrong act, provocatively while undergoing analysis:

> Analytic work then brought the surprising discovery that such deeds were done principally because they were forbidden, and because their execution was accompanied by mental relief for their doer. He was suffering from an oppressive feeling of guilt, of which he did not know the origin, and after he had committed a misdeed this oppression was mitigated. His sense of guilt was at least attached to something. Paradoxical as it may sound, I must maintain that the sense of guilt was present before the misdeed, that it did not arise from it, but conversely—the misdeed arose from the sense of guilt.[52]

For Freud, in such patients, the Oedipus complex was hard at work.

Yet the guilt of those Althusserian innocents who'll readily respond to an interpellation, although they haven't committed a mortal sin and pray that they never will, is of a somewhat different order. Indeed, if you were intending to steer scrupulously clear of wrongdoing, you might, dispiritingly, feel worse because you realised that you'd forbidden yourself any prospect of relief through commission for your anticipatory guilt. Perhaps something shallower and broader is at work for those whose stubbornly persisting disquiet defies the fact that, rationally, their consciences should be quite clear. But that's the usual effect of being accused: to be made to feel guilty, irrespective of whether or not you actually are. Then doesn't any critical interpellation, with its syntactical structure of an attack, automatically produce a reflex guiltiness in even the most sanguine? So do we next decide that a certain temperament, an especially anxious soul, will shiver under this grammar of the accusative case and its pointing finger, while another spirit, more robust, will easily brush it aside? But if there really is a linguistics of guilt to be distinguished from a psychology of guilt, then the former can't rely on any such finer specification within the distinctly psychological.

Let's turn back again to the threatening double syntax of aggressive interpellation, which simultaneously demands consent and incites refusal. This paralysing demand is enacted almost at the level of language; the individual subject can't quite either be or not be in the collective category, can't coincide with it or easily escape it; these aren't genuinely open linguistic alternatives. Then is Althusser's idea of interpellation blind to the facts of its provisionality? No; a degree of failure is quietly built into the model. Because it announces 'you are this category', it's structured as accusing, yet as soon as it's pronounced, the way is thrown open to partly refuse it, because no one can always quite so smoothly submit to subjectification. Interpellation has to falter almost as often as it succeeds, and for both linguistic and historical reasons, but not inevitably for idiosyncratic depth-psychological reasons. Perhaps a certain disquiet is a necessary concomitant to categorisation. As an 'I' sidles into a category, it both gains and loses. Both 'being it' and 'not being it' can cause unease. Demurral about not being a wholehearted deviant or an unflagging nationalist may follow from the unlikeliness of either, settling with satisfaction into a category, or cleanly evading it. For either way, guilt can accrue at having to disappoint the boss Language, refusing its dictates whichever way you jump, whether to obedience or to rebellion. But such apprehensions are not narrowly linguistic. They are properly rhetorical.

'You are an x' does, as I've mentioned, possess the outline of an accusation, which it almost always is. Especially in the ears of anyone who has a history of being bad-mouthed, interpellation never signals any good. Still, one possible retort to the cry of 'Hey, you! You bad x!' is 'Who, me?', uttered with a raised eyebrow to cross-question the would-be conscription. Or someone may hesitate because she can't authentically enter in to an attribution, can't internalise it. As a way of answering back, to refuse an interpellation can occasionally be faintly reassuring. Yet to back away from something so apparently reasonable as a liberal self-indictment can produce a stubborn wilfulness and a guilt that one can't wholeheartedly sign up for a club. A stammer of disengagement can follow some invitation, a guilt at refusing guilt, for not agreeing to acknowledge one's coresponsibility for the Third

World debt, say, or for not taking on collective blame for racism. There's the 'But I . . .' which wants to slide away from the invited confessional, to retort, 'But actually I'm not a criminal; I'm not guilty'. Yet we should also remember the guilt attendant on a too-easy enrolment in the ranks of those making their confessions. Then must becoming a subject always be linked with a helplessly unhappy subjectification? Interpellation isn't usually a benevolent invitation into a good category, but it can be refurbished as a sardonic entry into a bad one, such as those 1968-ish slogans of militant empathy: 'We are all "undesirables."' One can always flounce. The importance of inventive irony here can never be underestimated, touching as it does on the long history of 'progressive' identifications, of how emancipation movements have reworked and parodied themselves rhetorically—as, say, the history of the designation 'homosexual', half recaptured and half jettisoned as 'queer'. Are there always costs to be paid for the adoption of a collective identity? Yet to what extent was there ever a choice? Each collectivity necessitates its own answers. So I can cheerfully argue that sometimes I am and sometimes I'm not a woman, because of the historicised and politicised nature of that category's deployments. But is it harder to agree to say, 'I am a poet', because—disregarding the matter of vanity—of the lack of much critical historicisation of that category? It's sometimes easier to overcome such an occupational hesitancy by replacing the categorising noun with a verb— 'All right, I am engaged in x-ing, but that doesn't make me an x'. This, though, is reminiscent of that well-meaning advice on child management; don't say he's an insensitive boy; just tell him that you don't like him kicking the cat.

Such speculations have been refashioned by Judith Butler's powerfully illuminating discussion of subjectification, which goes straight to the nature of how authority anchors itself in those it addresses. She argues that Althusser's whole conception of ideology is filtered through a conception of religious authority, as a divine authority of naming, and asks, 'And how does Althusser's sanctification of the scene of interpellation make the possibility of becoming a "bad" subject more remote and less incendiary than it might be? The doctrine of interpellation appears to presuppose a prior and unelaborated doctrine of conscience, a turning back upon oneself in the sense that Nietzsche described in *On the Genealogy of Morals*'.[53] The subject's whole existence as social is secured by a readiness to be named as guilty, through a passionate onrush to the law. For Althusser, she continues, 'inter-pellation is essentially figured through the religious example'.[54] It follows that his own use of scriptural reference as an instance of interpellation can be reversed, so that interpellation in itself becomes theological. Here one wonders whether interpellation as near-divine injunction still preserves in amber some stiffened traces of Heidegger's sense of language as an invoca-tion, with the edenic power to bring into being what it names, even though Althusser's version has lost all optimism and is black: naming as threat. Still, there's a potentially brighter rendering of this iconography of God's index finger descending from the sky to seek out, with unerring aim, its unresist-ing subject for baptism by interpellation's fire. That is, that interpellation can't restrict itself as a grandiloquently normative marker, since then there'd be no critical politics of social categories, no persistent badness, and no at-tempts at the flip side of dodging a category, by not having an orthodox conscience.

An aura of the doctrine of original sin enshrouds Althusser's account. If we give a scriptural embellishment to Butler's analysis, we find that the chief speaker in the Book of Genesis, God himself, was a well-versed Althusserian. For Adam and Eve were forced to recognise that they were guilty; in the in-stant that they ate the fruit of the tree of knowledge of good and evil, they immediately acquired a conscience-ridden fear of God and became self-conscious where no shame had been. Some might be tempted to suppose that their abrupt knowledge of good and evil coincided with the first cate-gorising in human history of sexual differences—but faithfulness to the scriptures instructs us that a partition of the sexes by designation in fact pre-ceded the Fall. God was, naturally, chief namer, but Adam also named what God had allowed him to, the beasts and fowls of the air and also Woman. What distinguished the Fall was not names but shame: 'And the eyes of them both were opened, and they knew that they were naked; and they sewed fig leaves together and made themselves aprons'. Among the punish-ments visited on the pair was to become godlike in a depressing sense: 'to know good and evil'. As God had warned in respect of the fruit of the tree, such knowledge was also a killer, 'for in the day that thou eatest thereof, thou shalt surely die'.[55] This warning the serpent had twisted to insinuate that not death but divine knowledge would ensue. Giving chapter and verse for interpellation's 'essential religiosity' implies that its prime site, the Book of Genesis, is preoccupied with the naming of species and the bestowal of Christian names. The dawning of guilt coincides with the acquiring of conscience as the capacity to differentiate, not just nominally but ethically, to know good and evil. To be sure, in the New Testament, the Gospel of St John economically identifies Logos and authority: 'In the beginning was the Word, and the Word was with God, and the Word was God'.[56] This recipe is quick, and does omit any intervening guilt. Althusser, though, was no evangelist, but a decidedly postlapsarian philosopher.

The structure of guilt embedded in his concept of how subjects are made is theological, after the example of the Divine Interpellator. Yet Althusser expounds what he simplifies as the 'Christian religious ideology' by drawing on Peter, leader of the apostles, as his first exemplary subject, named and interpellated in one fell swoop by God.[57] Again Althusser has offered a perverse illustration for his thesis. He has curiously evaded his own Catholic indoctrination, for he could not have escaped knowing that Peter, meaning 'the rock', was merely rechristened as such by Jesus, for the solidity of his faith—'upon this rock I will build my church, and the gates of hell shall not prevail against it'.[58] Peter, then, was hardly submissive in the face of an originary designation. Banally, he'd already earned his new appellation in advance. First he was it, and then he got to be called it. Once again, a suspicion of retrospective knowledge settles in, and this time it's dictating the facts to Jesus. And this illustration of the supposedly perfectly interpellated subject is more uncertain still than Althusser's theory avows. For it overlooks Peter's career of frequently departing from his rocklike attribution to be pigheaded and wavering, shaken to the core with grave doubts at the time of Gethsemane, even to the point of thrice denying any knowledge of Christ, his namer. Interpellation didn't do too well with Peter. In general, its grammar is hardly monolithic; it remains practically ambiguous; so as well as the submissive guilt that makes me walk in to an interpellation with my hands held high, there's the plain misgiving or the defiant guilt that retorts, 'Actually, no, I'm not an x as you understand it, and I don't like your terms'. That retort makes possible, and is also produced by, those objections to collective identifications which both shape and erode political movements. Not that these reworkings ever proceed straightforwardly, privately, in a linear fashion, or without emotional costs; they can also possess a tactical element. Knowing that others will find it less of an irritant if they can characterise and then pigeonhole your tendency, you may, while preparing to undermine their rhetorical base camp, adopt an identity satirically. Or you might elect to do so for the time being—a measure which, unlike poor Althusser's future, is certain not to last long.

What I was really trying to say was . . .

Why should these remarks have moved, under the cover of a concept of linguistic unease, from poetic writing to being picked out as a subject? They run along this chain of connection: that a shared and retrospective externality is native to the three affairs touched on here. These three all come 'from outside themselves'—the business of being named and taking on a social category; the working experience of writing; and the guilt which wonders what else it might have done. All entail puzzles about agency; if you look at them as evincing purely psychological anxieties about a lack of control, you could rapidly dismiss them as of interest only to, in that unpleasant phrase, a control freak. I persist, though, in suspecting that there is something more engaging here, which is to do with their common anteriority, their temporal characteristic of inclining backwards—of being externally given, right at the heart of a supposed inwardness. In those very areas where I am in theory most sharply and inimitably myself, where my originary capacities might most be held to reign—in what I freely write, in what I am, in what I will take responsibility for—there's instead a task of retrieving from the outside whatever I can for my own domain, yet only after the event has handed me the materials I am to work with, or against.

Self-description is endemically inconclusive; this is its nature, not its weakness; neither an 'identity' nor a nonidentity can ever quite convince. But the stronger case for its unease to be linguistic lies, I think, not in this very necessary hesitancy about being or failing to be anything, but in its common structure, shared with guilt, of a peculiar anteriority, a reversed and anticipating aspect. Merleau-Ponty comments that 'all our experiences, inasmuch as they are ours, arrange themselves in terms of before and after, because temporality, in Kantian language, is the form taken by our inner sense, and because it is the most general characteristic of "psychic facts"'.[59] Yet psychological guilt tirelessly modifies this psychic fact in its constant impulse to take responsibility for something that hasn't yet happened. I repeat my less than elevated suspicion, voiced at the start of this chapter: The greater the intensity of guilt, the more swollen the ego that it masks. It abrogates too much responsibility to itself and for matters well outside its domain, not only because it suffers from an admirable conscientiousness but because it also suffers from omnipotence. Guilt's unwilled but determined megalomania must repeatedly survive the agonies of its own near-defeat. In this painful success, guilt is in itself very close to that property of writing, where what you 'want to say' you discover not through prior deliberation but only over your shoulder, and humiliatingly late in the process. I've taken the writing of poetry as an acute exemplar of such retrospective knowing, which it isolates and exaggerates. Words are brought forward as things, even if their semantic element is not completely overthrown. Stuff predominates, but sense insistently wells up through it later. This generates awkwardness at being called a writer, because really I am largely written. Writing, my writing, has got to know far more than I know for it to be of any interest whatsoever. It knows superficially—at its surface laid bare to scrutiny. I wrote it, but more interestingly I didn't; yet I am not its agent or vice versa. As writer, I must be the ostensible source of my own work, yet I know that I've only been the conduit for the onrush, or for the rusty trickle, of language. I'm pinned in a position of 'I did and didn't do it'; there's oscillation at the heart of authorship. For the resulting lyric, Adorno extracts dignity here:

> Hence the highest lyric works are those in which the subject, with no remaining trace of mere matter, sounds forth in language until language itself acquires a voice. The unself-consciousness of the subject submitting itself to language as to something objective, and the immediacy and spontaneity of that subject's expression, are one and the same: thus language mediates lyric poetry and society in their innermost core. This is why the lyric reveals itself to be most deeply grounded in society when it does not chime in with society, when it communicates nothing, when, instead, the subject whose expression is successful reaches an accord with language itself, with the inherent tendency of language.[60]

For the author at one remove from the brief tranquillity of accomplishment, the thing is less serene. The temporal oddities of how, according to Althusser's interpellation, you become 'who you are' aren't far removed from those of writing, where you find out 'what you know' through a backwards process in which you, the author, are at best the editor of whatever language has forcibly dictated. Your status as originator is vacuous; you are 'a writer' only insofar as you consent to struggle with what has already been carried to you from the underbelly of words and sounds and as you skirt the mined field of involuntary plagiarism, where nothing is ever for the first time. Your writing arrives on your page largely from the outside—as your identification does. In both instances, questions arise of what you may take on with any sense of integrity. Who, me? I couldn't have written that—well, all right, my wrist and hand did, but it wasn't my self at work. It was my ear that had a field day, and the accidents of rhyme in time raced through their pathways in my passive skull. To refuse to be a 'creative' writer is to recognise the emptiness of the usual hope of linguistic originality. Such an acknowledgement is not in the least assuaged by meditations on the anarchic virtues of the signifier's free play, a conception which only mystifies the figure of the writer; nor on the delightful communality of this vociferous culture, in which who first wrote what is well beyond retrieval.

What now seems most apt for this chapter's subdued speculation as to whether guilt may be linguistic is—an equivocal answer. No, if by that some battle for supremacy against other claimants for chief marker of guilt is imagined. There are far more devastating and bitter pretenders to that dark throne. Yes, but only if that adjective 'linguistic' can suggest that guilt is also structurally given by its peculiar retrospective temporality which itself generates such uncertainty about agency, responsibility, culpability, subjecthood, identification, composition, and authorship. On balance, then, it seems better to speak of a linguistic 'unease' rather than of a linguistic guilt. Then to consider that this guilty disquiet also drifts at the broad level of language is also a dedramatising move in that it partly restores it to ordinariness, lifting it away from a purely idiosyncratic psychopathology of omnipotence, and reinstating it in the commonest place. This place is emphatically not the collective unconscious. It willingly lacks depths, yet is also truly historical, because language is historical, and is truly materialist, because language is solid. Following this line of musing, then, there are common and unexceptional effects which operate strongly and directly on a terrain pitched somewhere between emotionality and language in their conventional demarcation. That is, an individual if languagelike 'psychic unconscious' need not be rigorously opposed to some impersonal 'linguistic unconscious'. No inflexible ridge would separate them. Instead one would, ideally, reconcile both via a subtle alteration of each. But here I'm ineluctably reminded of the fate of Doris Lessing's heroine, shifted from a youth of espousing communism to a middle age of professing marriage guidance.[61]

Lyric selves

> Filled with joy and pride, we come to believe we have
> created what we have only heard.
>
> L O N G I N U S [1]

Some speculations which run throughout these chapters are put directly as
prosaic verse here. It's doggerel, to flesh out questions of the self's presence
to itself that might, in a more laboured way, be raised in critical prose; and
it would be a sticky sanctity which, glamorising 'creative writing' as unassailable, insisted on an unbridgeable demarcation between the poetic and
the analytic. My two exhibits here continue some of the suggestions already
advanced. The first sifts through ideas of lyrical self-presentation as they
emerge in some contemporary dilemmas and compulsions of style. The second separates Narcissus from his recent adhesions of 'narcissism' and returns
him back to his roots in Ovid and to his roots as a dried bulb once used for
healing 'affections of the ear', afflicted hearing. It also includes some special
pleading for Echo, too, and it proposes her role, fleshed out in my last chapter, as an adjunct of irony.

The Castalian Spring, a first draught

I

A gush of water, welling from some cave, which slopped
Down to a stone trough squatting stout and chalky as a
Morning sky: I plumped myself on lizard-ridden stone to stare
Into its old truth square that struck me as perhaps another lie
So serious did it look while it promised me, oh, everything.
That honest look of water nursed in stone excited me. Under
The generous trees, tall splotchy planes and brittle ilex, their
Dark flopped down, sun-glare and dust spun through it.

1. The spring lies close to Delphi, on Mount Parnassus. Not that the reader can know this yet, but we're at the start of a fable of self-presentation; it's going to resemble an ancient book of conversations between species likely to undergo metamorphoses, although here it's a bestiary populated with only one beast. The question of the speaking 'I', and of its possible egotism, arises immediately here. Is the lyric 'I' an irretrievably outdated form, as some would argue, a poetic version of that overthrown omniscient narrator we used to hear such a lot about and shouldn't much like to meet? But you can also have an impersonal lyric 'I', not at all confessional or self-aggrandising. Lyrical self-presentation distils all these worries, which are old enough.[2] The less that the poetic work is taken to be only consciously generated by its author, and the more archaic and dubious aspirations to technical control begin to sound, then, paradoxically, the more important the actual figure of the poet may become. Presenting the self and its fine sensibilities reaches fever pitch within some contemporary poetics. Poetry can be heard to stagger under a weight of self-portrayal, having taken this as its sole and proper object. Today's lyric form, frequently a vehicle for innocuous display and confessionals, is at odds with its remoter history. What might transpire if this discontinuous legacy in self-telling became the topic of a poem itself? Attempting this, the 'I' above has adopted a chatty conversational tone, yet the listener suspects this is some imaginary scenario flanked with venerable stage props. All we know so far about this speaker is that she possesses an odd psychology, some fixed anxiety about truth and appearance.

2

I sipped that cold and leafy water tentatively, lost lipstick
Dabbing my mouth, gulped down a little slippery grit I hoped
Was not ferny mosquito larvae; then sat on, guidebook-learned
To get gorgeous and pneumatic in the throat, my bulk deflating
Slowly until the sunset, when the last coach parties slid away.
The heat of the day peeled off, the light got blurred and hummed,
Pounding dusk struck up then a strong swelling rose in my throat
Thick with significant utterance. So, shivery in my cool and newly
Warty skin, I raised this novel voice to honk and boom.

2. The narrator knows, because she's read her Blue Guide, that if she drinks
some water from the Castalian Spring, she will automatically turn into a poet.
In this poem, however, she also turns into a toad, though she's perhaps surprisingly unfazed by such a strange translation. But what justification can
there be for the cod antiquarianism of this piece? 'The history of the imitation
of ancient poetry, especially as practised in foreign countries, is among other
things useful in permitting us to derive most easily and fully the important
concepts of unconscious parody and passive wit', observed Schlegel.[3] Unfor-
tunately the writer of this piece, like its imagined narrator, can discover only
an inverse ratio between knowingness and confidence. The matter of having
the confidence to make a noise at all continues to vex her in the next stanzas.

3

I was small enough now, and stoical, to squat on the slabs of rock
Edging the trough, splashed with the spring that welled steadily into it
Shaking its stone-cupped water. I wear yet a precious jewel in my head,
I mused, this line of old rhetoric floating back through me, as quite
Unsurprised I settled to study the night, flexing my long damp thighs
Now as studded and ridged as the best dill pickles in Whitechapel.
Into the cooling air I gave tongue, my ears blurred with the lyre
Of my larynx, its vibrato reverberant into the struck-dumb dusk.

3. Lyric poetry was, originally, simply words accompanied by the music of
the lyre. 'Dill pickles' are gherkins. This sanguine tourist-toad somehow re-

calls her school Shakespeare's lines from *As You Like It*, 'Sweet are the uses of adversity, / Which like the toad, ugly and venomous, / Wears yet a precious jewel in his head'. One inescapable and deeply disconcerting effect of writing is such unwanted intrusions. Your own automatic 'intertextuality', to give it a misleadingly dignified name from the lit-crit lexicon, drives you spare. Quotation as white noise can be maddening. But this is a bookish amphibian, whose preoccupations are largely with what she can do with her new voice, so I let this one stay in.

'Picking up other people's ideas like dead birds'[4] can be replaced by an uncomfortable awareness that all writing is derivative: a truism in, say, the history of ideas, where an acknowledgement that you are at best going to manage a cut-and-paste job is the minimum you require to proceed at all. But if poetry is also an affair of high speed autodictation and half-conscious gluing, then the concept of the poem as a protected reservation for the unique personal voice is torn apart. Catching my borrowed rhetoric at its work on the page, I suddenly realise what I've been up to, and my whole bag of tricks, once exposed to me, becomes unusable. I append my signature sheepishly because I know I am a sounding chamber in poetry, even more so than in prose, since more than the content of the poem is derived. Its style is also a set of mechanical effects which spring up, felicitously or miserably, as that inescapable unconscious of language. I'm left with a peculiar new status of my own, now not so much the author as the editor of my own work but an editor inevitably so conscious of the automata which have leapt into life without her active consent that she must become a sharp censor. When the work still fails (as it does fail), that marks a lapse of retrospective vigilance rather than some shortfall of authorial 'originality'.

4
What should I sing out on this gratuitous new instrument?
Not much liking minimalism, I tried out some Messaien,
Found I was a natural as a bassoon, indeed the ondes martenot
Simply oozed out of me. Or should lyric well up less, be bonier?
So I fluted like HD's muse in spiky girlish hellenics, slimmed
My voice down to twig-size, so shooting out stiffly it quivered

In firework bursts of sharp flowers. Or had I a responsibility to
Speak to society: though how could it hear me? It lay in its hotels.

4. The she-toad rehearses some familiar debates using as analogies the
sounds of particular instruments. She skips through simplified versions of
some positions in contemporary poetics and, as will happen all the way
through this poem, abandons each in turn. So here she wonders about how
full-bodied and gorgeous a contemporary lyric writer can allow herself to
be—or whether something bleaker and bonier is in order, especially if the
writer is female, and here she invokes the precedent of the poet HD. Is the
very demanding labour to produce beautiful utterance enough in itself, or
should she make some extra, violent effort to get through to some audience?
What if it's asleep, or out having a perfectly good time somewhere else?

5

I spun out some long lines, let them loop in sound ribbons
Lassoed the high branches where they dangled and trailed
Landing like leathery bats in vacancy; alighted, they pleated,
Composed themselves flawlessly, as lifeless as gloves.
The silence that hung on these sounds made me sheepish.
I fished for my German, broke out into lieder, rhymed
Sieg with Krieg, so explaining our century; I was hooked
On my theory of militarism as stemming from lyricism.

5. She has a go at working with pure line, and so she runs straight into the
problem of the apparent self-sufficiency of the aesthetic object, here of decorative sound and its strange excluding quality of finishedness, when what
you have made stares back at you like an angry adolescent. The insistent
theme of 'social responsibility' can never be held at bay for very long,
though, and she is briefly entranced with her idea that some common
rhymes that a particular language generates might have a powerful effect on
ways of writing and of thinking in that country. 'Sieg' is German for victory,
and 'Krieg', for war. This isn't far from the way that the wild French linguist,
Jean-Pierre Brisset, reasoned. (He's appeared in the previous chapter.) He
also held that humans were descended from frogs, and this historical fact
partly explains the amphibious nature of my narrator here. Another German

rhyme, 'Herz', meaning heart, with 'Schmerz', meaning pain, facilitates the concept that love lies very close to sorrow in the lyric tradition, as it so often lies in life. Once you could have had that same rhyme and meaning in British English, too: 'heart' with 'smart'. But in modern British English, 'smart' now means well turned out or flashily dressed, while in American English it means acute, clever; although this usage, originally from early English, is drifting back again across the Atlantic. The older sense of a 'smart' as a burning pain is now lost. Still, you could invent the argument that cleverness and elegance are stalked by feelings of apartness or loneliness, and so you've caught a shadow of that original meaning of a stinging pain, preserved forever in amber at the heart of hipness.

6

I'd crouched close by a cemetery; at twilight its keeper
Lit oil lamps in shrines on the pale marble graves, each
Brandishing silver-framed photographs; fresh flowers
For the well-furnished dead shone out amiably, while
The scops owl in residence served up its decorous gulps.
Lights burned on steadfastly in this town of the dead,
Each soul in for a long night, their curtains undrawn.
My monotone croaking rang crude in such company.

6. Graveyards in Greece are often tenderly kept, and at dusk, once the little oil lamps on the tombstones are illuminated, they take on the aspect of a glowing village. In the face of this company of the dead, the speaker forgets her theories of poetics for a while in the face of grave matters, and must recognise that she is coarse and inelegant of expression. She's tacitly feeling a serious lack, that of any useful contemporary notion of Rhetoric—which is, arguably, desperately needed for understanding how languages work. Meanwhile, no way of rising to the elegiac occasion is open to her since there is now no available tradition of civic song to which she has access, so now she feels herself small. Which indeed she is.

7

Black plane trees bent over me, crouched in the night breeze.
For hours I called out on a sonorous roll, growing somewhat self-

Conscious I'd nothing to do but to sound: yet sound was so stirring
And beauty of utterance was surely enough, I thought I had read this.
A wind rose as I tore out my ravishing tenor, or sank down to throb
On my pitted hindquarters while my neck with its primrose striations
Pulsated and gleamed. Then beauty sobbed back to me, shocking,
Its counterpoint catching my harmonies; I had heard a fresh voice.

7. Here she temporarily abandons her worries about the social responsibility of the performing artist and the vacuum that her cemetery experience has just painfully revealed, and instead simply sings out alone, still wondering whether a purely aesthetic approach to lyric noise is adequate and if 'purity' is the best she can realistically manage; and then wouldn't that be a lot to achieve, anyway? Yet she's feeling cut off; until, as in an ancient device, out of the darkness emerges another voice, miraculously in tune with her own.

She is seized briefly by the romantic solution to the problem of how she should speak, because her conviction of the arrival of that sole addressee who will completely understand her words has temporarily put paid to her earlier anxieties of audience. This dazzling immediacy has for the moment stilled her problem of knowing that to speak is to settle to be heard under some designation. Speaking as a literary social subject carries a consent to be it: Someone appraised for marketing purposes as 'a Yorkshire writer' knows, when he too takes up this designation, that he's doing something beyond letting his home town of Bradford, or a sepia dream of the West Riding, sell his novels. Under his breath he has said to himself, Right, from now on, this is what I'll be. This personal agreement could conceal many undertones, perhaps an angry determination, a satirical concession, or a gracefully ironical resignation. But I cannot peaceably and quiescently inhabit a literary social category, any more than I can be an original author, and for analogous reasons. I am prey to whatever noisy inscriptions have run in advance of me. If the notion of 'integrity' conveys an originary wholeness, then writing, quintessentially derivative, must find some quite other basis for its truth. I might try to substitute the resigned compromise of collage for the impossible integrity of originality so that, for any assembly of fragments, it is those acts of selecting, pasting, and reshaping which bestow virtue on my effort. Yet even this thinned-down 'integrity' of the collagist remains a disappointingly slight notion.

8

No longer alone, not espousing Narcissus, I answered each peal
In a drum of delirium, recalling with shame the dry white thighs
Of frogs like baked chicken wishbones, sorely in need of a sauce.
Our calls clasped in common, as heavy as love, and convulsively
Thickened by love—until ashamed of such ordinariness, I wailed
In sheer vowels. Aaghoooh, I sloughed off raark, aaarrgh noises,
Deliberately degenerate; exuded ooeeehaargh-I-oohyuuuh; then
Randomly honked 'darkling blue of Dimitrios': I had dreamed that.

8. Here the toad, having on the instant fallen for the call of a creature who
sounds just like her, a common enough provocation for falling in love, suffers from memories of having, in her human shape, eaten a dish of baked
frogs in a restaurant. Guilt fires her embarrassment at finding herself in the
supremely ordinary predicament of being so captivated, yet having nothing
original to say or write on the subject. Her fruitless search for originality
leads her to zip through a few current theories in poetics; so she tries to use
pure noise like some contemporary sound poets may do, sometimes to get
rid of the supposed imperfections and corruptions of signifying language by
jettisoning semantic meaning. Next she goes for big, random sounds. Then
finally, harking back to earlier surrealist experiments, she has a go at incorporating verbatim into her song work a fragment from one of her dreams.

Common hesitations shadow her closely related uncertainties of writing and
of self-description. Both share a frustrated longing for resolution through an
ideal of integrity, which itself sits close to that of originality. While I may
have my doubts about the virtues of either ideal, nevertheless I can't fail to
realise that while I can't be original, I nevertheless need to discover some
helpful way of understanding the nature of my failure. The author who ac-
knowledges herself a plagiarist—that, however much she strives for originality, she's merely parroting the accumulated insights of others—is she relying on a sickly charm to get her through, the old 'frank admission'? Every
time I open my mouth, I'm insinuating myself into some conversation
which preexists me and to which my contribution is only a rustle of echoes
—on paper, which is where we all must live. Nevertheless, writing moves
through its own simulacrum of originality; for even if its 'creativity' is con-

ceived as really a matter of endless refashioning and involuntary plagiarising, it still retains, in the lonely fact of the signature, its final flourish of individuation. Then it's a question of how one takes on responsibility for the text in all its weaknesses, while in the same breath avoiding the gorgeous mantle of 'being a writer'.

9

The voice hears itself as it sings to its fellows—must
Thrum in its own ears, like any noise thumping down
Anywhere airwaves must equally fall. I was not that
Narcissus who stared stunned by his handsomeness;
Or I was, but not culpably, since as I sang, so I loved.
In that instant of calling hope out I embodied it, got
Solemn and swollen ushering in my own utterance.
I rang florid yet grave in my ears, as I had to.

9. Noticing the workings which accompany overhearing yourself write can produce effects on the page that you may need to distinguish from an undesirable self-attention or conceit. The toad has an optimistic line here on thought as echoing in the ear of its originator, although it's treated somewhat ironically. Distinguishing blind self-regard from that devotion to another which must always aim for the clearest address, she attempts a tranquil reflexivity. Yet she totters on the brink of being jarred by noticing herself doing so.

10

Did I need to account for myself as noise-maker?
I had stared in the windows of Clerkenwell clock shops
At dusty brand oils for the watchmakers' trade, made for
Easing the wound spring—some horo-prefixed, and so close
To my horror of time ticking by—brown bottles of clock oil
Labelled Horolene, Horotech. Should I wind up my own time,
Chant, 'I was dropped on the Borders, a poor scraplet of
Langholm, illegit. and state's burden, lone mother of three'?

10. Clerkenwell is a district in inner London where all the watchmakers had their shops; many hang on to this day, although their windows are dusty

and funereal, some still full of bottles of the oil labelled for 'easing the wound spring' of the clockwork mechanisms. It's almost impossible not to pronounce this piece of the innards of a clock to yourself as 'woond' spring, with the sound of a wound as a hurt rather than what it means, a mechanism to be wound. And then the Greek-derived prefix 'horo', meaning time, easily slides into 'horror' to become a compacted shorthand for the fear of time passing, of mortality. This is one of those inescapable echolalic effects that worry the lyric toad, because they crop up so forcefully in the act of writing, whether or not they are wanted, and are yet another instance of language speaking you. Then at the end of the stanza, there is a movement from thoughts about time slipping away, implicitly towards death, to thoughts about presenting a conclusive autobiography (a deathly preoccupation) and how, if at all, the modernist, let alone the postmodernist, creature can speak accurately about her life. A homely example of these troubles of presentation and self-presentation returns to her mind from a memory prior to her metamorphosis; bookshops' shelving policies groan under them. The best-intentioned classifications can result in obscurantism and comedy. The class, for instance, of 'woman writers' will swell for just as long as this marketing device might work commercially without bursting, and meanwhile it forcibly embraces those who'd spin in their graves at being so designated, such as Edith Sitwell, boxed as a 'woman poet'. One side effect is that shops are lined with neutrally labelled 'poetry' shelves, yet these contain only the work of men poets as an unadmitted—and deeply uninteresting—category, since the generically captioned shelves are flanked by a smaller quantity of weeded-out and separately designated 'women's poetry'. If 'Black writers' and 'Asian writers' are by now bracketed with some attempts at a greater refinement, nevertheless, under these headings, Guyanese and Ghanaian sports journalists may rub shoulders awkwardly as 'Black', and Chinese and Indonesian novelists must coexist unhappily as 'Asian'. Meanwhile the yards of nonethnically designated shelves are, by implication, heavy with the work of nonblack or 'white' writers, who are never thus specified, thereby silently exposing the weakness of the catch-all category of 'Black'. Admittedly all such classifications must be approximate and nowhere near those of the library; the absurd end result of the demand for precise specification would be an individualised classification for each title. For finer and finer subdivisions will arise ad infinitum, yet always obscuring someone else beneath them. Granting this, the failure of categories to keep pace with their claimants can still result in dark humour. The label of 'Irish writers' may readily be affixed to London bookshelves yet will not always differentiate between those who'd make furious neighbours, whether as Ulster opponents of Stormont or devotees of the Red Hand, as Anglo-Irish golfers or as mystical Fenians, or as solitary modernists dreaming internationalism in Dublin.

The pretender to lyric worries with reason, then, about espousing self-presentation within the conventional categories, about tying herself up or winding up her story of her own case, subjecting herself to subjectification and loudly inhabiting her potential identities, including having been born in an area so long fought over between Scotland and England that it was designated only as the blurred 'Debatable Lands'. She senses that she nevertheless can't erect her minuscule tale into any consoling identity, not even into that pleasing identity of being 'debatable'. Is that apt matter for lyric poetry—the presentation of a self, within such received groupings, as pitiful or as proud? But much contemporary work does exactly this, and its defences and damages do need to be debated. In the next stanza, she goes on wondering about this, so revealing more of her webbed hand.

II
Could I try on that song of my sociologised self? Its
Long angry flounce, tuned to piping self-sorrow, flopped
Lax in my gullet—'But we're all *bufo bufo*', I sobbed—
Suddenly charmed by community—'all warty we are'.
Low booms from the blackness welled up like dark liquid
Of 'wart' Ich auf Dich'. One Love was pulsed out from our
Isolate throats, concertina'ed in common; 'Du mit Mir' was
A comforting wheeze of old buffers, all coupled, one breed.

11. This stanza lets rip sound echoes, for instance of 'buffer' with '*bufo*'—the Latin name for the main toad genus. And there are more echoes between 'warty' and 'wart' ich'—German for 'I wait', implicitly for You. Anyone who works in a medium which uses quotation, in words or paint or celluloid or sound, will be all too familiar with this phenomenon of irrational as-

sociations arising spontaneously, crowding in, generating a constant headache of self-editing. There's a characteristic excess in working with lyric, that
buzz of ramifications through sound-echoes and not, in the first place,
sense-echoes, and which resemble forms of speech disturbance as described
in the literature on aphasia or schizophrenia. You need to process them into
a controlled mania, but you exert such control only after they have arrived;
you may be able to cut through the blur of sound associations, but only retrospectively, after you've detected them swarming on your page. Do they
stay or do they go? There's a feeling of being seized by too much language
or of being inscribed by language, as not their meaning but the aural resonances of your words very often determine what you'll say next, in an untidy vacillating process, after which you have to dust yourself down, to realise 'what's really been going on here' only in retrospect. But the experience
of retrospective knowledge that floats up at you from the surface of the
freshly written page, when you suddenly see something of what you've actually written, may be alarming.

Back to the content of this eleventh stanza, where happy song arises. Lyrics
of the 1960s espouse this cheerful communitarianism, although some may
suspect these echoes on the grounds that popular music is rankest com-
merce, it cheapens the emotions, and so on. Still, the narrator's prejudice is
solidly in favour of such lyrics on the grounds that if her amphibian emotion is at once very powerful and very ordinary, popular song can encapsu-
late the coincidence of both, which is reassuring. 'Du mit Mir' just means
'you with me'. These words are kept in German, in part because that's the
language of the early nineteenth-century song cycles, in which words and
notes hang intimately together. By now the toad has given up on her string
of self-pitying self-presentations and stumbles instead upon an ideal of social identification. It's a hymn of togetherness, not only the togetherness of
the couples joined to each other in their affections but beyond that, for they
are linked in a feeling of unification with every other member of their
species, such as the old Coca-Cola television advertisements with people
clasping hands to chorus about 'one world'. The myriad selves volunteer for
a happy self-alienation, a merciful release from solitariness into unison. Her
stanza is rude about this. There are more worrying undertones here because
it's not yet possible to use the German language to talk about group emotion

and identity without recalling, in Reich's contentious phrase, a mass psychology of fascism—even if there are now all too many contemporary claimants for this unhappy association.

12

But then I heard others, odd pockets of sound; why wouldn't these
Claim me to chant in their choir? As I grew lonelier, I got philosophical,
Piped up this line: 'Don't fall for paradox, to lie choked in its coils
While your years sidle by'. Some hooted reproachfully out of the dawn,
'Don't you stifle us with your egotist's narrative or go soft on "sameness",
We'll plait our own wildly elaborate patterns'—they bristled like movies
By Kurosawa. By then I'd re-flated, abandoned my toadhood, had pulled on
My usual skin like old nylons. I drifted to Delphi, I'd a temple to see.

12. The she-toad, now restored to her original condition of being a tourist, goes off, surprisingly unshaken by her metamorphosis, to Delphi, the small town where the oracle-containing temple of Apollo lies. There's a reference to the Japanese director Kurosawa in here, only because I happened to see a movie of his, 'Ran', based on the *King Lear* story, which is so full of bristling arrows and lances and spears that the screen is frequently a mass of spiky diagonals. This jump-cut brings up an etiquette of private allusion: Suppose you have odd associations which your audience aren't necessarily going to catch, do you cut these out in the interests of intelligibility or accessibility? Here I let Kurosawa and his bristling arrows stand, not because of their weight but because of their slightness in their context; it makes no difference if you miss them, and if you don't, they might entertain you by recalling the movie. The others who chorus in this final stanza are vexed with the speaker for having, during her phase of professing One Love, occupied a position which seemed to obliterate their real differences and had homogenised them into a mass. The speaker toad has had enough by now, as this writer felt that this doggerel was too slight to bear any more weight. So she becomes human again, and we abandon her at the point of resuming her tourism. The problem is how to end such an unresolved composition. Do you just give up on it, maybe wishing you'd somehow tried harder? Does it walk out on you—do you both somehow know when things are irretrievably over between you?

Affections of the Ear

I

Here's the original Narcissus story: The blue nymph Leiriope, called the
        lily-faced,

Clear blue as any Cretan iris, got the river-god, summer Cephissus, so on
        the boil

That lapped by his skeins of water, soused in them, spun round, twirled,
        interlaced

Until made pregnant, she had Narcissus. Stupefied well before he was
        pulped to oil

What future did he ever really have, with that slight azure mother of his
        embraced

By slippery Cephissus, insinuating himself everywhere to flatter, linger, and
        coil?

Leiriope chased Tiresias to set him his very first poser: would her boy be
        effaced

By a rapid death? The seer said No—just as long as he didn't know himself.
        Recoil

From the goal of self-knowledge! That maxim, chiselled in temple rock,
        gets erased

By the case of Narcissus who came to know himself to be loved water.
        Philosophy

Recommends a severe self-scrutiny to us, while a blithe self-indifference is
        disgraced:

Yet for gorgeous Narcissus to know himself was sheer torment, and his
        catastrophe.

II

He did know he was beautiful before he ever caught sight of himself in the
        water.

One youth he didn't want died cursing 'Let him love, too, yet not get what
        he'll love'.

(I should explain myself, I sound derivative? Because I am, I'm Echo, your
        reporter.

I'll pick up any sound to flick it back if it's pitched louder than the
> muttering of a dove.
I am mere derivation, and doomed by Mrs Zeus to hang out in this
> Thespian backwater.)
He pushed into the surface of the lake; when push had come, as come it
> will, to shove
Narcissus had to know. Then deathly recognition drew him, lamb-like, to
> his slaughter.
His object was no wavering boy beneath the water, he was far more than
> hand in glove
With what he saw. I know his problem, though at least I do have Iynx my
> bird daughter.
To love himself was pain precisely when he came to understand that truth,
> most bitterly.
I got hurt too, by ox-eyed Hera as they call her although I'd say cow,
> recumbent above.
For me, Echo, to forcibly repeat others' words is my ear torment, my own
> catastrophe.

III
I told stories so Zeus' lovers escaped, as under cover of my chatter they'd
> slip past Hera.
I did things with words until she caught me, to rage 'False fluency, your
> gossip's untrue
You've always wanted the last word—see what good it'll do you'. I was right
> to fear her
For now I have got it. So exiled, I fell for Narcissus. I had no voice to plead
> so I'd pursue.
He called 'I'd die before I'd give myself to you!' I shrilled 'I'd give myself to
> you!' ran nearer.
If he'd cried 'I'd die before I'd fuck you', at least I could have echoed back
> that 'Fuck you'.
Sorry—I have to bounce back each last phrase. Half-petrified, I voice dead
> gorges. Dearer
My daughter Iynx, a wryneck, torticollis, twisted neck, barred and secretive
> as any cuckoo,

A writher in the woods—as a mother I am, and am merely, responsive;
    still, I keep near her.
My body goes rocky when I hang round Narcissus. Numbed to a trace of
    ruined articulacy
I mouth words I can't voice; half-turned to stone, am rigid with memory of
    what I could do.
So for lonely Narcissus fruitlessly knowing himself as his object was torture,
    a catastrophe.

IV

He saw truth in fluidity, was an offshoot of water; he dreamily propped
    himself prone
Beside his reflection; the image that shone yet broke at his touch he did not
    misconstrue.
He lay dumb in the daze of himself by the glaze of the lake with his face set
    like stone.
If your mother was blue and your father was water, then mightn't you try
    to be true?
'Only the thinnest liquid film parts us; which is why, unlike most lovers', I
    heard him groan,
'I long for more distance between us; only then could I start to get near
    him'. Narcissus knew.
In the end, he was not misled by vanity. He saw it was himself he loved,
    and not his clone:
In just that lay his torture. I've said that as a bulb he got pulped down to
    oil, mashed to a stew.
Narcissus oil's a narcotic, both stem from the same root *narcos*, numb; the
    bulb was known
As the botanical root to cure 'affections of the ear'. (I'll need that oil on my
    tympanum, too,
If thought is truly a bone.) His becoming a herbal remedy concludes
    Narcissus' biography.
Dying by water in knowing misery, he's recycled as unguent to drop on the
    sounding tissue
Of sore ears to heal their affections. Affections of the ear, not of the heart;
    familiar catastrophe.

V

'Ears are the only orifices that can't be closed'—though force may get some
    others to succumb.
My inward ears will jam wide open to internal words that overlying
    verbiage can't smother.
Boated over the Styx, Narcissus' shade peered in its black waters just in case
    his image swum.
Numbed by affection of his heart, now dried he'll cure the ear affections.
    Son of his lily mother
His beauty drove me deeper into repetition as a sounding-board, a ringing
    rock, a mere eardrum.
A rhyme rears up before me to insist on how I should repeat a stanza's
    formal utterance—other
Than this I cannot do, unless my hearers find a way of speaking to me so I
    don't stay semi-dumb
Or pirouette, a languid Sugarplum. Echo's a trope for lyric poetry's
    endemic barely hidden bother:
As I am made to parrot others' words so I am forced to form ideas by
    rhymes, the most humdrum.
All I may say is through constraint, dictation straight from sounds
    doggedly at work in a strophe.
'To make yourself seen reflects back to you, but to make yourself heard
    goes out towards another'.
That's all I, Echo, ever do. Occasionally diverting, it stays my passive hell
    and small catastrophe.

All these details of the story of Narcissus and Echo are taken straight from Ovid's *Metamorphoses*, book 3. It also incorporates Robert Graves's claim that narcissus oil, crushed out of the bulb, was used as a cure for 'affections of the ears'.[5] The word 'affection' is an archaism for 'disease' (as an example, the *Oxford English Dictionary* says that to possess 'an affection of the heart' was, in 1853, to suffer from heart disease). These lines have resurrected Ovid's antihero, who perfectly came to realise his mistake of falling in love with his own reflection, and so they disinter the first Narcissus, aeons before our popular psychology of 'narcissism'. That original Narcissus, though, was not so short on self-knowledge as his later version implies. And self-knowledge need not, anyway, inevitably induce self-absorption. As Nietzsche remarked, 'A thing explained is a thing we have no further concerns with. What did that god mean who counselled: "Know thyself"? Does that perhaps mean "Have no further concern with thyself! Become objective!"'[6] 'Knowing one-self' can be a catastrophic undertaking—yes, but only if that Socratic in-junction is taken in its modern deployment, to mean the introspection of individual self-consciousness. Then the risk of self-knowledge becomes that of complacency: 'How many people know how to observe something? Of the few who do, how many observe themselves? "Everybody is farthest away —from himself"; all who try the reins know this to their chagrin, and the maxim "know thyself!" addressed to human beings by a god, is almost ma-licious. That the case of self-observation is indeed as desperate as that is at-tested best of all by the manner in which almost everybody talks about the essence of moral actions—this quick, eager, convinced, and garrulous man-ner with its expression, its smile, and its obliging ardor!'[7] Classical writers, too, were often sardonic about the famous injunction. So Lucian's amiable cynic Menippus runs out of patience with the complaining shades of Croe-sus, Midas, and Sardanapalus and lambasts them: 'You, for your part lament and weep and I will accompany you and occasionally join in with the refrain "Know thyself": for it would be quite a suitable accompaniment to such howling'.[8] But the injunction is saved if you agree with Hegel that self-knowledge implies a knowledge of Mind itself, rather than of the quirks of any individual idiosyncratic psychology.[9] Or that, as in Kierkegaard's gloss on Socrates, you should come to self-knowledge as an act of helpful differ-entiation and separation from yourself.[10] 'Knowing yourself is valuable, so that the self can be removed from the process', as Mark Rothko, a man sadly all too good at removing himself, observed.[11]

Although later he was compelled by Freud to undergo yet another meta-morphosis into the emblem of his concept of narcissism, Narcissus' original mythological dilemma was profoundly different from that sketched in that familiar modern characterology. Narcissus suffered not error but horror. No ignorance through vanity tormented him at the last but rather his horrified and transfixing knowledge of the true nature what he loved. If he had to en-dure his own impenetrability as he withers, Echo, his companion in Ovid's story, has to endure a passivity which, nonetheless, has its marked effects.

Lacan offered the line, 'In the field of the unconscious the ears are the only orifice that cannot be closed', while his assertion that making oneself seen 'comes back towards the subject', but 'making oneself heard goes towards the other' repeated his own extension of Freud.[12] The verses above, however, wonder aloud about both these assertions and are not convinced by them. They suggest instead that Echo might be taken as a figure or a trope for the troubled nature of lyric poetry, driven on by rhyme, and condemned to hapless repetition of the cadences and sound associations in others' utterances. This piece also deploys such a long line itself that any listening ears will not catch its structure of rhymed alternating couplets. There seems to be a 'natural' length for the heard line, beyond which the ear cannot stretch, so that here an elaborate structure has turned out to be a workup for nothing. In that respect, it's in a rather worse position than poor Echo's enforced repetitions of others' endings. But in the final chapter, she'll make a more constructively passive appearance.

Yet how can I defend my flippant doggerel and its tongue-in-cheek exegesis here as having anything much to do with the serious question of how political subjects are consolidated? Only thus: Calling out, calling myself, and being called are all intimately related incarnations of the flesh of words. This materiality of language is packed through and through with its own historicity. Such a materiality isn't some antiquarian's decorative piecrust of orality or of etymology to garnish the real meat of what is being said, its meaning-content. The linguistic materiality lies rather in the reiteration, the echoes, the reflexivity, the cadences, the automatic self-parodies and the self-monumentalising which, constituting both being called and calling oneself, constitute the formation of categories of persons. There is nowhere beyond interpellation for us. Not so much because any speaker is also spoken by language and trapped, but rather because we do not and cannot have naming's full measure (indeed that 'we' is interpellation's measure of us) as it runs across and through us to go beyond itself. There is, in effect, a will to name. Often it pursues incalculable directions; it may run wild, or may look less anarchic altogether and appear to rein itself in or even make a display of its own historical sense. To attend to the inherently rhetorical nature of its calling, so often a latent political calling, wouldn't mean policing or cleaning off its rhetoricity, but trying to track both its effect and its affect. (And this kind of attending isn't so far removed from the experience of writing lyric as might first seem.) The materiality of words isn't the secondary but the immediate stuff of the political, while what's assigned as rhetoric bleeds and seeps so steadily into ordinary language that its boundaries are of degree and convention, not of kind. Yet though being named and self-naming happen from the outside as well as within any speaker, as exteriority as well as interiority, this doesn't imply that their affective temporality is an undistinguishable blur between verbal outer and verbal inner which renders these always the same. (A claim that sameness does exist here—which is also a claim to that 'successful' interpellation which indeed never fails—is what defines the ideological.) It's exactly in the lack of such a homogenised linguistic temporality, and instead within naming's very differences and repetitions, that for good or ill the possibilities of politics constantly arise.

FOUR

'The Wounded Fall in the Direction of Their Wound'

> *Socrates*:   And what do they think about me in Athens?
>
> *Menippus*: Ah, you are fortunate in that respect. You pass
>   for a most remarkable man, omniscient in fact.
>   And all the time—if the truth must out—you
>   know absolutely nothing.
>
> *Socrates*:   I told them that myself: but they would have it
>   that that was my irony.
>
> LUCIAN[1]

Tales from the river-bank

We are in hell. Or almost there; the destiny to which all travellers must come lies beyond the river of Lethe. These are sluggish waters, according to Plato, and sluggish, too, the recall of their past lives by the freshly dead who crowd its banks, waiting for their lots to be drawn for their next time round.[2] Striving to remember, fighting for adequate recapture of blurred detail, is usually a precursor of the will to be, and one kind of *amor fati*: What exactly was I, so that I can be it all over again, and be it better? But Plato recounts the vision told by Er, set on the river-bank, which undoes this wish. Here, to remember what one was runs closer to the will to not be it, to not repeat— but instead to assume a new destiny as a corrective to the past. In this drive to liberation through recall, it's remote from the stoicism of *amor fati* (but comes closer to Freud's conviction of the failure to remember, which is lived as a drive to repeat). Plato's dead souls, awaiting reincarnation, don't elect to repeat themselves by entering lives similar to those they have relinquished. If they choose rationally, they may settle for future lives of sharp contrast, therapeutic opposites. So Orpheus elects to become a swan in order not to be born again of woman, the sex which had just seen him out of one existence by tearing him limb from limb; so Odysseus, worn out by voyaging, plumps for a next life of restful obscurity. On the plain of Lethe, although your choice is narrowed to that range of futures to which your character inclines, you do have some scope to choose on the basis of whatever wisdom your past has managed to accumulate. You will have learned at least something, which may cloudily penetrate the amnesia-inducing river waters that you sip. Plato's own directive, to know how to distinguish the good from the evil life, and how to effect this critical choice, has its most profound test here on this river-bank.[3]

His dead, waiting in line for their sage or ill-chosen futures, still have some capacity to colour their destinies in their next reincarnation. But in Lucian's savagely witty burlesque, his *Dialogues of the Dead*, the freshly expired, queuing on the bank to be rowed across the Lethe by Charon, are forced to first lighten his boat by jettisoning each quirk of individuation: their titles, their characteristics, their foibles. Such differences weigh heavily, and would rock the boat. Everyone is forcibly stripped of each burdensome particularity; 'They must leave all this nonsense behind them, and come aboard in their skins'. The messenger of the gods and the ferryman of the dead together patrol their clientele; Hermes, surveying his fresh crop of punters, complains about the recent falling off in the quality of the customers: 'After all, Charon, in the old days, men were men; you remember the state they used to come down in—all blood and wounds generally. Nowadays a man is poisoned by his slave or his wife; or gets dropsy from overfeeding; a pale, spiritless lot, nothing like the men of old'.[4] It's Hermes who enjoys the task of frisking each shade for his attributes, to lighten the boat. So the famous good-looker, Charmoleos, is briskly received; 'That beauty must come off—lips, kisses, and all; the flowing locks, the blushing cheeks, the skin entire'. The tyrant Lampichusis is denuded of his wealth and his diadem, his cruelty and his folly, until he too stands bare. Crato's very reputation and pomp are peeled off, and any boasting from him brusquely checked; 'and you need not tell us what size your tomb was; remarks of that kind come heavy'. Most weighed down with his luggage of intellectual quackery, of 'prickly arguments, intricate conceptions, humbug and gammon and wishy-washy hair-splittings without end', is an anonymous philosopher who must submit to the unceremonious shearing of his beard and even of his bushy eyebrows, 'trained up all over his forehead, for reasons best known to himself'. A clutch of dead rhetoricians are ordered to junk 'your verbosities and your barbarisms, your antitheses and balances and periods' before they are allowed to embark. Only Menippus, the cynic, is permitted to hang on to his attributes of high-spirited independence and speedy wit. As Hermes remarks, 'useful commodities, these, on ship-board! light and handy'.[5]

Lucian's celebs, marooned in the underworld, furiously lament their lost glories, their failed scheming in life, their withered heroics, and their trickeries, which had sometimes enticed them to fall into their own traps, thwarted by a precipitous end. Or their great beauty gone: Helen boiled down to a bare skull. The great Achilles remarks morosely that among the dead, it is dead level. All skulls, denuded of flesh, now bear the common 'snub noses' of skeletal facial bone. There is a relentless democracy in being dead. Only the love-tormented Protesilaus is allowed to go up briefly to earth, to glimpse his bride again, for he cannot endure the urgency of his longing for her. 'Did you miss your dose of Lethe, man?' inquires Pluto severely; but frustrated love had proved stronger than even that liquid opiate. Lucian gives the final sardonic say to the pirate Sostratus, who points out that the dead wrongdoers were merely the slaves of fate's impersonal ordinances and so were hardly personally culpable. He's abjured by the judge, Minos, to keep this insight prudently quiet.

But one modern embellishment of Plato's recounting of the myth of Er makes the dead will to next become that which has already been allotted to them by destiny. An account of *amor fati* as the determination to repeat, is, in Klossowski's gloss on Nietzsche, sanctified with a mythology of its own.[6] Here Lachesis, the Fate whose province is the past, keeps a sharp eye on those directions the freshly dead may take in the light of their past experiences. Their choices are policed. If the dead drink only a little of the waters of forgetfulness, it allows just enough memory traces to remain intact to let them reminisce about their pasts, yet their recall is benign enough to ensure that they'll wish for that 'new' destiny into which they are, anyway, about to be reincarnated.

Such an amiable anaesthesia of a forced choice, an interest in being that which one is already condemned to become, is different again from another speculation on *amor fati*. Nietzsche's own rhetorical challenge is 'Do you really want this all over again?'[7] A daemon offers a man the chance to live his life in replica, to do it again in minute detail; 'This life as you live it and have lived it, you will have to live once more and innumerable times more; and there will be nothing new in it, but every pain and every joy and every thought and sigh and everything unutterably small or great in your life will have to return to you, all in the same succession and sequence—even this spider and this moonlight between the trees, and even this moment and I myself'. Contemplating this scenario he's devised, Nietzsche wonders, as he might, at that impassioned affirmation needed for a glad acceptance of such a highly ambiguous prospect: 'If this thought gained possession of you, it would change you as you are or perhaps crush you. The question in each and every thing, "do you desire this once more and innumerable times more?" would lie upon your actions as the greatest weight'.[8] But he doesn't make it clear whether the man who elected to relive his life as an eternal return would, throughout, continually realise that he was embarked on a series of relentless repetitions. Such an awareness, or its lack, would be crucial to the question of whether such a life might, on the far side of the initial yea-saying impulse, still remain bearable.

For knowledge of oneself is no panacea. That unfairly treated emblem of ignorant vanity, Narcissus, knew his plight of self-love perfectly well and died rooted to the spot in the torment of this very self-awareness. The injunction to 'know thyself' enacts its ambiguities in these different scenarios on the bank of the Lethe. For Plato's long queue awaiting reincarnation, a blurred and limited memory of what one once was casts a forward shadow over what one may become. For Lucian, all attributes of the self are gleefully unpeeled in the great democracy of the dead. Those garrulous dry bones who people his dialogues have been flayed of their attributes and have become literally featureless. Their 'will to be' is reduced to a furious nostalgia. Yet, satisfying the needs of burlesque, they still contrive to remain as characters. On Nietzsche's river-bank, there's a heroic plunge into wilful repetition, towards being it all over again, with a happy vengeance. In their different ways, all these dead souls take up attitudes towards what they have been and may next become. But in a twentieth-century corner of the world devoid of reincarnation, the attitude I bear towards myself has no prospect of a beyond, no anticipation of anywhere else to go. This may result in my electing to be it, deliberately and heavily, here and now.

An unhappy kind of *amor fati* may anchor itself in vengefully deter-mined being: 'The settling scar agrees to voice / what seems to speak its ear-liest cut. / A rage to be some wholeness gropes / past damage that it half re-calls— / where it was, I will found my name'.[9] Can the adoption of a societal or a national self-depiction sometimes mark a violent determina-tion, even an anger to be, even though this may be awkwardly allied to some calmly calculated aspect to the decision? This 'rage to be some whole-ness' is an inflamed inversion, perhaps, of Iago's strategically cool definition of love: 'It is merely a lust of the blood and a permission of the will'.[10] A will to be some entity could become an act of petrification. Just as too long a sacrifice can make a stone of the heart, so too rigid a self-conception could make a rock of the self, to which its own limpet shadow of self-portrayal must cling. And whatever allows a category to solidify must also include this drive towards inhabiting it—a drive not, though, to be neatly opposed to history, since in itself it's also historical.

Bad faith

This 'will to be' may reverberate through some acts of self-description. Vi-carious as these adopted categories are, that's not remotely material to the force of the drive to dwell in them. On the contrary, the more impersonally sociological and the duller the category, the more vehemently it may be viv-ified with its wearer's will. When such a will becomes entangled with a no-tion of inauthenticity, as is easily done, then Sartre's 'bad faith' furnishes one outcome. This bad faith he characterises as 'a certain art of forming contra-dictory concepts which unite in themselves both an idea and the negation of that idea',[11] while at the same time they carefully insist on preserving their differences. (This very characterisation could, neutrally, be applied to irony.) But Sartre's speculative psychology, in the grip of this logic, is always vacil-lating between transcendence and factity. To put a spoke in the wheels of this ceaseless oscillation is risky, for it may result in 'the man who deliber-ately arrests himself at one period in his life and refuses to take into consid-eration the later changes'.[12] Then to avoid such wilful self-paralysis (which recalls that overzealous keeper of promises suspected by Nietzsche), must some determinedly inventive self-fashioning ensue, and need this take the form, Sartre asks, of willing to be? The reader might cheerfully reply in the negative. Sartre, though, needs to hang on to his rhetorical question in order to introduce his famous character-type of twentieth-century philosophical psychology, the person who is 'in bad faith'. He asks, 'But what are we then, if we have the constant obligation to make ourselves what we are, if our mode of being is having the obligation to be what we are?'[13] This ushers in his celebrated puppet, the café waiter so zealously intent on being a waiter that he impersonates what he already is, in order to be quite certain to be seen as it. He is bad faith in a white apron.

But there's a counterpart to this waiter in a rarely cited and even less comfortable example of bad faith: 'the homosexual', unblinkingly glossed in Sartre's text as 'the paederast', who refuses the apparent sincerity of acknowledging that this indeed is what he is. This insufficient being is produced to set against the waiter's excessive being: 'Here is assuredly a man in bad faith who borders on the comic, since, acknowledging all the facts which are imputed to him, he refuses to draw from them the conclusion which they impose. His friend, who is his most severe critic, becomes irritated with this duplicity. The critic asks only one thing—and perhaps then he will show himself indulgent: that the guilty one recognise himself as guilty, that the homosexual declare frankly—whether humbly or boastfully matters little—"I am a paederast." We ask here: Who is in bad faith? The homosexual, or the champion of sincerity?'[14] Sartre's homosexual of the 1940s (hence not armed with a later diction of sexual liberation, yet certainly still faced with problems of what came to be termed 'being outed') is elided to a wilful 'paederast' who will not agree to interpret his mistakes as his crushing destiny: 'He does not wish to let himself be considered a thing. He has an obscure but strong feeling that a homosexual is not a homosexual as this table is a table or as this red-haired man is red-haired'.[15] For he intends to hold his future open, in suspense. To retain some hope to be born anew,

> he needs this perpetual rebirth, this constant escape in order to live; he must constantly put himself beyond reach in order to avoid the terrible judgement of collectivity. Thus he plays on the word being. He would be right actually if he understood the phrase 'I am not a paederast' in the sense of 'I am not what I am'. That is, if he declared to himself 'To the extent that a pattern of conduct is defined as the conduct of a paederast and to the extent that I have adopted this conduct, I am a paederast. But to the extent that human reality cannot be finally defined by patterns of conduct, I am not one'.

Sartre's caricature is not, though, permitted by his creator to become quite so reflective; more passive, he deceives himself by falling into straightforward denial.

But his fictional interrogator-friend is also in a weak position. Demanding 'sincerity' from the homosexual, he wants the latter to agree to treat himself as a thing, to allow his every act to stem from a core of identity. Then, after owning up to what he really was, the abject homosexual would be ripe for rehabilitation by his friendly critic—a supposition which Sartre denounces: 'Who cannot see how offensive to the Other and how reassuring for me is a statement such as "He's just a paederast" which removes a disturbing freedom from a trait and which aims at henceforth constituting all the acts of the other as consequences following strictly from his essence'.[16] For one can be too vigorously, as well as not be adequately. And an act of confession alone will not entail salvation: 'The man who confesses that he is evil has exchanged his disturbing "freedom-from-evil" for an inanimate character of evil'; he is evil, he clings to himself, he is what he is. But by the same stroke, he escapes from that thing, since it is he who contemplates it, since it depends on him to maintain it under his glance or to let it collapse in an infinity of particular acts'. So the harm, if once avowed as such, may be disarmed. A virginal future hovers, released from absolute characterisation. 'Thus the essential structure of sincerity does not differ from that of bad faith, since the sincere man constitutes himself as what he is in order not to be it. This explains the truth recognised by all, that one can fall into bad faith through being sincere'.[17] Both bad faith and sincerity alike can lift the self out of its own critical reach.

To be and not to be itself is self-consciousness's founding predicament. This ambiguity must always be fought out, for the ordinary relation of any self to itself can't escape this post-Hegelian restlessness in which the pursuit of self-definition, a will to be, is also its own undermining. 'If bad faith is possible, it is because it is an immediate, permanent threat to every project of the human being; it is because consciousness conceals in its being a permanent risk of bad faith'.[18] Despite this risky ordinariness, Sartre exhibits his own tableau of waxworks censoriously: the young woman who decides simply not to register the fact that her hand is, across the table, being held by her companion; the exaggeratedly waiterish waiter; and that most unconvincing pair of buddies, the homosexual and his hearty critic. An injection of irony would have enlivened and relaxed the stiffness of these vignettes, but Sartre had no time here for irony, deeming it a neighbour of bad faith and an instance of what he considers attitudes of negation towards the self. Despite his own shading of these figures to imply that some twist of a deficient psychology animates them, it nevertheless follows from the logic of his account that bad faith is not so much an inherent psychological failure but a risk of an ontologically premature arrestation in one condition. It's almost a problem of bad timing, as if the temporal dialectic of being has jammed at a certain stage. As such, it is an exaggerated form of a common hesitation endemic to being alive. Bad faith is what haunts the dialectic of self-description and others' descriptions. Bad timing goes with the territory.

Yet we could compare Sartre's discussion here of the classification 'the homosexual' with that of 'the Jew' in another interesting and worrying analysis he makes, in a sort of wartime revisiting of Marx: 'Thus, to know what the contemporary Jew is, we must ask the Christian conscience. And we must not ask, "What is a Jew?" but "What have you made of the Jews?"'[19] Being constructed from the outside can be no source of relief: 'The anti-Semite reproaches the Jew with being Jewish; the democrat reproaches him with wilfully considering himself a Jew. Between his enemy and his defender, the Jew is in a difficult situation: apparently he can do no more than choose the sauce with which he will be devoured. We must now ask ourselves the question: does the Jew exist?'[20] And in Sartre's own eventual reply, a confidently pluralist nationalism of Paris in 1944 speaks its strengths and its weaknesses:

> What we propose here is a concrete liberalism. By that we mean that all persons who through their work collaborate toward the greatness of a country have the full rights of citizens of that country. [. . .] This means, then, that the Jews—and likewise the Arabs and the Negroes—from the moment that they are participants in the national enterprise, have right in that enterprise: they are citizens. But they have these rights as Jews, Negroes, or Arabs—that is, as concrete persons. In societies where women vote, they are not asked to change their sex when they enter the voting booth: the vote of a woman is worth just as much as that of a man, but it is as a woman that she votes, with her womanly intuitions and concerns, in her full character of a woman. When it is a question of the legal rights of the Jew, and of the more obscure but equally indispensable rights that are

not inscribed in any code, he must enjoy those rights not as a potential Christian but precisely as a French Jew. It is with his character, his customs, his tastes, his religion if he has one, his name and his physical traits that we must accept him. And if that acceptance is total and sincere, the result will be, first, to make easier the Jew's choice of authenticity, and then, bit by bit, to make possible, without violence, and by the very course of history, that assimilation to which some would like to drive him by force.[21]

I've quoted Sartre at length because just here, his version of 'the will to be' has been deflected from its familiar psychological colouring and nudged towards its own latent question of the social and political consequences of 'being it'—although this question is, in the passage here, clearly ruined by its classically unhappy topography of the 'we' in here set against the 'him' out there. Today we often hear a supposedly liberal version of this partition of ourselves versus the stranger, but now rendered in the plural as 'them out there'. Sounding sensibly forbearing, this argument, made in modest defence of others' unpromising assertions of new identities, runs; 'But I can't object to their chosen way of identifying themselves, since they have every right to call themselves what they like'. (For example, 'they' want to declare themselves separatists in the exclusive group that they have willed into being.) Yet what this attitude tacitly does is altogether less liberal than it thinks. For it imposes an almost certainly false unity and consensus on the new 'they' and its claimed constituency, while next it cuts corners by excluding the resulting 'them' from the interrogation of serious debate. It's an argument which, having concurred with this 'they' as a radically separate entity, and then installed it as such among its own range of collectivities, inevitably fails to treat its creation in the egalitarian manner it likes to imagine.

There is one cousin of the notion of bad faith which will justify some degree of blaming the victim as, up to a point, quite correct. It's an argument which retains the flavour of a borderline psychology and which, half-realising this uncertain status, strives to present itself as fully distinctive. As an example of how it works, we could turn to Slavoj Žižek's rendition of Hegel's dialectic of form and content (here, the content is behaviour) where the truth of the matter comes to settle in the form. Žižek's scenario invokes Hegel's 'beautiful soul', the conscience so helplessly entrenched in contemplative abstractions that, isolated and yearning, it cannot grapple effectively with the world. 'It lives in dread of besmirching the splendour of its inner being by action and an existence', says Hegel,[22] and it collapses, swamped in this conception of itself, only to fade out into the sad light of its own transcendent purity. But this beautiful soul is wrenched instead towards an earthily sexed sociology in Žižek's vignette (which itself keeps a flavour of Sartre's limp-handed girl 'in bad faith'). A professionally long-suffering mother is abandoned by her family to do all the housework single-handed. This she undertakes with loud and prolonged complaint. She 'identifies' pleasurably with her own misery as a fragile victim of her ruthless relations, but in this, comments Žižek, 'her real identification is with the formal structure of the intersubjective field which enables her to assume this role'. So the explanation for her inability to let go of her own self-sacrifice is that 'by means of a purely formal act, the "beautiful soul" structures its social reality in advance in such a way that it can assume the role of passive victim; blinded by the fascinating content (the beauty of the role of "suffering victim") the subject overlooks his or her formal responsibility for the given state of things'. This responsibility demands that the subject exert an intervening will to grasp the world not as simply and 'objectively' there but as posited. This the lamenting mother has systematically failed to do. Again in Žižek's gloss, 'on the level of positive content she is an inactive victim, but her inactivity is already located in a field of effectivity [. . . .] For the reality to appear to us as the field of our own activity (or inactivity) we must conceive it in advance as "converted"—we must conceive ourselves as formally responsible–guilty for it'.[23]

Perhaps this analysis affords us an accidental cameo of Hegel in a black beret, abruptly Sartrean, and not for the first time. More seriously, it could imply that somehow I have to envisage myself, and quite without pathos, as held in a structure which is not of my own making but with which I tacitly concur; yet this formal situation should not generate an unadulterated psychological guilt in me, indeed my recognition of its impersonality is the precondition for my possibility to act. Persuasive though this scenario is, we're left with the problem of exactly what weight to accord to a guilt which must, then, be formal or 'structural', and as such may nurse some emancipatory hopes. Where, if anywhere at all, does some residual element of psychological guilt lurk within this structural guilt, which, as the quotations above intimate, can nevertheless carry its own injunction to me to act better? And then am I not even more bound to behave myself flawlessly within this structure, since having relieved me of my starring role as villain, it is so generously

carrying all the guilt for me? But at the same time, structural guilt does indeed 'put me in the wrong', by displacing me inside it. It's when I'm completely innocent that I feel especially uneasy, since then I am doubly put
awry, first by my dethronement at the hands of accusing interpellation and
then by my failure truly to be able to occupy even this position of skewed
blame. Then even the most structural of guilts cannot usually feel itself to be
quite clean, and must strive in vain to seek relief in its own formality. Constantly flooded by emotional guilt, that promise for change which is consequent on the structure's impersonality maintains itself with the greatest difficulty. If, for instance, I continue to dwell inside an arrangement which,
despite the affectionate intentions of both its inhabitants, is objectively and
structurally sadistic, and in which my own painful disappointment is both
guaranteed and endlessly renewed, then my disabling culpability will seep
back to me in the guise of my tenacious compliance, so hard for me to maintain as my 'only formal' guilt. On the other hand (to put it more optimisti-
cally), the very formality of the structure might now begin to address its own
demand for change, carrying me along with it; my properly depersonified
grasp of the form is a prerequisite for disentangling myself—if not, unfortu-
nately, a sufficient cause. The intricacies of structural guilt (or structural
sadism) don't readily concede to the interrogations which desperately seek
their ethical advice; but if there is an affect of language which includes its
syntactical structures, there can be a structural emotionality, one fit to be
cross-examined further. In the ensuing tussle to establish what pertains to the
category of psychology and what better fits the category of language, it might
help to view the psychological not as purely personal interiority and depth
but as an overarching structure: a turning inside out, to make it convex. And
then, although I have not yet managed to extract much practical instruction
out of that Hegelian notion of my 'formal' responsibility, it's clear that the
question of how wide a scene of effectivity I can come to envisage around
myself is critical for how I can grasp my agency. From this broader perspective, I might be sanguine about my own relative displacement. Again the
scope of my self-depiction, my own case history that I set forth, immediately
takes on (as it does in so many traditions) an ethical character.

Yet it follows that so, too, does my impulse to ditch all self-description.
Then I will want to quarrel with a set ascription, not by refusing the aptness
of its particular content as applied to me but by cross-examining the range

of suppositions about identity in the first place. Meanwhile, if I have to be fingered at all, then I will insist on being got right. In this spirit, Gilbert Sorrentino has issued a snappy warning:

> Whatever has made you
> The defendant you are
> There is no metaphor save specific.
> Don't associate
> Things on me, ever.[24]

One way of dodging inept attributions as they come showering down around my head is to be alertly tuned to the task of instead fixing in place the ones I do want. Still, that noun 'defendant' is all too apposite here. It's as if I stand before some bar of Being, where I am accused of being what I am. My defensive demand may ultimately come down to this: that what really needs to be got right, to be made exactly specific enough, is that very ontological charge against me.

'The Wounded Fall in the Direction of their Wound'

Lucretius writes: 'The body makes for the source from which the mind is pierced by love. For the wounded normally fall in the direction of their wound: the blood spurts out towards the source of the blow; and the enemy who delivered it, if he is fighting at close quarters, is bespattered by the crimson stream. So, when a man is pierced by the shafts of Venus, whether they are launched by a lad with womanish limbs or a woman radiating love from her whole body, he strives towards the source of the wound and craves to be united with it and to transmit something of his own substance from body to body'.[25] Shot by a bullet, the modern wounded body would spin and fall quite differently, not towards but away from the source of the attack. Lucretius made his observations at a time when the design of hand-to-hand weapons, such as the spear, would have ensured that you would collapse in the direction of the blow and of your assailant. Ignoring, with some difficulty, the entirely amorous thrust of his metaphor,[26] I'll instead wrench it around towards the figure of the wounded self, wounded by an aggressive description which it may then itself take on.

The wounded fall in the direction of their wound in the sense that the injury, if narrated enough and without transformation, has the terrible capacity to embrace and to infiltrate the whole person. Willingly or not, I advertise myself as scarred. Mechanically come the lines of 'Show your wound; ah yes, mine's deeper'. I can easily become not just 'the walking wounded', but in myself a walking wound. Walking, and talking too; and once I am a talking wound, I am at grave risk of being heard only as a scar on legs. There is a bleak impartiality in the fact that the grammar of the unconscious-as-language (like some theories of the unconscious of dreams) will apparently admit of no distinction between the subject and the object of injury. Experimental psychology has offered us a sound reason for not gossiping, in its demonstration that those who indulge in hostile gossip only have its unpleasant terms rebound on them, instead of attaching to the objects of their talk. But it rains, though, on the unjust and the just alike. With nothing at all by way of poetic justice, perhaps a similar, and morally indifferent, syntax of blame operates in the matter of 'being a victim'. This condition may be widely despised partly because the stuff of the lamentation will adhere like tar to the lamenter; that's one argument (beyond that of discretion) for never mournfully reflecting aloud, for example, 'I only ever attract sadists'. One beauty of steering clear of having any qualities at all is the freedom it confers from any attributes that might boomerang upon their owner.

'I am an injured self' freezes and perpetuates the injury, marks me as quintessentially wounded. It is boring to be always wounded, and it is especially boring to the self. One wants to put a statute of limitation on this kind of self-description. If I recognise, for instance, that I was what would now be called 'an abused child', then I cannot rest in that realisation, both gloomy and emancipating. I have to do something more interesting with the description, and, if I can, productively transform it. And then to adopt these public designations of being hurt may not, in fact, offer me the consolation that they purport to bring. They can act, paradoxically, to conceal the real persistence of the distressing memories of the condition they describe. Yet doesn't some effort at honesty entail my taking on some harsh name that I've been called, even if that naming was in itself a part of what might be designated as abuse? And in any event, my painful recall of any hostile description may induce self-interrogation as to whether I am really an *x*, as an ex once described me. Am I that name? It doesn't quite ring true, even under my severest self-examination. Yet the authority of angry calling is such that I can never be confident that it's mistaken. My hopes of redemptive integrity might lie in musing conscientiously as to whether I really was that thing, if I was once called it. (How easily one might resign oneself to fading away under the power of angry calling is evident through the success of the curse. Here an unsurprising anthropology of magical naming has been documented: I shall indeed die, because I have been named as about to die.)

Suppose, though, that my living self is made vivid to me largely through my bad name. Here Judith Butler has speculated,

> But what lets us occupy the discursive site of injury? How are we animated and mobilized by that discursive site and its injury, such that our very attachment to it becomes the condition for our re-signification of it? Called by an injurious name, I come into social being, and because I have a certain inevitable attachment to my existence, because a certain narcissism takes hold of any term that confers existence, I am led to embrace the terms that injure me because they constitute me socially. The self-colonising trajectory of certain forms of identity politics are symptomatic of this paradoxical embrace of the injurious term.[27]

Yet a chance of release from this painful embrace may be detected in the penumbra of the bad name itself; some relief may be retrieved from among its shadows if the deliberate flaunting of a harsh term can render it usefully queer to itself: 'An aesthetic enactment of an injurious word may both use the word and mention it, that is, make use of it to produce certain effects but also at the same time make reference to that very use, calling attention to it as a citation, situating that use within a citational legacy, making that use into an explicit discursive item to be reflected on, rather than a taken-for-granted operation of ordinary language', as Butler elaborates.[28] Irony possesses just this skill in making mention of something by displaying it, holding it aloft to view in a pair of tongs. It makes a curio out of the bad word, a proper object for dispassionate investigation. My last chapter will suggest how irony may operate as a responsible forensic pathologist.

I might steer clear of taking up any ironic attitude to my interpellative fate by quietly submitting to it. Alternatively, I could also be enacting my irony thoroughly, in exactly the same show of submission. Or else I could resolutely be the thing I am charged with being; I might pursue that destiny,

THE WOUNDED FALL IN THE DIRECTION OF THEIR WOUND

with or without some ironic edge to my resolve. For a comfortable and gratifying suffering can abound. Some unhappiness is suffused with a glow of
Gemütlichkeit. The charms of being an injured soul, the powerful pull towards the most florid language of suffering, need no special pleading. A
redemptive religiosity swells readily. So Flora Tristan, contemplating the passion of Christ on the cross, could reportedly declare: 'When I see Thy griev-
ous sufferings, Thy crown of thorns, and Thy most bitter trials, O Lord, how
trivial do they seem compared to mine!'[29] But such a witty and properly vig-
orous self-regard will often assume less direct and creepier forms. There is an
ostentatious aspect to self-portrayal. What Merleau-Ponty characterises as
the 'gesture' of the spoken word is apt enough, too, for the placing of the
self; a powerfully directing gesture, which waves its enunciator onward to
some greater whole.[30] It drags the body of its speaker in its wake. Studied
self-redesignation abjures isolation and launches headlong upon a tide of
communality. The speaker may even take decisive pride in surrendering all
presupposition of linguistic autonomy. There is a comfort in inscribing myself among the excluded, dwelling inside an unjustly treated category; here I
can make myself at home and contrive some domestic comfort inside my espoused estrangement.

For there are, admittedly, cheap pleasures in naming oneself as a bad
thing. Some dubious popular psychologism, such as, 'Of course I'm para-
noid' or 'I'm so neurotic' is often uttered with a winsome satisfaction. Near-
masochistic submission may flower in the adoption of a mildly derogatory
category. It is the narrow gate one enters with a bowed head, as in Althusser's
maxim about the subjection attendant on subjectification. Or it's a walk
through the saloon door with one's hands in the air before they start shooting, for shoot they will. I am taking on something given to me and which
assigns me. I step into it, surrender to its designating embrace. Isn't to take
on a lowering description sometimes a pleasurable resignation, an eroticised
and treacly submission? It makes me up, as I've consented to let it. And by
now, my account is starting to become heavy with an aura of sado-masochis-
tic exchange. There is worse. Film footage from a New York fetish loft shows
a chamber of descriptive sado-masochism and systematic verbal humiliation.
Literal as well as metaphorical tongue-lashing includes injurious epithets,
purchased dearly by those driven to buy them: 'Yes, yes, I'll say it, I am a
nigger, worthy only to be your slave, oh my dominatrix' and 'Degrade me,

my mistress, as I deserve, for I am a disgusting Jew, a foul faggot'.[31] More encouragingly, we can note that the will to be, whether or not pursued with a vengeance, need not necessarily be straightforward within its submissiveness. As Deleuze observes of Sacher-Masoch's *Venus in Furs*, that conventional fusion of conditions embodied in the word 'sado-masochism' is quite misguided, since the one is not the mirror image of the other: 'While the Sadeian hero subverts the law, the masochist should not by contrast be regarded as gladly submitting to it. The element of contempt in the submission of the masochist has often been emphasised: his apparent obedience conceals a criticism and a provocation. He simply attacks the law on another flank. [. . .] We all know ways of twisting the law by excess of zeal'.[32]

What is the nature of this act of taking on that which is already laid out for me? If it need not be masochistically humiliated, it's often masochistically defiant in this zealous manner. *Amor fati*, though literally and simply the love of one's fate, may be poised anywhere between a desperate and a nobly Stoic resolve to accept what I cannot avoid anyway, 'by taking on deliberately what I am fortuitously'.[33] Not as a quiet assumption of what's happened, but as biting the bullet to make sure for myself that it has already happened. Or to submit to futurity only through militantly abrogating to myself the dictates of fate. Mayn't there be a furious overreaching in vowing to be it, in naming oneself the monster of others' florid imaginations? Or some quieter self-will may decide on an announcement which is both retrospective and anticipatory: 'I will become this thing, which I recognise that I already was then, yet without quite realising it'. Differently again, Merleau-Ponty's drive to extract some moral exercise out of an unhappy tangle settles on an ethic of seizing on a contingency to appropriate it: 'For the value is there. It consists of actively being what we are by chance, of establishing that communication with others and with ourselves for which our temporal structure gives us the opportunity, and of which our liberty is only the rough outline'.[34] Actively being what we are by chance, not in order to discard it—but to run with it. This has an echo in Sartre's notion of taking on as my own whatever hand fate has played me, assuming it, and so (in theory) mastering its brutal contingency by making it my own. But this resolve is quite distinct from that 'being with a vengeance' which will seize on my public description, to wield it as my weapon. Its insistence that you must come fully to inhabit the events of your life is something quieter and yet more strenuous. As a demand, it is close to Kierkegaard's recommendation, 'It then requires courage to want to be glad'.[35]

The thought that your injuries are what you must come to take on, as only by this means can you calm your own self-damaging resentment, resonates among the Stoic philosophers. Epicureanism (a tendency horribly traduced by its much later champagne-and-truffles association) included the ethical duty not to be unhappy—especially the duty not to fall under the mournful sway of any philosophy of 'necessary' suffering. A Lucretian spirit refused to grant any charm to the negative: 'One of the most profound constants of naturalism is to denounce everything that is sadness, everything that is the cause of sadness, and everything that needs sadness to exercise its power'.[36] Deleuze, continuing in stoical vein, announces briskly, 'Either ethics has no sense at all or this is what it means and has nothing else to say: not to be unworthy of what happens to us. To grasp whatever happens as unjust and unwarranted (it is always someone else's fault) is, on the contrary, what renders our sore repugnant—veritable *ressentiment*, *ressentiment* of the event. [. . .] What is really immoral is the use of moral notions like just or unjust, merit or fault'.[37] But this reader, for one, fears that while this view might well be bracingly applied to, for example, one's upsetting divorce, it would have proved less instructive at Srebrenica.[38]

Ambiguous gains in categories of the self

> For personal uncertainty is not a doubt foreign to what is happening, but rather an objective structure of the event itself, insofar as it moves in two directions at once, and insofar as it fragments the subject following this double direction. Paradox is initially that which destroys good sense as the only direction, but it is also that which destroys common sense as the assignation of fixed identities.
>
> GILLES DELEUZE[39]

The injured self may have been further enticed to fall heavily in the direction of its wound by the personal politics of recent decades—an observation which by no means forgets their strengths. Here Wendy Brown, introducing her study of the production of social injury and its risks of becoming rigid within an ostensibly progressive politics, has argued tautly that 'Politicised identity thus enunciates itself, makes claims for itself, only by retrenching, restating, dramatising and inscribing its pain in politics; it can hold out no future—for itself or others—that triumphs over this pain. The loss of historical direction and with it the loss of futurity characteristic of the late modern age, is thus homologically refigured in the structure of desire of the dominant political expression of the age: identity politics'.[40]

This 'dominant' political expression (dominant at least in some places), conceived in great trouble, remains troubled itself. It's hard to determine exactly what is being asserted within its air of overall assertiveness. Within it, there may well be irritated identities. This is not far from the reflection that, as Butler has ventured, the subject is 'a kind of crossroads of identification, identifications that are carried by language'.[41] Yet even this may in the end be too purposive a metaphor, not ruthlessly casual enough. Crossroads are witnesses to past effort: prominent intersections, useful sites to bury your vampire, a stake skewered through his heart, whereas subjects may be more haphazardly pinned down. Their confinement may have an unpredictable duration, with their components knotted off with a slack loop or no more than clustered threads, filaments fanned out.

Even when this bundle of effects has been tied and unified under its appellation, there's little hope of tranquillity. 'I am downwardly mobile', 'I am postsexual', 'I am deracinated': from the most sociological to the most idiosyncratically adjectival, the self-descriptions are susceptible to upheaval. What geological surveyors term settlement, heave, landfill, and subsidence are everyday hazards of categories of the person. Intricately energetic classifications may become dully stiff, impacted masses, slowed and hardened like cooled lava. More fluid names of a self can spill into namelessness; others thicken to slip into the drift of descriptions until submerged, perhaps to bob idly to the surface again, but now in unrecognisable shapes. Others sink into a sluggish taxonomy. Few self-descriptions aren't themselves the unrecognisable residues of a forgotten deposit and aren't open to a creeping politicisation.[42] More muscular categories such as 'class' may periodically strangle others in the Darwinian struggle for the survival of the fittest identification. This is no fight among contestants of comparable vigour; no gentlemen marshal on an agreed terrain with their seconds to exchange pistol shots at dawn. As Foucault has it, 'Rather, as Nietzsche demonstrates in his analysis of good and evil, it is a "non-place", a pure distance, which indicates that the adversaries do not belong to a common place. Consequently, no one is responsible for an emergence; no one can glory in it, since it always occurs in the interstice'.[43] Yet while the identity which emerges in the cracks of such a rough contest is rarely a rounded thing, nevertheless its contemporary invocations conspire to suggest exactly that: that it is something finished, a desirable purchase to be held up to the light, patted, inspected, and, if desired, carried home. Against such commodification, Zygmunt Bauman has declared instead that 'identity' is really the name given to attempts at escape from the uncertainty of not quite belonging:

> Hence identity, although ostensibly a noun, behaves like a verb, albeit a strange one to be sure: it appears only in the future tense. Though all too often hypostatised as an attribute of a material entity, identity has the ontological status of a project and a postulate. To say 'postulated identity' is to say one word too many, as there is not nor can there be any other identity but a postulated one. Identity is a critical projection of what is demanded and/or sought upon 'what is' with an added proviso that it is up to the 'what is' to rise, by its own effort, to the 'sought/demanded'; or more exactly still, identity is an oblique assertion of the inadequacy or incompleteness of the 'what is'.[44]

If we pursue the direction of Bauman's thought here, then the common urge towards identity itself becomes an implicit social critique. It is a testimony to a felt lack, which may explain its tenacity, even if identity does announce its own solution in the form of a wish fulfilment. It is in this respect magical thinking. Still, we are left with the puzzle of why such an uncertain testimony to life's unsatisfactoriness should retain so driving a resonance. (One answer, that identification forms the indispensable foundation for a politics, will soon be queried here.) It's remarkable that something which is so evidently mutable and plastic as an 'identity' should be periodically invoked and hunted as if it had the hard permanence of diamonds.

Some compound identities, such as that of being, say, Irish-American, can offer well-established niches to inhabit. But if I am Irish-Somalian, I might well end up not only unable to settle inside either component but also unable to occupy any settled interstitial identity as a 'hybrid', either. To make up some 'positive identity', when as accident has it I cannot occupy either a majoritarian identity or a majoritarian hybrid identity, is hard indeed. I could try spiritedly announcing myself a mongrel, a mulatto or a half-breed—seizing on the old pejorative terms to refashion them as mine. But all this returns to the question of need: Under what historical circumstances do I come to feel sure that I need to find an identity as an aura over and above the facts of my parentage? The cruel aspect of identities is their frustrated promise of an identification for everyone; but while slots of possible description may feverishly multiply, they still remain as mass-produced slots into which thousands, in their rare specificities, can never neatly fit. The tinier the club, the more restrictive the conditions for membership it lays down. A site where the minutest classifications seem to proliferate most freely is the names of sexual behaviour. That a catalogue of something called 'sexual preference' can be tabulated at all seems strange; that it offers such rapidly dating colours and transient flavours to its fluctuating schools of consumer, from 'vanilla' to 'snow queen', only underlines its ardent power of purchase; arresting, too, that this diction of having can now extend to saying that someone 'has sex', rather than that—as seems closer to the truth of the matter—sex has that person.

A category has its political life long before I sidle up to wrap myself in it, and whether my advance is made in a spirit of glad militancy or in a spirit of dejected resignation isn't material to that. But it does become material to me, if I become paralysed by the dilemmas of contemplating my own status on its threshold. If what's held out to me as an apt political rhetoric of self-description, as a progressive self-historicising, also happens to encourage a study of the self as liminal, that doorway can be a very cold place to lean for long. The repetition that I am an injured self would chill me to myself, but it is dull to be always hurt, and I bore myself in my dullness. The self cannot just relax into its knowledge, simultaneously gloomy and emancipating, of its own past harms. I may be unwillingly drawn to my old injuries; but if I become a case history to myself as I leaf carefully through my pages, I shall get stuck. My identification as disfigured becomes something that I recite to myself over and over; and while this may be almost comforting and unassailably secure, it leads me nowhere.

But aren't such musings straying from the critical point that it is often politically necessary to assert an identity? And then my hesitation on this score may be read as tantamount to a wish to 'get rid of the subject', which is often taken to be politically reprehensible, a mark of a somewhat old-fashioned light-mindedness. For someone today can find herself standing accused of advocating 'feminist poststructuralism' much as Marie Antoinette stood accused of advocating cake. I imagine a reader vigorously out of sympathy with the persuasions of the pages here. She slams them shut, retorting, 'It's all right for this author to produce her naïve and ivory tower objections to identities—white and privileged as no doubt she is, she hasn't even begun to grasp that there's a political imperative to what she calls self-description among those less fortunate than she is, because the lever of social change is the occupation of an identity, so that any serious and realistic political engagement must mean struggling to construct and assert one's own identity as a member of an oppressed group, and taking it on—not pussyfooting around in this misguided and idealist manner of hers'. As is usual with such rhetorical devices of imaginary debate, I am offering something of a caricature of my spectral opposition, with the design of fetching up shortly with a compromise of such overwhelming moderation that not even my spectre could disagree. Meanwhile, as a preliminary counter to her objections, I'll first recall that identity is not the same as solidarity. This point is extended in my last chapter, but I'll anticipate it here somewhat. Much must depend on what kind of identity is sought; so, for example, my claim to territorial autonomy as political emancipation may pass through an expression of nationalism in the course of my country's liberation struggle. Can I query this in the way that I might want to reproach the erection of some idiosyncratic trait into a personal identity—can the same structures of doubt conceivably be applied to both, without conflating the political and the trivial? Impertinent though this reflection may sound, they may. It is here, in their inevitable juxtaposition, that tensions are fiercest. In a calmer civil context, the rediscovery of identity's ceaselessly double-edged nature still hits hard and creates anxiety: 'In the specific context of contemporary liberal and bureaucratic disciplinary discourse, what kind of political recognition can identity-based claims seek—and what kind can they be counted on to want—that will not re-subordinate a subject that is itself historically subjugated through identity, through categories such as race or gender that emerged and circulated as terms of power to enact subordination?'[45] As Brown's answer to her own inquiry implies, we can reply only specifically and locally. What becomes of those designations, freshly minted, that do spread? Ideally we could electronically tag some new identification, like a bird of passage, to trace its flight paths. This assumes its lift-off. But a category which had once sounded neatly useful, like an essential oil or a distillation boiled down and strained off, may soon become noisily ripe for derision, scarcely to be pronounced without a groan. It may suffer the corrosions of parody on the way to its repository in the long home of the archive. Meanwhile, curious or grotesque discursive coincidences will constantly spring up across political vocabularies. So Bauman points to some odd congruences, across the political spectrum, of the advocacy of 'difference':

> postmodern times are marked by an almost universal agreement that difference is good, precious and in need of protection and cultivation. In the words of that towering figure of the postmodern intellectual right, Alain de Benoist; 'We see reasons for hope only in the affirmation of collective singularities, the spiritual reappropriation of heritages, the clear awareness of roots and specific cultures'.[46] The spiritual guide of the Italian new fascist movement, Julius Evola, is even more blunt; 'The racists recognise difference and want difference'.[47]

In France, it has been easy to hear Jean-Marie Le Pen, in the name of the Front National, praising 'cultural differences'. So both right and left, the traditional and more recent theorists of separateness, now agree on the desirability of living with strangers by keeping them apart in all their rich diversity—but now in the name of the pluralist and multiculturalist community.[48] Common causes may indeed be dangerous where their insistence on an identity of 'difference' serves to guarantee the expulsion of those they single out.

Isn't this example irrelevant, though, because we were not debating such cultural identities which, bestowed from the outside, become political counters, but those self-chosen personal identities springing from the new acknowledgement of some hitherto repressed harm? But these too are open to similar, if lesser, risks. I'll flick through some of the drawbacks and gains in a few commonplace identities of the hurt self which accident has laid open to me. These are innocuous indeed on any serious scale of damage—but enough already! Where newly shaped or more often reshaped categories such as 'the abused child' describe some once-buried ill which has been brought to light, or where they recognise unadmitted needs, then their formation is profoundly helpful. Yet their installation within those they portray is also ambiguous in its effects. These new characterisations may eventually become sources of damage in their turn—to someone who inhabits them for too long and vengefully, as a mode of life—although evidently they will cause a very different and usually less acute harm than the original wrong. There's a fine but vital line to be drawn here—between taking on a self-description as if it both delineated and guaranteed my very soul, and taking it on as transient, as contingent, as able to be superseded and not definitive of me. At this point in the argument, it's often retorted that only someone 'with a secure identity' is in the luxurious position of being able to afford *not* to espouse the concept of identity. That, at least in my understanding, is simply not true. There's a world of difference between settling some context for yourself— and discovering 'an identity'. For instance, to be brought up as the child of one set of parents, then much later to stumble upon the fact that these were not one's original parents at all, might well be assumed to generate 'a crisis of identity'. Yet it can do the very opposite—the previous long years of unease become immediately explicable, and the suddenly revealed genealogical lacuna ushers in an illuminating confirmation as to why things were as they were. As is often the case, this 'lack' is really a kind of plenitude—not mournful, but a positively productive lack. This distinction between acquiring historical knowledge about oneself and acquiring a new identity isn't mere semantic fussiness. I underline it because it underpins this example: The promise of an identity was a consolation prize held out to those born in England and debarred (under more restrictive terms than Scots law) from knowing anything about their original parentage before the legislative reforms of 1975.[49] But this newly proposed identity involved a prospect of 'being reunited' which could be dashed, while its inevitable disappointments would then become hard to acknowledge in a culture of originary identity which so emphasised its curative powers to heal the torment of blankness. Hard-won realism may dictate a scepticism towards identity, since it may, in all honesty, be able to locate its truest identity only within its dispersal. This is not to imply that to have access to one's personal history isn't crucial. Its earlier legal suppression was certainly a cruelty. But the cruelty lay, not in its refusal of an identity, but in the obliteration of a history.

A collectivity of illegitimates as such is indeed implausible; it's the felt need for information about their past which has brought people together to question the laws of concealment—a need which will only take the form of association for as long as its satisfaction is blocked by legislation. Pressure groups flourish for mutual aid in the hunt for ancestors; there are Web sites for a 'Bastard Nation', since US state laws vary in the access they allow to records of birth, and the great majority remain thoroughly restrictive.[50] This need to unearth some history of yourself is hardly belittled by its consequence: that what you may establish, through discovering background facts and perhaps some living relatives, may not be an 'identity' so much as a short history of the impossibility of having an identity. To mention that the search for an 'identity', with its glowing promise of fullness, might eventually prove to be a chimaera is no chilly and high-handed reproach to those who are ardently in search of one—but only (and this observation does smack of the benevolent parent's tone) that identity's promises here may turn out to be misleading. Yet, more significantly, the object lesson that one gains about its elusive nature does nothing whatsoever to detract from the real imperative of knowledge about your past. On the contrary: There may be a measure of relief in tracing the actual extent of your own historical dispersal, rather than struggling to be able to cup some newly consolidated and satisfyingly fully rounded identity in your hands. In fact, this idea of a consolation to be gathered among the very facts of one's dispersal will need to be justified and supported rather rapidly, since the burgeoning new technologies of birth are fast making archaisms out of the conventional bases for one's familial identity. To know and to live with two biological parents of different sexes may become even more of a rarity as the number of children who result from casual and vanishing fathers, or from careful but nameless donor insemination, perhaps becomes outstripped by those whose laboratory conceptions are wholly extrauterine. Then many infants will, in future, be cloned directly from cells. When there are no warm bodies at all, and not even the anonymous penis in the dark, then what will become of that notion of personal identity which has for centuries rested on genealogy?

To announce today that 'I am illegitimate' could resonate with the anxiety or the piety of someone fishing up an old injury, or could just be an innocuous statement of legal fact (which is becoming drained of consequence in more countries, although the legislation remains uneven and its future extensions uncertain). As a self-description in England, 'being illegitimate' has a quite other ring for my children's generation than for mine, as it had meant something violently different again for the generation before mine. So my newly discovered elderly relatives will tell me that I 'need not be ashamed of what I am'; theirs is a kindly reassurance, because it marks a recent capacity to separate the status of illegitimacy from the person of its bearer. Injurious vocabulary, fortunately, does have its own history of decay; it withers on its feet, and the old term of abuse slowly becomes dust. A quarter of a century ago, I bridled at 'bastard' used as a handy piece of abuse, while feeling that it was prissy to object, as on occasion I did, to its casual use in the mouths of those who had no quarrel with the class of illegitimates and who were surprised to have the meaning of their reference pointed out. Now in Britain it's easy to detach the old sting from the word 'bastard', thanks to the numerical rise of single mothers who keep their children and to the legislative changes which have allowed these children better claims (in theory) to maintenance. So the ranks of candidates for the annals of victimhood are reduced, and the armoury of aggressive terms, which in one decade could devastate its targets, can in succeeding years mercifully dwindle.

The emergence of 'the abused child'[51] adds another story of the person, a freshly available category of being, previously submerged under other forgotten codes (such as the regulations against 'overcrowding', in effect a euphemism for incest, in nineteenth-century public housing records). This emergence of the group condition can shift the old burden of private badness away from its hitherto isolated subject. To become able to say to oneself, 'So that's what I was: an abused child', yet only to consider it at all because this description has been coined and circulated during one's lifetime—what, for its new human subject, does this sudden linguistic resource achieve? That the category of child abuse has been established is an advantage and a relief, even though its histrionic risks in self-description are patent and one might well not want to wear it. Its good effects are clear: ammunition for the defence of those at risk and practical protective outcomes. Its glaring weaknesses as a self-description are its potential as a final destiny, its enticement to fatalism. But by means of this recently produced sociology, at least a helpful impersonality can ensue, in that I am suddenly freed from that ascribed burden of my uniquely bad nature, which previously meant that I deserved all I got. For instead I am released into a new collectivity of those who are no longer themselves held culpable for the violence they received. Nevertheless, I learn that I must pay for my ambiguous emancipation in some other currency. I discover that the culture of victimhood can also inadvertently de-monise those victims it has kindly identified, so that, in a legal context un-scrupulous enough to disregard all evidence to the contrary, I find myself charged with being a likely perpetrator of child physical abuse because I was once its victim. But although the gains I may make through this category's articulation are thus sharply double-edged, this is typical enough of those in-escapable historical ambiguities which mark so many rising identities. Even if these are voiced and chosen from within the group (although language cannot have such an originating and clean 'within'), that moment of an ap-parently self-selected description does nothing to arrest the volatility of its subsequent movements and cannot secure it somewhere politically benign and always adequate. That does not mean that any identity is to be shunned absolutely (a vain proscription), but it does mean that its strategic risks as well as its campaigning uses need to be scrupulously anticipated. Such an an-ticipation may demand a stance of sympathetic impersonality both towards and within an identity, rather than the determined embrace of some personal identity which will ultimately recoil against its wearer. This analytic imper-sonality can in itself constitute a critical solidarity. By no means indifferent to its situation which is also that of others, it understands that it's heavily im-plicated, it studies itself keenly as positioned and societally named; but it will use, distort, and return that name with a scepticism which has closely ob-served its categorical consolidation and, in laying this bare, plans to acceler-ate its decay. But should this critical solidarity periodically require the adop-tion of an externally imposed label as strategic pathos, then so be it. As there can be no room allowed to holy identities, there can be none for sacrosanct or forbidden 'unethical' tactics.

Let me labour this point with a third familiar example, that of the emer-gence of the 'single mother', a catch-all category marked out for critical at-tention by the current British government of New Labour as well as its con-servative predecessor. To declare oneself a single parent carries a mechanical note of defiance, springing from the vilification of this thoroughly com-monplace condition.[52] The vast group of single parents are designated as a social condition defined only negatively, by what you do not have (even though 'the double parent' is, in Britain, such an endangered species as to at-tract governmental conservation). Because it masks a range of circum-stances, blending those alone from the onset by preference, or alone intermittently, or consequent on abandonment, the grounds for shaping a coun-teridentity of single parents 'from within' are limited. For every unhappy family is indeed always differently lived, if in a common ordinariness of feel-ing; whereas for those contentedly alone, their condition, exactly because it is untroubled, need not urge them towards 'identifying' with others. Perhaps the main impulse leading to identification is indeed unhappiness. Then any potential for solidarity would lie in a capacity to look out over the parapet of one's self-description and to generalise it, yet not on the basis of exact replication. If, identified as a single parent, I also decide to take on this cat-egorisation, however vexing it is, as my own project—if I also want to make something out of it—then something very different is happening through my act of consent to that bracket, as distinct from my assignment to it by others. To make it into a productive difference would need an emerging and energetic solidarity to run counter to, or right across, the boundaries of the officially bestowed and homogenising identity. But here diffused oppro-brium is hard to counter, since its true targets are never openly specified, hiding in an unadmitted distinction between the 'deserving' respectable ca-sualties of marriage breakdown who cost the government nothing by way of support, and the 'undeserving' welfare claimants who draw on state funds. Then some wider solidarity might, across this divide of economic differ-ences, seize back and prise apart the withering designation to expose its eco-nomic basis—and in full anticipation of that designation's pitfalls if instead it were to slide, as everything entices and provokes it to slide, into a defen-sive identity.

And yet of course one cannot abjure self-telling altogether, and no clean line can ever be drawn in practice between the ambitious sense of lack which transforms itself in the direction of altruism, and the lonely sense of lack which collapses into abjection. Nor is there an innocent language here. The need for strategic self-description is familiar to much political campaigning, where it rapidly becomes evident that a bad rhetoric may draw people to-wards a better cause. An antiracist sensibility, for instance, may be generated through a sentimentalised racial rhetoric. The ambiguities in its develop-ment are illustrated by the example of the early 1930s international agitation over the trial in Alabama of the Scottsboro Boys, who were accused of the rape of two white women. The Communist Party's defence campaigns in-voked, and produced with great success, 'the Negro mother'; while the ascription to the young defendants of letters of appeal intended their diction to be identified as black vernacular speech because it was couched in an established 'darkie' syntax of pathos, of 'us poor boys': 'Working class boys, we asks you to save us from being burnt on the electric chair. We's only poor working boys whose skin is black'.[53] The authors of this study, James A. Miller and Susan Pennybacker, have commented that

> The various voices within which the Scottsboro Boys and subsequently their mothers spoke—or were spoken—all reflected various attempts to convey black vernacular speech—some to be sure more accurately and authentically sounding than others. In an important sense, these attempts to render black 'authenticity' go to the heart of the strategic and rhetorical decisions which shaped the Scottsboro campaign. Any attempt to render black vernacular speech was bound to be highly-charged, carrying with it as it did the possibilities of replicating deeply entrenched racial stereotypes that derived from minstrelsy as the dominant mode of representing black life in the United States.[54]

The dialectic of progressive feeling may move along gratingly and with deep embarrassment. This is borne out in any sentimentalised diction of sexed specificity which has knowingly and instrumentally been echoed by its subjects, such as that of the woman who should be granted the vote in order to humanise the rigour of the masculine electorate with her different softness and her domestic tenderness, or of the homosexual who was fashioned askew by his Creator and who consequently shouldn't be blamed for his condition, but accepted. Here one is also struck by the speed with which the supposed biological determination of homosexuality has shifted in some quarters from being a slur to constituting grounds for its liberal defence, because the condition is 'genetic'. Something analogous happened with the rapid reversal of English policy on closed adoption records. An assertion of 'the right to know' one's parentage—somewhat vacuous as a rhetorical claim, and slipping dangerously towards a mystique of blood—nevertheless still chimed in well enough with other new assertions of human rights to enable these once rigidly sealed records to be released, although gingerly and with mandatory counselling. That practical development has made clear the mercifully transient nature of any claim to be wounded through one's systematically obscured birth alone. Yet if we transpose these questions to Argentina and to

Chile, where thousands of adults and children, *los desaparecidos*, were systematically 'disappeared' under the regimes of the 1970s, then we set them within an infinitely harsher history and its rigorous demand for clarity.

Linguistic healing

On the road to Emmaus, Saul becomes Paul, in a blow of light. Being is sentenced into being at the Annunciation, the instant at which the Angel Gabriel informs a distraught Mary that she's to become the mother of God. Potent in itself, that announcement could not bring about the conception; that 'the Word was made Flesh' was, according to the gospel of St Luke, the work of the Holy Ghost. But the power of naming is emphasised in the wide phenomenon of ritual renaming, writing anew on a clean slate. Baptism is such a redesignation, claiming the soul for the church; a child's new name, bestowed on adoption, was held to obliterate its past; and a second and compensatory adult baptism in which an African name replaces a 'slave name' makes restitution, at least rhetorically, for a bad job. All this rather resembles the venerable work of dissociation again: In the same spirit that by failing to register some aggressive description I defuse it (at least somewhat), so I may refuse to give house room within linguistic memory to some damaging history. Even the moment of damnation can resemble an unholy baptism. There is a frequently screened scenario in television drama where the angry, wretched youth, perched on scaffolding or poised on the parapet of some tall building, cries out furiously to the cop trying to cajole him down, 'Tell me I'm a loser!' and the cop, who's long since had enough, obligingly replies 'You're a loser'. The youth jumps.

So the subject becomes shot through with descriptive arrows fired from many angles and is left as perforated as the martyred St Sebastian. But must it simply hang there, limp and gorgeous? The sacrificial iconography of 'the wounded subject' forgets that arrows can be gingerly plucked out, resharpened, and slung back. Whereas that old chant of bravado in the school playground always did ring hollow: 'Sticks and stones may break my bones. But words can never hurt me!'—a defiant bromide in which no one could ever have placed much faith. For toughing it out in the face of verbal hostility is a lonely last stand, which ultimately needs to call on reinforcements from the cavalry of more generous and alternative descriptions. Meanwhile, the very reception of injury may also save itself by elaborating on the aggressive word. Repeatedly called 'bad', I could strive to extricate myself in several ways: by quarrelling with the ascription itself, or by querying the motives of my accuser, or by accepting it just long enough to parody it, or by refusing to accept any characterisation and instead insisting on being nothing at all. Each device has its uses as well as its drawbacks. Certainly effective recovery for the word-wounded won't result from tossing back the bad name at my attacker, as war movie heroes do with the enemy's hand grenades—a gesture never too efficacious outside the film studios. The literary method of being with a vengeance, being a stubborn and gloriously seductive bastard, as espoused by Violette Leduc or Jean Genet, bears witness to its own suffocations.[55] The utopian tactic, espoused by some idealists within the 'caring professions', reinvents the self as a dispenser of wisdom, a 'wounded healer' like the mythological centaur Chiron, a notable teacher elevated after his death to gleam on as an asteroidlike heavenly body. Such grandiose reincarnation aside, how could there be a linguistic healing for the linguistically wounded? Oleaginous 1970s song lyrics about 's-s-sexual healing', as performed by Marvin Gaye, explained to their listeners just how that particular outcome was to be achieved. By analogy with their instruction, 'linguistic healing' should come about through a better (more extensive and more sensitive) use of language.

As a domestic illustration, I'll put myself in the linguistic position of a child, regularly called 'evil', who must cross-examine herself daily as to whether she really is. I have to study the interpellation closely, not because I feel especially guilty, but because of its awe-ful authority. Here it is the interpellation's authority that works and not just the parent's, because the power of that language on anyone's lips would give me pause. Soused in the diction of Christianity, I hear that a terrible metaphysical inheritance is being evoked and brought to bear on me. How might it ever become possible for a child in this position to begin to query this attribution of badness? To deploy deliberated irony couldn't help, and anyway is well beyond my reach. But that peculiar thingness of repeated words, which in its fully fledged form may produce irony, is always available to me. It emerges as the comical effects of reiteration. 'Boll-weevil, evil, evil boll-weevil', I mutter inaudibly to myself, having once encountered this exotic insect in a story of Southern cotton fields inside some imported American children's magazine. Or again, when I am habitually referred to only as 'she' by those around me, I soon begin to call myself 'she' too. Not because I seriously imagine that is really my first name, but rather as a low-grade kind of irony, which is spontaneous and needs no acquaintance with adult ironic devices. This automatic 'making strange' of the word through subdued repetition is quite safe to practise because it will not be detected as ironic by the grown-ups; and it's also safer for me in another way, because it parodically naturalises my less than gratifying manner of being named. Such intuitive strategies, silently rehearsed through many twilights, may indeed induce a state of psychological 'dissociation' in me—but where there are no other sources of help at hand, to distance oneself is an effective mechanism, if ultimately limited. The mechanical iteration and reiteration of harsh words has in itself generated at least this everyday and cheap anaesthetic of dissociation.

There is what we could name as a trauma of iteration and reiteration—that involuntary and hypnotic repetition to oneself of the worst interpellations, over and over, compulsively, as they flash unbidden across one's mind, perhaps years after their original articulation. This is a verbal version of post-traumatic stress disorder. There is nothing remotely comforting in such a reiterative misery. Nonetheless the question becomes, at what point might the helpless repetition of the aggressive word start to take on another quality, to become a phenomenon in itself, and to emerge in its full strangeness as an arbitrary echoing sound held in my mouth and in my inner ear? And next, at what point, if ever, might this thingness of the word become invaded with a further degree of detachment, which can then query what both this object of a word, and its utterer, are actually up to? This is the analytic stage, which will lead it towards an emancipating irony. Before the next chapter returns to this topic, my provisional answer as to how this might transpire must be stiffly formulaic: that the capacity for that flip into irony is highly historically specific. Yet it is not so rare.

What may also help someone trying to deflect an aggressive description —insofar as I succeed in extricating myself very far at all—is the presence of alternative and competing descriptions, but which still lie within the same rhetorical tradition that accuses me. Given that a harsh utterance will often serve to distract its target's attention from the motives of the attacker, so that I am unlikely to be able to deflect some antagonistic naming by speculating on the psychology of whoever has voiced it, then some recourse to a different, yet proximate, speech becomes critical. In the case of the child called evil, mantras useful as protective charms could be extracted from the very same metaphysics that had furnished the denunciation. This is the time-honoured device of consolation, drawn from the ambiguous armoury of religion—the pathetic 'Christ might still care for a child, however bad it is' or the Lutheran 'if I do my honest best, then I am answerable only before God and not to man'. So, following my practice of self-examination, a clear enough conscience confers relative invulnerability before my accusers. I may end up with a severely inflamed sense of justice, but at least I will still have a potent defence, because I have found a diction which is an enlarged version of that which has attacked me. Without this battery of protective saws, picked out of the stockpile which furnished the original onslaught, all would be much harder.

It follows, then, that there's a simple salvationist argument for establishing as wide a discursive field as possible—that it provides more directions in which to run.[56] If my self-scrutiny results in my incorporating fresh linguistic possibilities which would also be sanctioned within the discursive community of my accuser, then immediately I am less alone in the teeth of rough speaking at home. If the limits of my language are indeed those Wittgensteinian 'limits of my world', then acquiring more linguistic resources will afford me a protecting extension of my territory. Such additions to my ways of talking can also helpfully dedramatise my position by rendering it less idiosyncratically private, and reinstating it within a wider and common range of speech. It's sounder to extract some means of self-defence by enlarging the existing rhetorical formation that surrounds me, rather than relying on simple repudiation, 'No, I'm not!'—for my sheer denial leaves me out in the cold, backed up only by my defiance. But if from some broader range of speech I can begin to extract some protection against aggressive interpellation, I have at least begun to draw on a great democratic source of liberation: the very mutability of the words around me. The element of historical vulnerability can then begin to pass away from me, to *the* language—which, being infinitely greater than I am, can bear this burden without strain. Then, in its turn, it will become transformed again, back into *my* language. And perhaps this movement affords a concrete example of taking upon myself unapologetically the weight of my previous verbal injuries—yet doing so lightly, and through the ultimately liberating agency of words.

To return to Lucretius's dazzling metaphor for the painful condition of love, that 'the wounded fall in the direction of their wound': Neither the love nor the hurt can be in the least assuaged by this brutally mechanical collapse and inclination towards the source of their excitation. This stark fact offers us little that is consoling for the possible political advantage in assuming an identity founded in distress and not converted to solidarity. A pragmatic approach, however, does furnish a rough answer. In short, it may be strategically necessary to wield an identity to approach some desirable outcome. Later, it may become imperative to fight one's way out of that identity if it has come to characterise the entirety of the person in a manner which inhibits and distorts its earlier emancipatory impulse. Such a train of political-linguistic events (to repeat the venerable marxist maxim) 'History has shown us'—and copiously.

FIVE

Echo, irony, and the political

> *Fiorilla*: In Italia certamente
>
> non si fa l'amor cosi
>
> *Selim*:   In Turchia sicuramente
>
> non si fa l'amor cosi
>
> ROSSINI, *Il Turco in Italia*[1]

> everything is all right, and difficult
>
> FRANK O'HARA[2]

Irony's poor reputation

No one appears to have produced a full history of irony; a wise inhibition, since its incarnations appear so alarmingly dissimilar.[3] However can it have it come about that both these matters can be termed 'ironic'—first, wearing (say) a pair of beige mid-1970s flared crimplene trousers, and second, failing to realise that you have just murdered your father and slept with your mother?[4] The taxonomies of irony don't elucidate much here. Verbal irony, standardly distinguished from the dramatic or situational irony of theatres or events, is an infamous riddle: Exactly how does it work, linguistically? And however do we realise in the first place that there is something there to be deciphered? It's not that verbal irony is 'expressed in' language; the relation between these two is far more intimate. Or better, to mimic the celebrated Lacanian aside that there is no sexual relation—there *is* no ironic relation, because this irony is already the language in its tone and cadence, and immediately so. Lying in a simple inflection of the voice, or of the voice slipped onto the page, it generates puzzles of recognition and of knowingness. For if verbal irony states the opposite of what its speaker or writer means, the listener or reader must 'get it'—but must already have grasped enough of something to realise that something does need to be got. The history of irony, insofar as it can ever possess such a unitary thing, is marked by altering attitudes to how we come to see the true nature of things. There is both an ethics and an aesthetics of irony, and in this, it resembles the fate of ambiguity. But irony's question is no longer of how you tolerate or admire uncertainty, but how you tolerate or admire knowing, as it tips dangerously towards knowingness.

Irony has its periods of being respected, and its longer periods of being despised as a slight, enfeebled thing. As a rhetorical device, it has drifted well away from its etymological anchor in the 'simulated ignorance' of *eironeia*. Yet its poor reputation harks back to the enemies of Socrates. The Socratic practice—cross-questioning someone to clarify what he didn't know, in order to enlighten him, yet as if this was partly self-revealed—is the irony of knowing. Secretly understanding what it's really after, it operates by handing the suppositions of its victim back, presenting his own utterances afresh to him as mildly absurd things. Socrates' feigned ignorance was designed to expose confusions under the confident certainties of those it engaged. Yet this irony was also self-disparaging and no mean-spirited trickery; he himself observed, 'It isn't that, knowing the answers, I perplex other people. The truth is rather that I infect them also with the perplexity I feel myself'.[5] His advantage is that he knows that he doesn't know; his discussants usually don't know that they don't. Socrates enacts the clinical irony which clarifies a true perplexity. Yet later Aristotle downgraded *eironeia* as dissembling understatement, in effect telling lies: If admittedly better than boastfulness and at least 'more gentlemanly than buffoonery', it was no virtue.[6] Irony for Aristotle leaned towards the hopelessly low-life, despite its dignified location within Rhetoric which, embracing 'a knowledge of the emotions', was 'an offshoot of Dialectic on the one hand, and of Ethics on the other'.[7]

Such a suspicion of interrogative irony as a cunning pursuit, dear only to those who ought really to be more serious, encounters a further doubt: Isn't it somewhat sadistic? Some genres of irony do indeed require a clear victim; so situational irony in a drama lets the audience know something that the actor doesn't. When Oedipus prays that the killer of Laius should be cursed, we onlookers know that he curses himself. Revelation in dramatic irony is often an unveiling, revealing Hermione's marble statue as real warm flesh, or the hated corpse as the remains of someone loved, where the stage instruction to 'uncover the body'[8] sounds the note of sadism, the audience itself staged as voyeurs supposed to take pleasure in anticipating a character's shocked humiliation. Manipulation, or else superciliousness: Under such clouds, irony was in dire need of rehabilitation. That came when it hit the moral high ground; and a little history of irony would encompass its enactment as satire, its high moment in the eighteenth century.[9] Later literary irony moved well away (to make a crude generalisation) from attacking worldly corruption and folly, to drift to the softer and wistful irony of circumstance, towards an everyday pathos, to what Thomas Hardy called 'Life's little ironies'. A late eighteenth- and early nineteenth-century twist produced the notion of romantic irony, entangling romanticism with detachment in an extraordinary and uneasy alliance. It stemmed from the supposed predicament of the artist in the modern world, to offer a positive self-consciousness redeemed as desirable self-awareness: You should present the chaos of the modern world in your work, for you needn't try to reconcile its clashing elements. You will realise, painfully, that while your imagination is free, your capacities and your circumstances are limited. This irony approaches a dogma of heroic failure; you may be up against the wall, but you make a virtue out of knowing that you are there—a stance which heads in the direction of Samuel Beckett's utterly reliable saw, 'Fail again. Fail better'.[10] For, as Friedrich Schlegel neatly noted, 'Irony is no joke'. Or, irony is no laughing matter.[11] To escape the bitterness of a crippling realisation of our limits required a deeply ironic detachment; by giving up on any notion that the world was either moral or rational, you abandoned not only hope, but also (logically, at least) you abandoned despair. Well realising the limits of this logic, you could dispassionately observe yourself. That would, strictly, have entailed a curious return to a Stoic position of impersonal resolve, but romantic irony ground to a halt well short of this; it supported the significance of the expressive individual in a way that would not remotely have concerned the Stoic philosophers. It believed in that highly irritating creature, the Artist.

Schlegel's wittily elaborate, if violently fluctuating, concept of irony emphasised its staging as a verbal exchange; entwined with conscience, it was no aesthetic contemplation of the romantically isolated self, but an ethical one.[12] It's indeed death to irony once it becomes a declared aesthetic stance, which is perhaps why today's superficial ironisation of everything is itself so scorned that it's largely deployed with a jeer. Charmed with its own psychology, 'the ironic attitude' implies an urbane onlooker with a lightly twisted smile or a sardonic gaze upon the ills of contemporary life. But irony, if lived as a virtually permanent style, turns listlessly back on itself. As Schlegel observed, 'the most fundamental irony of irony is that even it becomes tiresome if we are always being confronted with it [. . .] if irony turns into a mannerism and becomes, as it were, ironical about the author'.[13] That other devoted student of irony, Kierkegaard, was also transfixed by Plato's Socrates as at least occasionally up to no good, his interrogations negative: 'One may ask a question, not in the interest of obtaining an answer, but to suck out the apparent content with a question, and leave only an emptiness remaining'. Irony retained too, a dubious urge towards escaping, for with it, 'the subject is always seeking to get outside the object, and this he attains to by becoming conscious at every moment that the object has no reality'. And Kierkegaard brooded over irony's exclusive nature; not everyone might crack such a riddle, which relied heavily on hearers wise to its tone of voice: 'The ironic figure of speech cancels itself. It is like a riddle and its solution possessed simultaneously'. This élite aspect of irony gave it a high perch from which to peer around. It 'looks down, as it were, on plain and ordinary discourse immediately understood by everyone: it travels in an exclusive incognito. . . . [It] occurs chiefly in the higher circles as a prerogative belonging to the same category as that *bon ton* requiring one to smile at innocence and regard virtue as a kind of prudishness, although one still believes in it to a certain extent'.[14] And Kierkegaard had little time for floridly romantic irony, either. Then could irony, thus suspect, still be a candidate for rehabilitation?

In his deeply Hegelian dissertation on the concept, which soon overarched its father's meditations, Kierkegaard held that the latter had taken even Socrates to be a merely negatively free subject. Hegel, at times himself a relentlessly ironic thinker, had consequently disliked professional ironists. By the 'universal irony of the world' he meant its propensity for internal destruction and dissolution, whereas irony as a private stance was the mark, he feared, of a lapse of seriousness congenital to a languishing nature. The vagaries of 'dissemblance' exercised him[15]. 'So I am not really *in earnest*', he concluded in respect of that artist who lived a self-composed life 'of mere *semblance*', for whom 'earnest can never come into being, as nothing has validity ascribed to it but the formalism of the I' and for whom 'skill in living an ironical artist life apprehends itself as a *God-like geniality*, for which every possible thing is a mere dead creature, to which the free creator, knowing himself to be wholly unattached, feels in no way bound, seeing that he can annihilate as well as create it'.[16] Such artistic irony, lived as a corrosive negativity was, again, inauthentic. In his own study of the ironic, Kierkegaard was dancing an elaborate *pas de deux* with Hegel. As choreographer of the whole work, he could allow himself periodically to spin off in a pirouette of his own:

> In this [the Socratic] sort of irony, everything should be playful and
> serious, guilelessly open and deeply hidden. It originates in the union of
> *savoir faire* and scientific spirit, in the conjunction of a perfectly instinctive
> and a perfectly conscious philosophy. It contains and arouses a feeling of
> indissoluble antagonism between the absolute and the relative, between the
> impossibility and the necessity of complete communication. It is the freest
> of all licenses, for by its means one transcends oneself; and yet it is also
> the most lawful, for it is absolutely necessary. It is a very good sign when
> the harmonious bores are at a loss about how they should react to this
> continuous self-parody, when they fluctuate endlessly between belief and
> disbelief until they get dizzy, and take what is meant as a joke seriously and
> what is meant seriously as a joke.[17]

And, he continued, Hegel had been unfairly confirmed in his bleak assessment of the ironists around him by the flaws of the postromantic philosophers: 'Hegel, in one-sidedly focusing on post-Fichtian irony, has overlooked the truth of irony, and as he identifies all irony with this, so he has done irony an injustice'.[18]

Kierkegaard himself did hold tight to a concept of the real thing, however much it might tease, and he worked towards mounting a passionate defence of it. This plunged him into a bathing metaphor of irony's oceanic revitalisation: 'As philosophers claim that no true philosophy is possible without doubt, so by the same token one may claim that no human life is possible without irony. When irony has first been mastered it undertakes a movement directly opposed to that wherein it proclaimed its life as unmastered. Irony now limits, renders definite, defines and thereby yields truth, actual-

ity and content; it chastens and punishes and thereby imparts stability, character and consistency. Irony is a disciplinarian feared only by those who do
not know it, but cherished by those who do. He who does not understand
irony and has no ear for its whisperings lacks *eo ipso* what might be called
the absolute beginning of the personal life'.[19] This is a strong claim indeed.
How can this most forceful advocacy of irony have evolved, despite Kierkegaard's earlier doubts? His *The Concept of Irony* eventually attains it wholeheartedly only by way of several dazzling glissades and somersaults. We will
sneak up on just one of his unlikely loopholes which does open a way to seriousness here—that is, irony as a form of dress.

Irony as costume

How far will the contemplation of irony as costume strain the metaphor, as
well as straining a garment? Perhaps not so far as it first looks. 'A man clad
in a condition': One can wear one's social being lightly, avowing its contingency. But if the impulse to characterise myself is supposed to indicate a will
to truth, what could it be to inhabit a self-description 'authentically' if the
thing is really only picked out like a fashion item? If I hold my self-portrayal
to be a reliable report on my interiority, it commits me to some effort at authenticity. It embodies some idea of bearing witness, even though I also realise that I'm an amateur sociologist of my self. But then this entire business
of taking on a personal category must at first sight lack integrity, since this
tailored costume which, obediently or triumphantly, I pull on, is off the peg.
It is hardly couture made expressly to fit me. Nor is it the expensive em-
broidery of some poetic self-fashioning where furbelows are indulged and
pleating allowed to run riot. It is mass marketing. Off the peg is desirable
enough, if I can afford the designer I want; but even if I can't, these days the
market in high-street copies is booming. A particular self-description might
suit: 'Do I look good in this one?' It's one of this season's, but won't quite fit
me at its seams and there's no decent hang. Still, it'll show off the newer
identificatory modes if I give it a whirl. And after all, a fashionable bagginess
is de rigueur. Self-descriptions, including those of 'identity politics', are indeed costumes, whether avant-garde or hopelessly outmoded. To wear one
means first trying it on—and sometimes in both senses. It's a suit, a fancy
dress which is pronounced: a label on the lapel. Even that familiar dis-

avowal, which never quite works as its speaker might hope, 'I refuse to be labelled', aims for an air of studied déshabillé; but its state of undress may turn out to possess all the deliberation of the nudist colony which only ensures that no one goes truly naked.

The 'art clothing' made by Stephen Willats has recently offered some gaily literal renditions of this metaphor of self-labelling as costume.[20] His tunic dresses in geometric shapes have clear plastic pockets stitched onto their fronts. Flash cards in white paper, printed in black type with adjectives—such as Rash, Bright, Smart, or else with the names of qualities, such as Idealism—are displayed in these pockets. The dress promotes the wearer of the clothes in whichever characteristics she selects to hang out to view. She becomes a walking advertisement for herself. All this is heavily ironical in its display of the knowingness which intends to be seen to know all about self-attribution. It understands that describing is potentially endless, for a further selection of adjectives waits in a wad of flash cards, stashed in one dress's breast pocket, to be pulled out as wanted by its imaginary wearer—imaginary, for this is clothing now in existence only as art. But it need not be. This dress of attributes could perfectly well be worn, as indeed are those sweatshirts which advertise the wearer's espoused qualities or convictions in far less knowing slogans altogether, such as 'Born to Be Wild' or 'Acid Head'. Such display is not too remote in spirit from the banally 'ironic' wearing of some dated fashion. You might, if you were a young woman in 1998, wear an electric blue nipped-in jacket with gilt buttons and large shoulder pads to satirise a 1980s notion of Whitehall power dressing; but if you couldn't contrive to get your entire setting right, your intended sartorial irony would crumple and you'd look merely bizarre. Irony dates as rapidly as style (perhaps it's a tribute to its fleeting temporality that an entire new range of a modish brand of watches is named 'Irony'[21]). Highly vulnerable to both its context and its onlookers, it easily turns embarrassingly arch in performance, yet this very vulnerability can also afford it a claim to protection. If you can put your irony on or off at will, it looks congenitally unserious and flippant, and Kierkegaard, acutely aware of this, goes for the demanding defence which turns this very contingency into a virtue. He exploits it. His catwalk notebook of 1841 credits the ironist as a sharp dresser: 'What costs the ironist time, however, is the care he lavishes on selecting the proper costume for the poetic personage he has poeticised himself to be. In

this matter the ironist has great skill, not to mention a considerable assort-
ment of masquerade costumes from which to make a judicious selection.
Now he strolls about with the proud mien of a Roman patrician in trimmed
toga, now he is sitting in the *sella curulis* with weighty Roman seriousness,
now he disguises himself in the humble cloth of a penitential pilgrim, now
he crosses his legs like a Turkish pasha in his harem, flits airily about like a
bird, a lovesick cyther player. This is what the ironist means when he maintains that one should live poetically, and this is what he attains by poetically
producing himself'.[22]

Yet if we strip this exquisitely ironised figure of Kierkegaard's bare of his
wilful and florid personage, we will end up with an uncontroversial description of the everyday processes of adopting a self-description. Sign up under
some popular slogan of identity and you have indeed bought the T-shirt.
But in any event, you must have something to put on. There is a will to become which is so endemic to this ordinary morning's act of getting dressed
that it becomes innocent. (Or rather, it becomes trivially linguistically guilty,
hence its faint unease.) It's true that this passage on self-invention as masquerade only reintroduces the old charge of irony's fatally light-minded passivity, as if to strengthen Hegel's suspicion. But Kierkegaard inches towards
irony's defence by presenting its air of arbitrariness as perfectly reasonable:
'All things are possible for the ironist. Our God is in the heavens; he hath
done whatsoever he hath pleased; the ironist is on earth, and does just as he
likes. Still, one cannot blame the ironist because he finds it so difficult to become something, for it is not easy to choose when one has such an enormous range of possibles. For a change he even deems it appropriate to let
fate and accident decide for him. He therefore counts on his fingers like a
child: rich man, poor man, beggar man, etc. As all these determinations
merely have the validity of possibility, he can even run through the whole lot
almost as quickly as a child'.[23]

The fact that self-fashioning may well exist in an uneasy dialogue with being fashioned, that the performing self may slide into being itself performed,
does cause Kierkegaard some misgiving: 'It is one thing poetically to produce
oneself, quite another to allow oneself to be poetically produced'.[24] But I'll
leave his teasingly ambivalent exposition of irony, for the time being, in order to chase elsewhere some ramifications of the metaphor of self-description
as costume. Others have taken a less ambiguously concerned attitude towards

the brutal contingency of those characteristics which one may assume or which may, on the other hand, assume the self. So Lucian's satires always play with the utterly disposable nature of human conditions, both material and temperamental. A personality is as tenuous and arbitrary a thing as a fortune. His light-hearted cynic, Menippus, has a story to tell about his travels in the underworld where he witnessed the figure of Chance doling out costumes to the living who, for a time, would wear whatever properties she had distrib-uted—properties in the senses both of attributes and stage props—until the accident of their death would recall them to her. 'And when the procession was done, everyone disrobes, gives up his character with his body, and ap-pears, as he originally was, just like his neighbour. Some, when Chance comes round collecting the properties, are silly enough to sulk and protest, as though they were being robbed of their own, instead of only returning loans'.[25] The democracy of the dead must hand back the props of those char-acteristics which alone had demarcated the living from each other. Here Lu-cian's wit pays profound tribute to the passive dictates of contingency.

Nevertheless, these several flirtations with, or upbraidings of, the ironic are all preoccupied with its least engaging variant: with irony as residing, treacherously, in the inessentials of personal style. Might irony appear instead in the service not of personality but impersonality? Arguably, it does need an impersonal character to be able to work at all. The redundant entrance of the uninteresting person of the ironist on the scene will at once make his at-tempt at irony appear as exactly that—at which point it must shrivel. Once irony is caught poking you in the ribs and nodding at you with a meaning-ful look, then at a stroke all is, hideously, up. Here Schlegel instead retrieves the properly anonymous ground: 'Philosophy is the real homeland of irony, which one would like to define as logical beauty; for wherever philosophy appears in oral or written dialogues—and is not simply confined to rigid sys-tems—there irony should be asked for and provided. And even the Stoics considered urbanity a virtue'.[26] One might want to amend this comment with the words, 'Especially the Stoics'. For there's a differently hopeful yet unassailably stoical attitude towards contingency, which doesn't bewail the fleetingness of personal identities as costumes and cloaks, but scrutinises them to reveal, phlegmatically, that behind the masks there are—more masks. So Foucault, in a grand rhetorical burst, joyously produced his long parade of possibilities in the course of discussing historical method:

First the parodical and farcical use [of history]. The historian offers this
confused and anonymous European, who no longer knows himself or
what name he should adopt, the possibility of alternate identities, more
individualised and substantial than his own. But the man with historical
sense will see that this substitution is simply a disguise. Historians supplied
the Revolution with Roman prototypes, romanticism with knight's armour,
and the Wagnerian hero was given the prop of a German hero—ephemeral
props that point to our own unreality. No-one kept them from venerating
these religions, from going to Bayreuth to commemorate a new after-life;
they were free, as well, to be transformed into street-vendors of empty
identities. The new historian, the genealogist, will know what to make of
this masquerade. He will not be too serious to enjoy it: on the contrary, he
will push the masquerade to its limits and prepare the great carnival of
time where masks are constantly reappearing. No longer the identification
of our faint individuality with the solid identities of the past, but our
'unrealisation' through the excessive choice of identities—Frederick of
Hohenstaufen, Caesar, Jesus, Dionysius and possibly Zarathustra. Taking
up these masks, revitalising the buffoonery of history, we adopt an identity
whose unreality surpasses that of God who started the charade.[27]

Before this flagrant charade of characters, parodied as paraded in this
dreamily monstrous procession, what kind of claim might we still make for
the more discreet and sober style of verbal irony? Only if we turn to its use
as a luminous felt-tip pen to highlight self-description's reiteration, and so
to generate a lively reflexivity, does it start to look very promising. For
irony's costumes do give it a quizzical air—but these costumes aren't cheaply
aesthetic. Irony has its own ethic of appearance, even though it can and
should have no ambition to be anything more than appearance. Irony has
to try things on (again, in both senses of that expression) because it is the
product of this impersonal integrity: Once it has heard and has become
alert to the harm in excessive reiteration, then it cannot any longer wear the
old formulae.

Echo makes possible the ironic

Hearing something said too many times will make it rise up out of its background, suspended in relief. But what goes to determine whether irritation
or boredom will be born of reiteration, rather than the saving grace of irony's

attentiveness to those categories which only unhelpfully apostrophise us? The nature of the categorical word's isolating is critical. Often this dawns during the archival work of feeling your way within the thickets of some strange discursive formation, where a growing sense of the peculiar intensity of its repetitions alerts you to the likelihood that something really is askew here. I'm not sure how forcefully a myriad archival reiterations of the word 'women' would strike a non-woman, who, probably possessing no brief here, might merely be bored. Yet officially being the named subject cannot determine a listener's response to reiteration, whether in the direction of captivation or suspicion; a woman sure of reiteration's neutrality might be quite unworried by reading a million invocations of her category. It is the presentation and the re-presentation of the category to its occupant that produces irony. But this is only a necessary, not a sufficient, condition for this irony to flourish. Reiteration may also give rise to nothing more or less than stultification in a clouded language, which, as George Orwell warned, obscures any political sensibility altogether.[28]

For the moment, though, let's push on in a spirit of subdued hope. There's an ordinary potential for irony to quietly interrogate damagingly rigid categories, including their predictable syntax. This has fuelled my excursion to Ovid's tale of Narcissus to retrieve the nymph Echo who shows that iteration can explode a category from within, and that language's parrotings sometimes do have a salutary agency. The word has the inbuilt capacity to interrogate itself, a latent capacity sparked into life by the truncated repetition which is both Echo's doom and her forte. A warning against assuming that good will always result from self-knowledge is plain in Narcissus' dilemma, outlined above in 'Affections of the Ear'. A related aspect of this story, discussed in Claire Nouvet's reading of Ovid, implies Narcissus' almost 'criminal responsibility' in not responding to Echo. His failure Ovid's text 'understands as it were etymologically (since responsibility comes from *respondere*, to respond), as the duty of responsibility to the call of the other'.[29] Yet, she continues, the tension between the text and its narrative then drain away any such a traditional 'ethical' possibility. For no echo, being automatic, can knowingly provoke any intelligible response, let alone constitute one in itself. Indeed poor Echo herself, disembodied into pure sound, can only ever respond—but she's compelled to respond far too much. She can never initiate any exchange. My own intuition, though, is to drag Echo back to the side of hope. But this is not offered as any ethic of 'intersubjectivity'. Echo's is a strictly solitary ethic of performance, and a largely impersonal and thoroughly decentred performance at that. Still, the proof of an ethics lies not in the humanity of its actor but in its results. Echo is unsparingly condemned to passivity—and yet her very passivity possesses its own strong agency. The effectivity I propose for Echo is that of initiator of the ironic.

This irony fingers strangeness simply through listening to what it over-hears being reiterated. It is hearing something said all too much, and that makes it uneasy. Unease, rather than boredom, grips it, as if irony must have some opinion of its own, to be alert to something which sounds to it in a wrong register. So how may it manage this: Might its sensitivities linger somewhere in its sense of historical timing? Yet irony's temporality would appear to be plain enough: a constant and synthetic present tense, which has the effect of stripping the history of the word away, to free it to appear as it-self, denuded of all its familiar and blinding accretions of 'context' which es-tablish its sensibly familiar meaning. It demands a careful stupidity to be successfully ironic. A determined will is needed to misunderstand the obvi-ous—to get hold of the wrong end of the stick, and, doggedly, not let go of it. Irony's studied incomprehension is what permits it to stop its ears to the content of what's being reiterated, and instead to become fascinated by the word made into a thing through the sheer fact of its reiteration. Now irony has made itself ripe to become the linguistic psychoanalyst of iteration. Condemned like Echo herself to listen attentively, irony hears and takes note when the language around it, like the lady, doth protest too much.

All this is only one solid aspect of the materiality of language, the fleshi-ness of words: the everyday opportunity for a sign to become present to it-self, to become 'the word as such'.[30] Iterability is no more than the ordinary capacity to be repeated. Its outcome, though, is not inert. If, like Narcissus to the frustrated Echo, you cry out to the apparent source of the words tossed back to you, 'Speak, so that I may see you!' then her reply is merely, 'See you!' The interrogator is thrown back upon the question or the plea. Echo does re-present, literally so. But what she presents back is no longer the original utterance. The word, now as thing, is wrenched into a novel sense or a nonsense, made strange by the brute fact of its re-presentation alone or because its context has been lopped off. Or, simply but forcefully, by the automatic irony of frequency. A word can crop up so often within a discourse that a groaning familiarity creeps in—and from then on, that word is on autodestruct.

Here we could glance at Deleuze's use of the term 'simulacrum' (he invokes this as alternative to the Platonic Idea and its reincarnations) and which sounds close to how you could begin to characterise a genetic clone: more of the same. It's not itself exactly a copy, but it queries that whole concept of the model plus its copy. It doesn't resemble; instead, he writes, it ironises.[31] Then it follows that what 'ironises' must be something within or about the very repetition that it enacts. Somehow it ironises by doing it again, over and over, yet nevertheless contriving to fall somewhere lively, poised between dullness and provocation. The raw stuff of verbal irony, this iterability, possesses the odd power to make strange that which it familiarly reflects. Repetition is never an inert affair, despite its mechanical fidelity. Say it, read it, echo it often enough and at short enough intervals, and the word suffers a mutation, its thingness abruptly catapulted forward. It begins to look somewhat comical or grotesque in its isolation—and this folly soon seeps over the reader too, who may feel sheepish to be so greatly struck by the repeated thing-word.

Is this strangeness only in the violent decomposition of the word, all meaning evacuated, into its typological clusters of characters in their graphic shapes? If one were to think, conventionally, of the word as animated solely by its meaning, then through the process of reit   .ion alone, one would be suddenly confronted by the word's corpse   .ts waxwork. Whether by the enforced prominence of its sounds or ·'   odd look of the letters themselves, to see a word printed many time=   .r on a page makes it start out, and this exposed arbitrariness is inde   ,ueer. This dizzied us as children. Sheer repetition exaggerates the ·   . into a wonder.[32] Waiting in the Underground, my eye is snared b·   e lettered name of the station, picked out in London Transport's sa·   crif at frequent intervals all along the platform. Its oddly strangul=   consonants, that bunched *ghg* in the middle of 'Highgate', mak   .e wonder anew how anyone can ever decipher English pronunciation. Some oral repetition could also do the trick; and then this station's name does have a vague similarity to Hecate, herself another dweller in the underground, but that is far less compelling. Such bemusement is an automatic product, not only of the slowness of the trains to carry away the gazer, but of the visual reiteration of the displayed word, multiplied fifty times along the platform wall.

That reiteration produces more than inert copies is clear, too, in the case of rhyme, but here it is yoked to systematic variation. Time enters strangely into this complex reiteration, for the time of rhyme cuts both ways. There's an uncertainty about whether any rhyme will actually materialise in the expected manner and where its arrival will throw the meaning of the line. Or at least there's a little suspension of belief in its coming, a string of doubts offset by its anticipation. In this, it resembles the affects of interpellation where, as my second chapter has suggested, some borderline linguistic guilt nurses its own anteriority. Like Echo, interpellation carries its affect as a distorted temporality. The retroversion of rhyme in the inner ear, after the quick uncertainty which might throw a listener forward into novelty or back to familiarity, complicates the homophone's power to reveal and exaggerate the thingness of words, to bring the language crashing down on itself. Is the direction of rhyme really 'undecidable'? I'd prefer to argue instead for an affective tension in rhyme between hesitation and confidence. Strict metrication dictates the latter because it establishes expectations and demands its aural satisfaction, whereas to know the fallibilities of the ear and voice and writer all incline towards uncertainty. Anticipation lives within prosody. It hovers as cadence—that overlooked yet omnipresent force to influence and to direct the meaning—and in the metrical patterning which mounts towards the crescendo or slips to the diminuendo of the rhyme. Yet rhyme, especially within a tight metrical structure, runs perilously close to the comical, where it may aim to be most serious. The more blatant the metre, the more obvious the rhyme, the greater the risk of being risible. Resemblance to the comedian's punch-line capsizes some attempted *gravitas*; and heavy closure, as in the clinching couplet of an awkward modern sonnet, will provoke titters.

The rhetorician Demetrius pointed to Sappho's decoratively replayed poetic clauses; 'for example, the use of repetition when a bride addresses her own virginity: "Virginity, virginity, why have you gone and left me?" and it replies to her with the same figure, "never again shall I come to you, never again shall I come." The idea clearly has more charm than if it had been expressed only once, without the figure'.[33] Charm is, somewhat perilously, credited to pure reiteration here. Absurdity is a commoner effect. As for the deliberate reiteration of rhyme itself, whyever should there be enjoyment in an echoed sound, trapped in the service of a different meaning? And what is it that can tip the gravely or sensuously pleasurable headlong into the comically inept? One could ask, what precisely is it that makes amusingly deflationary the rhyme which aspires to be elevated? We can readily think of Freudian answers. But there are aural scholars of humour, too. Bergson believed that comedy had a clockwork element: 'The comic is that side of a person in which he resembles a thing: it is that aspect of human events which, by a special kind of rigidity, institutes a mechanism pure and simple, an automatism, a lifeless movement'.[34] Such reiteration can culminate in an effect of mockery, and the risk of self-parody haunts any social category whose function it is to dare to speak its name over and over. Echo deflates, even against her own will—as in that seventeenth-century genre of echo poems where some swollen amorous discourse is wittily rendered absurd by the very truncations she is forced to impose on it. Kierkegaard himself becomes savagely humorous in the face of the merciless deflations of rhyme, whose unsparing echoes refuse to revere high feeling, turning it instead to bathos:

> Each time I wish to say something there is another who says it at the very same moment. It is as though *I thought double*, and my other self continually stole a march on me [. . . .] I will flee out of the world (not to a cloister—I have strength in me yet) in order to find myself (every other driveller says the same), no, in order to forget myself. Nor shall I go where some jabbering brook plods across a field. I don't know if this verse is by some poet, but I could wish *an inflexible irony* would compel some sentimental poet to write it, yet *in such a way that he himself all the while read something else*. Oh Echo, yes Echo, thou great master of irony! You who parody in yourself the highest and deepest on earth: the Word which created the world, since you merely give the contour not the fullness. [. . .] Yes, Echo, you whom I once heard chastise a nature lover when he exclaimed: 'Hear yonder, the lonesome flute tones of a lovelorn nightingale' (*Nattergal*)—and you answered; 'Mad' (*gal*).[35]

Thus satirically tormented, Kierkegaard advocates giving tongue to uncertainty and a curative prominence to irony—that we should, 'instead of giving constant assurances that doubt has been overcome, that irony has been vanquished, for once to allow it to speak'.[36] Speak it must, whether or not we choose to attend to it, since the formally helpless Echo is indeed the master of irony. She bounces the language off the rocks and back to itself.

Suffering a literal petrification, becoming rock herself, she is turned to stone until only her voice remains. Then how can her misery support the faintest optimism? Just as being repeatedly physically knocked around will rapidly teach you the anticipatory reflex of covering your head with your hands, so being verbally knocked around will also generate its avoidant reflex against the blow. The harsh word has somehow to be turned back on itself. It is irony which picks up the hurled word and holds it curiously aloft, to form a natural screen. In this action, irony always has to interrogate itself too, which is why it cannot ever have a clear conscience; and it must do so just because it is systematic reflexiveness. It is compelled to examine itself through the word that it scrutinises.

This action has its automatic quality, which does at least guarantee it a democratic potential. So even unhappy Echo attains to irony, admittedly outside her control, when she compulsively repeats the closing fragment of whatever last sentence she has heard. Even unwilling mimicry will achieve an effect of mockery. It's a moment of the impersonal—indeed, the trans-personal—unconscious of language itself at work: If the unconscious is understood as language overtaking the intentions of its speaker, then here's an example drawn from my lines above of a rough justice in the language that mercilessly outruns the feelings of its speaker. As a result of Narcissus' contemptuous speech to her, Echo, despite her ardour, is compelled to turn his words back against him through her wholly accidental retort:

> So exiled, I fell for Narcissus. I had no voice to plead so I'd pursue.
> He called 'I'd die before I'd give myself to you!' I shrilled 'I'd give myself to
>   you!' ran nearer.
> If he'd cried 'I'd die before I'd fuck you', at least I could have echoed back
>   that 'Fuck you'.
> Sorry—I have to bounce back each last phrase. Half-petrified, I voice dead
>   gorges.

A political necessity of irony

To begin with an invaluable exchange, from 1799:

Julius: I understand it. I even believe it. A joke can make a joke about
            everything; a joke is free and universal. But I'm against it. There

are places in my being, the deepest ones in fact, where for that
reason an ordinary hurt is unimaginable. And in these places a
joke is intolerable to me.

Lorenzo: So the seriousness of these places is probably not completely
perfect yet. Otherwise there would be irony there by now. But for
that very reason irony exists. You'll only have to wait awhile.[37]

These two speakers are among Schlegel's protagonists in his absorbing and
bewildering polyphony of a novel, *Lucinde*. It's impossible to match Schlegel's
clarity here, but I take it that what his character Lorenzo is implying is that
irony will arise spontaneously within that injury which has been compelled
into an intensity of self-contemplation. That irony is not an effect of any
leisurely distance, but of the strongest and most serious engagement with
hurt.

If in my violent unhappiness I once become abject, I forget all my capacity for self-irony, and then am truly sunk. Yet the province of irony should
not be limited to the consolation of a temperamental style any more than to
some charming personal quirk; then again, its meaning need not be reduced
to its supposed world-weary superiority, rendered by one quietly arched eyebrow. I cannot, obviously, declare that I am an ironist. There can be a politics of irony; it must lack a programme and a manifesto. By definition without predetermined content, irony can only be a practice without calculation,
or else an inclination. Kierkegaard, boldly echoing Christ, characterises it
better: 'Irony is like the negative way, not the truth but the way. Everyone
who has a result merely as such does not possess it, for he has not the way.
When irony appears on the scene, it brings the way, though not the way
whereby one who imagines himself to have a result comes to possess it, but
the way whereby the result forsakes him'.[38] Irony, once achieved, will always
sidle away from anyone's ownership. A public irony must flourish, for the
sake of the political and ethical vigour of language; lurking inside a self-categorisation, ideally it can inspect the limits of any expansionist identification, can check hyperbole, can puncture any overblown claims from within
to arrive at a sounder measure of them.[39] It guarantees a grasp of proportion.
As Kierkegaard observed, 'There is a different tendency in our age that
exhibits an enormous enthusiasm, and, curiously enough, what excites it
seems to be enormously little. How beneficial irony could be here'.[40] It can
expose a personal category's historicity and fragility by isolating it as both

real enough yet also as an artifact, eminently questionable. This irony is not ethical weakness, not vacillation, and emphatically not evidence for any failure of political commitment. Yet irony still periodically attracts charges of being evasive; but it will remain so for just long enough to recuperate its forces. For it can redeem, can defuse a hurtful description by deforming it so far towards the grotesque that it becomes a frank travesty and caves in. There's a virtue in the gallows humour which can do the work of resignification. Change, through the dynamic of word and named thing, protects against paralysis: Concerned that a post-Hegelian insistence on 'actuality' should not degenerate into a stiffened dogma, Kierkegaard proposed irony to make vivid a lived philosophy.[41] And as Jakobson rhetorically inquired, 'Why is it necessary to make a special point of the fact that sign does not fall together with object?' He immediately answered himself with his insistent claim that such nonidentity was productive of (in my gloss) any historical life: 'Because, besides the direct awareness of the identity between sign and object (A is A) there is a necessity for the direct awareness of the inadequacy of that identity (A is not A). The reason that this antinomy is essential is that without contradiction there is no mobility of concepts, no mobility of signs, and the relationship between concept and sign becomes automatised. Activity comes to a halt, and the awareness of reality dies out'.[42] Irony is the mark of such an active nonidentity.

If irony is the rhetorical form of self-reflexiveness, then through it, some sedimented category can achieve the happy status of becoming ludicrously thickened in its own eyes. Both being angrily named by others, and naming oneself through self-categorising, can be punctured or slowed in their tracks through their own reiteration. The exaggerated or outworn naming of selves has an inherent tendency to parody its own excesses just through the repetition which, catching its absurd diction in its own ears, may in the end become wryly amused. Yet the self might present its descriptions to itself very differently: as the glad recognition of some happy 'identification'; as triumph; as lassitude; or as frank repugnance, all depending on the timing of the volatile self-descriptions on offer. If irony needs its right moments to flourish, the very nature of the iteration which spins into irony is historically determined, and—for even the caged parrot may crack the kernel of the dialectic with its chattering—is itself also effective. As Marx almost wrote, 'Language makes history, but not under circumstances of its own choosing'.

There is indeed what could be described abstractly as a simple mechanical dialectic where quantity flips into a qualitative change, since sheer verbal repetition starts to bore itself and, released through its boredom, can turn to something different. But this dialectic lives its always elaborately solid life as the ironised sedimentations of societal groupings—as a dialectic of language which is 'in itself' both historical and materialist. That 'in itself' is in quotation marks, because really language is everywhere but in itself. Admittedly, such musings imply a mildly self-righting tendency in language, or rather its glorious indifference to manipulation, and as such they may well be naïvely hopeful. Still, better maybe to err on this side than to fall for that paranoia which sees only the bewitchment of a language which will constantly lead reason astray.

Some calcified solidarity or a decaying essence show some past lapse of irony. Any collectivity which can't examine its own massifications and their deployment enacts the risk of petrification, or worse. Suppressed irony can perpetuate frank racism. This is not always recognised. The Jewish person, determinedly anti-Zionist or not, who's fond of Jewish jokes may be vulnerable to criticism from those who believe they detect in his humour the mark of his condition as a 'self-hating Jew'. Assuming that his Jewish anti-Jewish jokes bear witness to his 'unconscious self-loathing', they may brandish that designation severely—a wooden response, in the face of language's highly effective powers to query the very identification that it will perpetuate only if its own latent irony is neutered. Suffice it to say that there are many ways in which those who are targeted by identity claims based on appearance can deploy these themselves, and not remotely in a spirit of self-hatred, and Jewish antiracist wit affords a myriad enticing examples here. To cite just one, the story of the Chinese rabbi: A traveller from Brooklyn is journeying through the wilds of China. In a remote country village, he is astonished and pleased to discover an open synagogue; he enters, and participates fully in the service. Afterwards he has a word at the door with the Chinese rabbi, who greets him pleasantly, saying how glad he'd been to see a stranger to the village joining so familiarly in the responses. Then the rabbi adds 'But if you don't mind my saying so, you don't really *look* Jewish'.

A 'cure' of the word is, though, never certain. This remains so, irrespective of whether a cure is envisaged through an aggressive term's elimination, or through its ironical capture and deployment. What lets the latter succeed?

Extrapolating from Engels's much-reviled assertion that the sheer quantity of a repetition must eventually spark off a leap into an altered quality, we'd arrive at an automatic dialectic of irony. That, though, can't ever be relied on, since the quantitative accumulation of a word is just as likely to grind to a halt in nausea as in critique. Ownership of the bad word can also drift to unforeseen quarters. So Hanif Kureishi, half English, half Pakistani, and from London, visits his relatives in Karachi and finds himself descriptively caught out whichever way he turns: 'And when I said, with a little unnoticed irony, that I was an Englishman, people laughed. [. . .] But I couldn't allow myself to feel too Pakistani. I didn't want to give in to that falsity, that sentimentality. As someone said to me at a party, provoked by the fact that I was wearing jeans: we are Pakistanis, but you, you will always be a Paki—emphasising the slang derogatory name the English used against Pakistanis, and therefore the fact that I couldn't rightfully lay claim to either place'.[43] For irony's outcome can't be guaranteed. Coming down neither on the side of language viewed as frothily superficial nor on the side of a 'realism' which is supposedly wider, grander, and earthier than language, irony is constitutionally incapable of settling, since it must adhere to its principled hesitancy and to its openness to revision. Irony as self-scrutiny is above all conscious of its own provisionality; this is what it stages, and especially in the conspicuous provisionality of the categories of social being. Self-reflecting identities will happily know themselves to be tentative, as irony eyes them finely from different angles and holds them up to the light between its fingertips.

But isn't it necessary for irony to sometimes give up, to defer to more grave matters? No consolation can be derived from the facts of political and linguistic violence. Repetition alone assists no one here. Indeed, incantation is the officially approved and enforced style for recanting. So film footage of obligatory self-denunciations at show trials, for example that of Rudolf Slansky, the secretary general of the Czechoslovakian communist party, and his fellow accused,[44] offers a great deal of reiteration, wooden confessions made in set phrases, along these lines: 'I came from a bourgeois family. My father was a wealthy villager. I carried over these erroneous beliefs into the workers' movement when I joined. I never abandoned those wrong beliefs even within the workers' movements'. Such compulsorily parroted phrases may well have rung bitterly within the ears of those uttering them in the dock but naturally did nothing to deflect their executioners. The massive invocations and reiterations of '*die Jude*' by antagonists in the early 1930s may have been at times deployed cynically among those thus targeted, but can hardly be said to have acquired resonances of irony. Even if linguistic irony at a far earlier stage would have aided a refusal—indeed in itself would also have constituted a refusal to take seriously the categorical racisms which led to that final devastation—conditions for those aggressively designated as 'Jewish' were (flatly to state the obvious) not such as to permit widespread irony as distinct from world-weariness and horror at the use of the category. Irony saves no one in the face of the executioner's bullet or the mutilating machete. Jewish humour would not have proved of much avail at Treblinka. It may or may not be possible to write poetry after Auschwitz: It may not be possible to apply irony to the characterisations invoked to incite mass murder. Then are there categories which should not ever be treated ironically, and are untouchable because of their history of trauma? Yet it's precisely those who are most profoundly affected here who may refuse to suspend an ironic attitude.[45]

But here I don't mean the irony adopted by those militants in the rhetorical struggle who will capture an injurious term to use it as a sarcastic self-description, so disarming it. I mean something else, in a way stronger, by suggesting that irony is politically advantageous: that irony is alert to history, that to be able to deploy a category ironically frees you to recognise its historical formation and consequently its potential to alter and disintegrate. To recognise that irony has in this sense an inclination towards the good is a part of acknowledging the historical vulnerability of any rhetorical language. This recognition can aid its critical reworking. But there are quite other recipes, naturally, for trying to rehabilitate irony. 'In the last analysis, irony is nothing more than a question designed to draw another subject into discussion of who and where one is', concludes Gary J. Handwerk, who offers this as evidence for what he benignly considers to be irony's 'intersubjective' social and hence ethical nature[46] arising from the fact that, born in linguistic division, the ironic subject needs to appeal to an interlocutor to recognise it as such and to confirm its constitutional split.[47] For irony, as he says, is not a solipsistic pursuit. Even if, as Paul de Man once dispiritingly put it, irony 're-captures some of the factitiousness of human existence as a succession of isolated moments lived by a divided self', nevertheless it does still need to be known and recognised.[48] But can this particular brand of optimism convince, resting as it does for Handwerk on irony's posited 'intersubjectivity'? Being a divided self is anyway not so very melancholic a condition, since it does possess the decided advantage of unapologetic reflexivity. I'd place my own relentless impulses towards optimism elsewhere altogether: in the actual operations of irony, rather than in any hope of its ultimate sociability as achieved through its 'intersubjectivity'—a thesis which seems prematurely to assume the best. Murder is equally intersubjective.

Irony as a strategy against verbal aggression must frequently deny even putatively progressive sociological groupings their integrity, and forget niceness altogether. In the spirals of late nineteenth-century and early twentieth-century suffragist feminism, a willingness to adopt or to discard at high speed an attributed 'femininity' made for an effective mobility.[49] Such elastic strategies must and do persist. (So while I can't think why I'd want to utter that chilling phrase 'speaking as a woman', I can think of situations in which it could be my lot to cough pointedly from the back row, 'But what about women here?') Today, too, a ferocious readoption of the old pejorative classifications runs everywhere. Some campaigning groups, tired of what they sense as a pussyfooting and patronising diction of 'disability' or 'handicap', now insistently call themselves 'cripples'. Such pointed bravado is no detachable rhetorical frill; it characterises the volatile linguistic politics of self-naming. Any catalogue of the reappropriation of derisive words would include 'rude' itself, re-emerging in 1970s diction to be brandished among self-proclaimed 'rude boys'. Then 'spade' was circulated in the 1960s by young Jamaican Fanonists, among others, as a hip term coexisting with their flirtations with the notion of negritude. Was the circulation of this noun 'spade' itself a sardonic play on the expression 'to call a spade a spade' and as such a piece of truly black humour about refusing racial euphemism, and which itself invoked that old figure of speech used to describe linguistic frankness? Disappointingly, dictionaries of slang cite 'spade' as an American usage, casually racist in origin, and merely derived from the printed colour of the suit of spades on playing cards; by the 1920s, the expression 'black as the ace of spades' was widespread. Still, the potential of 'spade' to recoil can't have escaped anyone's notice then. Tactically taking on verbal hostility includes the dark humour of those who elected to name themselves 'faggots'; and 'queer' as a denigration belligerently adopted by those it tried to humiliate is another instance of verbally flaunting it. But there's less evidence of, say, any proud

female society of 'fat slags' or 'cunts', at any rate outside of the land of eso-
teric cartoons. Is that diction of sexual contempt far harder to reclaim satirically? Some have tried archness as a tactic, but for others the words will stay
resistant to effective ironisation as attempts to recapture them remain awkwardly self-conscious.[50] For many others, the old diction of sexual aggression
may now have become untroubling, mere banter long since drained of any
venom. Without a survey (which would make a very odd document), one
can't tell; but certainly no one can speak confidently 'as a woman' about what
might or mightn't vex others. Perhaps the diction of sexual disgust must
creep, labouring along from being unspeakable towards becoming accept-
able, if only through inducing wearied indifference: Vulgarity can be worn
down by erosion, but can't flash into irony.

   Using the slur to recapture the offensive may be tried by those it attacks;
then, in theory, over time, it becomes anyone's property and is defused. So
in the East End of London, for instance, the classroom abuse of 'jungle
bunny' was adopted by those it thought to finger contemptuously and used
by British schoolchildren of Caribbean descent among themselves.[51] Or the
widespread salutation 'niggah' occurred as a parodic retrieval of 'nigger' by
those this noun once named (still names) dismissively, and it has indeed
been claimed by some aspirant white niggahs too. But what about the bad
flavour that it leaves in the mouth? Some have argued that irrespective of
your own blackness, the word 'nigger' is just too damaging for you to circulate among your friends, however teasingly and with whatever ambiguous
affection.[52] The smell of the offensive word will linger on horribly, whatever
its user's aims, for some language is so intrinsically bad that trying to recuperate it is virtually to share a slave morality's entanglement with its oppres-
sor. Others will hold a sharply opposing view: Given that the verbal hygienist's route of prohibition is hardly a practicable strategy, and even if one
unpleasant term could be cleared away, others would swarm in to fill its
place, then verbal contamination should instead be exaggerated to the point
where it will become exhausted and faint away through its own prolixity. A
practical consideration arises: How long might the memory of either the
word's initial aggression or its secondary ironic rendering remain alive in the
course of such redeployment by its original targets? Once the whole ironic
point has been forgotten, its bite is lost; and yet this very loss may also mean
that the hostility in the unironised term itself has withered away. But as lan-

guage seeps everywhere, it may well linger on in pockets in an unrecon-structed form. My attitude here would indeed be Whiggish if I saw an un-waveringly strong hope for the ironic dispersal of some injurious speech to end it once and for all. But the power of racial invective to resurrect itself is all too evident in its many resurrections in Europe today; hostility keeps its own incalculable geography of dispersion.

Is there a standard of taste in irony?[53] Need today's irony observe deco-rum? This is argued out incessantly among the linguistic militants of coun-terappellation. One quick example. In a British newspaper column, the jour-nalist Randeep Ramesh speculates about 'ethnicity's' new currency within 'political pop'. He numbers himself among those who are convinced that the gain in this fashion for ethnicity in music is not worth the pain. Illustrating this, he reports on the emblematic exchange that transpired when he inter-viewed a British musician from a Sikh background: 'Would for example Tjin-der Singh—Cornershop's leading light—call his band 'Paki'? His reply last month to my question was blunt. "Depends what the wog was feeling like. . . ." Initially I refused to record the remark, but he insisted and I re-lented. The problem I have with this use of language is that this freedom may lead to white people using the word, too'. Here, perhaps also teasing his in-terrogator's earnestness, the musician Tjinder Singh enacts a strategy of lin-guistic flooding: You mockingly defuse through saturation, so that the inju-rious words wash free from their intended enclave and are diluted into a harmless generality. The very name of his band, Cornershop, also pursues this policy of sardonic re-enactment, since corner shops all over Britain are run by Asian families. Where, though, might this process of defusing through diffusion stick? Are there no limits to this irony of dilution through over-use, limits which could arise especially from metaphor's ability to stubbornly re-assert itself literally, overwhelming its other ramifications? 'Bitch' may now have become inoffensively familiar through its currently heavy use, yet it might still unpredictably bite. If linguistic putrefaction rather than dilution should occur, its effects are incalculable. 'All satire is blind in the face of the forces liberated by decay', comments Adorno;[54] and here indeed the phrase 'ethnic cleansing', coined with a sardonic undertow, has by now become used flatly to name an ill. The main worry for those who are sceptical about the tactics of sardonically broadcasting derisive racial speech is what happens when it falls into the wrong hands—that it's one thing for an Asian person to call himself a 'Paki' but quite another for a white person to use the word. According to this line of thought, which Ramesh exemplifies here, the possibility of redemptive irony would all depend on who's speaking. This can never be policed, nor can the speaker's perspective be patrolled; an utterance's harm, or its recuperability, also depend on where it is situated.

According to the argument for linguistic flooding, however, the word's sting can become so weakened that it's eventually denatured, neutered. Then this last theory would constitute the homeopathic school of linguistic use within the medical philosophy of language: Here, that the wide circulation of the word 'Paki', diluted to the point at which no detectable trace of its malice remained, would make it impossible for its venomous racist strength to return. Historical semantics readily shows this kind of weakening at work—as well as, devastatingly and emphatically, its reverse. Then, too, some accusers will remain indifferent alike to linguistic prohibition or linguistic flooding, and oblivious to repetition's tedium. Instead, they may continue to enjoy a compulsively senseless reiteration of taunts, bound in a fetish of pleasurable stupidity. Reiteration can take the shape not only of an ironic exhaustion of hurtful speech, but elsewhere of its consolidation in a group cruelty which relishes its own monotony.

Is there a syntax of potential hostility?

Perhaps something more insidious than bad nouns alone is also involved in hostile naming. The grammar of self-description often arrives in assertive blocks, stout and plain as a child's building bricks: 'I am thin' or 'I'm old'. Is there something misleadingly innocent about the simplicity of this adjectival form, for doesn't the ease of it change significantly if a noun form is available to be substituted? The prototypical example here remains 'he is a Jew', as distinct from the seemingly more neutral adjectival form of 'he is Jewish'. Does the categorical noun set in apposition to the third person pronoun, 'he is a Jew', comprise an English grammar of antisemitism, which in its shape could extend to other antagonisms?[55] The adjectival form, however, as in 'he is Jewish', need carry no such decidedly aggressive ring, although and decisively this would depend on just when and in what country it's spoken. Is the noun form of identification frequently a pointer towards hostility? There seems to be a syntax of potential racism in the structure of a sentence which consigns some other sectoral or national party to any capitalised category of being: 'she is a (So-and-so)'. To become the subject of a noun ending in the suffix 'ee' can often be bad news to its bearer, who is thereby treated as if washed through solely and exhaustively with the condition: 'a refugee', 'an adoptee'. And the phrase set in apposition, over and against its subject, can sometimes underline some less than happy permanence. The preferred diction of disability has long since moved away from the dismissive noun form, becoming 'she has cerebral palsy' instead of 'she's a spastic', or 'their child has Down syndrome' instead of 'their child is a mongol'. It's noticeable that some self-consciously 'liberal' discussion about a man's homosexuality will also incline away from the noun and towards the adjectival form, tending to prefer to say that 'he is gay' rather than 'he is a homosexual'. Overt contempt inhabits other appositional modes, such as 'he's a faggot'. There's no great parity here between the sexes, since the noun form 'she's a lesbian' doesn't seem to carry quite the same strains, which pass instead to its contemptuous shorthand, 'she's a les'. These few examples (to which counterexamples could readily be adduced) are in English, and many more would be needed, and from many languages[56]—but where some putative aspect of the person sits as a clause in apposition to the pronoun, such as 'he is a Muslim', perhaps this is felt differently from an attribute lodged as the adjectival form, 'she's Anglican'. The bearer of the hostile identification can, quite literally, be sentenced into being as such. Not, of course, that syntax alone can of itself create this aggression. But it may act not merely as hostility's neutral carrier but as its reinforcement and its anticipatory reminder. That waiting classifying bracket of 'she's a (Such-and-such)' is primed to receive those to be set apart from 'us' and is already imbued with suspicion. It's as if the assigned characterisation has its own apt vehicle, all prepared to convey the hostility. The whole structure of the sentence of identification is already leaning towards it. In the way that a phrase of music performed within a passage carries its own memory and anticipates its own resolution, so the sentence's grammar is poised in readiness. There are cadences for antagonism. Cadences rise as syntactical forms, and there may be a syntax of both remembered and anticipatory hostility. But that need not, though, be imagined as overriding the force of the site from which an utterance is voiced; so 'he's a Protestant' might be empathetically murmured about another member of my tribe but will have a different ring on the lips of a militant Fenian. No empire of syntax as affect is proposed here; only that syntax does possess an affect which can demonstrably contribute its distinctive resonance and is prepared for its moment. At the least, we can, I think, safely identify elements of structural recall and anticipation in the syntactical form which is a frequent carrier of suspicious dislike, and as instances not just of description's temporality but also of its linguistic affect.

Is there some way in which irony itself can modify this grammar in its latent capacity for damage? This is just what does frequently happen, although certainly it cannot happen always. Syntax may operate as the structural engineer of memory as recalled affect, and it may do so to the extent that there's what we might christen 'syntactical memory'. It's a memory which (perhaps like all memories) cuts both ways, moreover, for it looks ahead expectantly. Further, this architecture of the syntax of apposition, readied to receive the thing which 'is' a certain attribute, may itself collide with that growing sense of absurdity which stems from enough reiterations of the word—and the result may be the dawning of irony. But at such points of speculation, one arrives swiftly at an ancient crisis of semantics. It's that Presidential conundrum (derided, but entirely reasonable) of 'what the meaning of "is" is'—here, of the degree of prominence to which the verb 'to be' now rises.

Let's briefly revisit that painful matter of interpellation, a mechanism apt to waver in its efficacy.[57] It has as its counter and its retort the phenomenon of counterinterpellation; the capacity of a hostile interpellation to be twisted back against itself. But this is too self-contained a word, not ragged enough at its historical edges if it implies a neat reversal. 'Counterinterpellation' could instead be supplemented with some thoughts on irony as not only historical and linguistic but also psycholinguistic, if in an unorthodox sense. (To repeat the recipe given in earlier chapters, it blurs the edges of what counts as psychological and what as linguistic.) For in practice, this aspect of counterinterpellation turns on language's irrepressible knack of becoming a phenomenon unto itself.

Irony is not antithetical to solidarity

It is not my detachment from my attributed condition that leads to my irony, but on the contrary my deep involvement in it. Do I cross-question my category as a ratio of how much of me it addresses, on whether I've also willed it as my mannerism, or on how inescapably saturated in it I feel myself to be? This notion of a quality which envelops the entirety of its bearer—the racism of appearance—was brilliantly parodied by a British press officer of Caribbean descent, when she was newly in the public eye. To the eager journalists who asked her, '*How* black are you?' she reportedly answered 'All over'.

If uncertainty in becoming a new social entity is a linguistic inevitability, this is no 'merely psychological' quirk of one who shies away from making a responsible commitment to collectivity, and who, caught in the neurotic grip of idealism and hyperindividualism, refuses solidarity. (That irritated question 'who does she think she is?'—who is she to back off from some identity category?—is somewhat ironic in its wording, since it's precisely the one who *can't* think who she is who is thereby rendered vulnerable to that charge of bossy overconfidence.) Should the notion of solidarity ever become identified with maintaining a bloc of likenesses beyond scrutiny, something has gone badly awry. 'Don't adopt the erroneous idea that the foreigner, just because he insists on his difference, is incapable of solidarity', wrote Edmond Jabès.[58] And this differing solidarity may well present itself in the very mode of irony.

Admittedly the tactical advantage in making a slogan out of an ironic generalisation isn't always clear-cut. President de Gaulle's echo of Louis XIV's '*l'état, c'est moi*', the state? that's me, is readily ironised by rendering it universal. Each member of the populace could insist instead that '*l'état, c'est moi* —no, *I* am the state'. So it is switched into a radically libertarian slogan of a mass of selves. But if de Gaulle's pronouncement is instead recast as a maxim of conventional solidarity, it becomes 'the state? that's us'. Which is preferable? Before deciding, let's first prudently invoke the notion of context once more and glance more closely at solidarity itself. Famously, this may lie in the repetition of a category originally uttered as a racist slur but later invoked as a gesture of common cause with its targets, such as the street slogans of 1968, 'We are all foreign scum', 'We are all German Jews'. In the diction of that day, 'it is no accident that' these are resonant maxims of the late 1960s, when solidarising could speak in a rhetoric of identification with others. Self-description appropriates a slogan for oneself; and if indeed 'the history of language is the history of a process of abbreviation',[59] then the language of the slogan is a most terse and concentrated form of politics. The entire trajectory of political thought could be read as a fight for the enunciation, the supremacy, or the redundancy of the slogan.[60] 'The term derives from the Gaelic compound *sluagh-airm*: *sluagh* 'host' or 'army', and *ghairm* 'cry' or 'shout'. Thus, a war-cry; the cry of a political party'.[61] Then 'we are all foreign scum' is the war-cry of a band of sympathisers who constitute themselves through this exuberantly sardonic overidentification.[62] And those kinds of slogan are parasitical on the supposition that there's a generous and inclusive human totality to assert. Such a solidarity with those jeeringly named by powerful others is largely replaced today with duller sectoral identifications. Here Jacques Rancière, contemplating the deliberately nonsociological nature of the new social identities,[63] notes the failure of the slogan as an index of a fall: 'In France, for instance, the new racism and xenophobia [. . .] are the effects of a void, of a previous collapse—the collapse of emancipatory politics as a politics of the other. [. . .] Now we have only right names. We are all Europeans and xenophobes. It is the demotion of the political form, of the political polymorphism of the other, that creates a new kind of other, one that is infra-political'.[64] But need this account of a rhetorical decline slide towards mourning some fatally lost solidarity? For where nostalgia can strike up, there historical thinking has already stopped. Yet it may be better to consider afresh the whole possibility of linguistic intervention, forswearing all longings and golden moments. But to complicate this tart observation, there really is historical and social amnesia, and, repeatedly, what is learnt is lost again.[65] One answer may lie in a closer look at the nature of this respectfully invoked solidarity. If you see everyone waiting for their sector to find its right local name, and you also envisage any undifferentiated concept of humanity as humanist in the pejorative sense, as distastefully blind to its own dominance, then the old slogans must become the archaisms that they now are. If, on the other hand, you do want to hang on to a solidarity which can run right across the identities of group interest and transcend them, but you also want to steer clear of regretful longing for a lost street leftism, then you are committed to attempting some contortions. These can just about be managed—but they can't do without the assistance of irony.

It's hard enough to be solid in myself. Or to put it formulaically, acquiring a subjecthood is always transacted in relation to others' positions. Here I may need to fragment myself, the better to map myself. There are cracks too within the self's past, traces of a sometimes compulsory incoherence. As Ryszard Kapuscinski has characterised the history of one woman whose course he had tracked throughout the 1930s famine in the Ukraine and after: 'The frantic acceleration and mutability of history, which are the essence of the times we live in, dictate that many of us are inhabited by several persons, practically indifferent to one another, even mutually contradictory'.[66] In calmer and more sheltered places, Rancière's phrasing still applies: 'the logic of emancipation is a heterology' which may entail 'a process of disidentification or declassification'.[67] The backward turn of decomposition can also be an aspect of solidarity. So to recognise internal differences within some larger grouping may entail what we could christen 'a solidarity of disaggregation': an insistence on the political advantages of reformulation. The observance of some great 'difference' may well be the outcome of a process which has silently subjugated all its interior differences within itself for the sake of its grand homogenisation. The recipients of this homogenisation will in time be driven to apostasy and will kick up against it. Then some ostensibly progressive collectivities may disable their intended inhabitants. A short but vivid instance was captured in a documentary film made in 1968: the discomfiture of some workers at a car factory outside Paris, when asked by unseen students clutching microphone and camera: 'What do the masses think?'[68] The workers thus interpellated shrugged uneasily and rolled their eyes, silently embarrassed to be pinioned by the well-intentioned question. They could not speak in reply, could not retort along the lines of, But we are not these masses; that collectivity owns no opinion which I as a worker can cite; we can't answer for these masses and not because we are shy or politically ill-informed, but just because it is an unhelpful massification. Nor, on the other hand, could they conceivably wish to dissociate themselves from their continuing workplace fight. So awkward shrugs ensued, until someone, schooled in the correct lingo, arrived to announce on cadre autopilot that the class struggle would continue 'right to the end', et cetera.

To any attempt at demassification, I'd want to add that the mechanisms of an ironic self-presentation, through which the category can confront itself, become crucial for a disintegrative liberty. In any event, ironising the self is pragmatically achieved in the course of a grand if subterranean 'heterology': by the route of comparing, realigning, uncoupling, disaggregating, and reshuffling the self's set components. In such a fury of sorting, nothing can stay tidily in place for long. Then to announce myself as 'a hybrid', for example, is to re-present myself as a little mass of entities now welded pleasantly together into some more accurate whole.[69] For a while, until it too becomes viewed in its turn as overinclusive, this hybridity may be an encouraging thing to be, a temporarily reanimating defence against too large, too solemn, and too static a notion of difference. But when irony is out of the picture, ossified massifications are common enough. The course of feminism can yield several strategically parodied uses of 'women' en bloc. Against this history of agility, one instance of a present unhelpful alignment, although it was conceived as a benevolent refinement, is that of 'Eastern European feminism' against 'Western feminism'. Not that there aren't marked differences between feminisms: But the fictitious unities of what is 'western' or 'eastern' obliterate, in the name of reverently acknowledging differences, any true historical differences. 'Eastern Europe' bespeaks a blithe *in*difference to, say, how variants of Stalinism or communism were or were not lived in the USSR or in Poland or East Germany or Albania or Hungary, or to what Titoism variously signified within the countries of the former Yugoslavia. Next this cartoon monolith of Eastern Europe is credited with a feminism which is itself impossibly unified, exactly as is that puppet of its counterpart, Western feminism. Yet once these imaginary entities are traded as coinage— often, dismayingly, in the name of some newly won grasp of 'cultural differences' to supersede a supposedly imperialist feminist hegemony—then they ensure stupefying effects of their own. Their solemnity makes them unassailable as they bask in their purported sensitivity. Where irony is in short supply, that dangerous 'realism' which is left bears witness to the need for greater artifice. Under some circumstances, this loss of any vocabulary for the complex subject may result in something rather worse than stultification: Rancière notes, 'The "new" racism is the hatred of the other that comes forth when the political procedures of social polemics collapse'.[70]

Solidarity need not depend on identity

One might well need a responsive solidarity—but it does not thereby follow that one needs to assert an identity as a club of souls. Not only is an identity no sound foundation for empathy, but some strong attachment to it may run directly counter to the development of effective fellow-feeling. Jettisoning any keen interest in my categorisation may be a prerequisite for much interest in others who don't share my defining condition: The more rigorously I adhere to my own name, the less empathetic interest I'll extend. The contented gleam of the fully rounded subject need have no concern with what lies outside it. Identities may first have to be loosened or laid aside for the sake of solidarity.

The following snippet of etymology is one instance of a vehement claim to individual standing, achieved through sheer negation of any solidarity. A mid-Victorian Texan cattle rancher has bequeathed us his surname in the word 'maverick': a roving oddball, hard to place, ornery, without settled allegiances. This original Sam Maverick had refused to brand his calves with his name. As Phil Cohen, who has recently resurrected him as an apt metaphor for the stray intellectual wandering out of his field, points out, 'Every rancher in Texas would have been able to instantly identify one of Samuel T. Maverick's steers, by the very absence of his brand name: but only on condition that no-one else followed his example, for then of course no-one would be able to tell whose runaway steer was whose and the very basis of private ownership of cattle or ideas would be placed in jeopardy. Mavericks are supposed to be loners, not hunt in herds'.[71] Sam T. was in the happy position of being able to give his name to any wandering bovine loner and of consequently himself occupying just that position of unorthodoxy among his fellow ranchers. He both had them and was them (whereas usually we find ourselves, less generously, reduced to trying to be that which we cannot have). Maverick's tale also offers some persuasive anarchic arguments. Refusing to name my calves, if they cause havoc, I escape the identity of he who is responsible. Refusing to name my calves, I cause havoc within an arrangement of mutually exclusive identities. No other ranchers could practise solidarity with Sam Maverick unless they were happy to hold all their cattle in common or were willing to risk a showdown by claiming that his animals were really theirs. We might conclude that they weren't happy, since Maverick's stance remained rare and impressive enough to have been mummified within the echoing halls of etymology. As for his steers, they would indeed have grazed and roamed 'beyond interpellation', genuine claimants to a strong possession of the identity of having no identity. The branding iron's searing work offers an indelible instance of interpellation, and we feel how the smoke rises from our permanently singed hides under the scorching impress of bad naming. Maverick's own tale shows the triumph of the inimitable. He affords one case of an unassailably decisive identity, which nonetheless makes solidarity not only unthinkable but totally impracticable. I'll sketch some arguments in support of the corollary, that solidarity need not depend on identity.

There is a clear advantage in the sometimes lamented fact that to be English is today to be unable to assert any 'positive identity', especially when compared with, for example, being Welsh. In the context of past and current European nationalisms, the stance of being devoid of any national identity has its attractions, if it only can be sustained. As a purely personal stance, too, to claim only the identity of having no identity need be no coy provocation or irresolute faltering of a properly spirited will to be. It is too self-consciously aesthetic to make a very interesting manifesto, but it has at the least the virtue of deferring to the ordinarily protean shape of identities, and it mimics their projected nature. Or, to echo Zygmunt Baumann's phrase again, they are 'postulated'. If my accredited identity begins to acquire a rancid taste in my mouth, where can my disenchantment reach? What I may next attain, if with difficulty, is no renewed identity with others but a confirmation of my rigorous separateness within some common dilemma or painful fix, together at last, though far apart. On this stony ground I may possibly begin to build something of use to those whose lot is so decisively not mine. There is indeed an ethics of decentring, one that pertains to solidarity.[72] The decentred subject need be no anaemic spectre of a conservative postmodernism, but the pulsating and elastic creature of a million circulating words, vulnerable to history while it speaks history. For whenever a new being is articulated, something is indeed always being split up; yet this subject constituted in division is not (or not exclusively) a psychic phenomenon or some purely philosophical partition.[73] Moreover, this disintegration of the names of selves need not hint at any mournful lack. It is also reintegrative. Or, like Marx's notion of the progressive 'decomposition of man', it tears apart only to reassemble anew.[74] As a quick emblem of this, William Carlos Williams's line 'Saxifrage is my flower that breaks the rock' in itself reintegrates, for both botanically (the mountain variety of this plant can spring from stony clefts) and etymologically (its Latin roots mean just what the plant's roots do, 'breaking rock'), this poetical disintegration of the name of the flower enacts a historical reinstatement of the name of the species.[75]

My exegesis here is perhaps also an example of that decomposition which breaks a butterfly upon a wheel.

Such unifying division is a commonplace historical-linguistic occurrence, at the public surface of the everyday. It's the unwillingness to tolerate constructive divisions which can cause the most strain. Unhelpfully exaggerated inclusions will accidentally obscure that which they earnestly seek to clarify. For instance, there is evidence of the detail of what happened when, say, the political-religious determination to be a Black Muslim clashed with newer forms of being a Muslim and black, but without that declared will to a fusion of those two loyalties; or how and why, for example, that self-designation of the 'Lost Nation of Islam' had shifted by 1976 under Elijah Muhammed's son to become the 'World Community of Islam in the West'.[76] But if the category of 'race' were made key to the account of this, then it would suffer the explanatory collapse attendant on any such internally complicated a classification, here one which is anthropological in origin but historically particular, and a frequently devastating political instrument. Other self-descriptions will be asserted from within that vaster classification, all the more militantly when they are incompatible with a taxonomy of racial essentialism; and here Evelyn Brooks Higginbotham has emphasised a need to 'expose the role of race as a metalanguage by calling attention to its powerful, all encompassing effect on the construction and representation of all other social and power relations'.[77] An anti-essentialism here, writes Paul Gilroy, could be both engaged and accountable; 'Its motto would be that understanding the radical contingency of racial identities does not diminish their power'.[78]

I am at the mercy of others' unsteadiness as well as my own. It is strange that it should be regarded as somehow unserious to query the constancy of the human subject when the most banal daily reflection forces its cruel and patent daily instability upon us. My babies grow up to leave me only the faintest gleam of any recall of their infancy, my sylphlike self has ruthlessly vanished decades ago, those who once loved me no longer speak to me, and my last remaining claim to some unification, my very memory, is dying at each moment in a faint crash of brain cells. In the teeth of all this merciless fragmenting, an exaggerated statement of connectedness can appear, as if to anchor the eroded self among others. 'To identify with' may well be a benevolently humanist drive. But well meant as it is, it can also be an unsubtle affair, this identifying with the oppressed. There are overinclusive or premature solidarities, too. The white Rastafarian, the lesbian-until-graduation, the male feminist, may be objects of deep irritation to those whose ostensibly exciting marginality they'd hoped, by means of an empathetic mimicry, to share. 'Meiosis' denotes some rhetorical understatement.[79] Is there a rhetorical term for its opposite, a deliberate overinclusiveness?[80] A massification may hold more vehemently, as sensing itself up against the wall of others' hostility, it gathers itself defiantly. 'It's not just you as one man, it's like one huge person walking', explained an Orangeman in Northern Ireland.[81] A lighter-hearted kind of vicarious identification is energetically displayed in football 'supporting'; simply through announcing your support, you become a small aspect of the team, and its vicissitudes are yours. To live in very real remoteness from the field of play is no obstacle to this identification, as anyone can testify who's witnessed her nine-year-old exultantly taking into herself her team's triumph as 'we won!' or weeping wild tears before the television set if 'we' were beaten. As Wyndham Lewis tartly remarked, 'An *esprit de corps* can be worked up about anything'.[82]

If taking up my place is always done 'in relation', as a social affair, this in itself cannot guarantee me any confidence in my new grouping. It can arise darkly. My self-identification can be a protective response reached through great fear: the core of negativity in identification, demonstrated in the defensive adoption of the name of the threatened ethnicity. Unhappy examples of a self-protective if reluctant self-identification are legion, such as decisively becoming Zionist in the face of European anti-semitism. Or, as sometimes instanced in the disintegration of the former Yugoslavia, first becoming that ethnic–religious type that one is told that one is, and then being attacked, or left undefended, for being it. This politicisation of the 'ethnic' is most bitterly debated among those it seeks to reassign, as in the deliberate manipulation of a presumed 'ethnicisation', some already imaginary ethnic identity becomes further contorted.[83] Lately it has been all too easy to hear the devastating effects of such enforced imagined identities transformed into political counters. The following is one out of a thousand possible instances of such a critique readily overheard in recent years (and to preserve it in its lucidity is hardly to pursue a mirage of some idealised multiculturalism, always to be lived out, come what may, elsewhere in the world and by 'non-Western' others). In late 1995 an open meeting in London was addressed by senior academics from Tuzla and Sarajevo.[84] A member of the audience inquired about the proportions of what he termed 'Muslim, Croat, and Serbian' students enrolled before the outbreak of war and how many of each remained now there. This question was answered with calm simplicity, any impatience well concealed: that it had never been found necessary to keep such statistics before the war, and that, at the end of the war, it was even more necessary not to keep such a count—'For if we begin to count now, we are lost'.

A useful nonidentity could appear, then, in a refusal of the 'realism' of groups in the name of a better understanding of solidarity. Rancière's related claim that emancipation entails 'a heterology' defends the idea of a useful distance between those figures which populate the space of democratic politics, and the supposed realism of some group identity. The arena of the political demands a necessary artifice. Even the initial articulation of some 'we' is no mark of a simple joint consciousness, for it names new subjects different from the old selves which enunciate them. This makes for a productive complexity: 'There is politics when the "we's" arrange by their words and acts the visible sphere of subjects who are not collective bodies or social groups, but operators who, under diverse names (citizens, patriots, workers, women) make visible and dispute the relations between inclusion and exclusion'.[85] Some distance between the speaker and the category under which that speaker ostensibly speaks becomes an index of a helpful mobility: 'If there is democracy, that means there are figures of subjectivation which are figures of a difference. The people is something which is not the population, race, blood and so forth. The proletariat is not a social group'.[86] Invoking his own historical work on the label of 'worker', Rancière holds that a politics with an adequate vocabulary will become anti-identificatory; not so much a confirmation of the self's status as a reaching out to others.[87] In a comparable spirit, Wendy Brown has eloquently set out this prospect of what we could name as an altruistic identification:

> What if we sought to supplant the language of 'I am'—with its defensive closure on identity, its insistence on the fixity of position, its equation of social with moral positioning—with the language of 'I want this for us?' [. . .] Such a slight shift in the character of the political discourse of identity eschews the kinds of a historical or utopian turns against identity politics made by a nostalgic and broken humanist Left as well as the reactionary and disingenuous assaults on politicised identity tendered by the Right. Rather than opposing or seeking to transcend identity

investments, the replacement—even the admixture—of the language of 'being' with the language of 'wanting' would seek to exploit politically a recovery of the more expansive moments in the genealogy of identity formation, a recovery of the moment prior to its own foreclosure against its want, prior to the point at which its sovereign subjectivity is established through such foreclosure and through eternal repetition of its pain.[88]

Isn't this programmatic hope, in effect, a reinvocation of the older ideal of solidarity, although this time with its formative archaeology instructively laid bare? And then how, as recommended here, to 'incite a slight shift in the character of political expression and political claims common to much politicised identity'?'[89] The engine of such a transformation waits to be specified (to put it in a leadenly marxisant manner). As for Rancière's own developing political subject, this is hydra-headed, in transition, and again thrown forward as 'a crossing of identities, relying on a crossing of names: names that link the name of a group or class to the names of no group or no class, a being to a nonbeing or a not-yet-being'.[90] Within such a laudable formula, we might unearth some slight implication that the business of subjectivisation is wilful and somewhat fantastical in its anticipations. Like wish fulfilment, it speaks its futurity, but it speaks through the magical device of christening its own actuality. And, conjuring trick though it may be, this is a thoroughly effective magic. It must have worked well enough, at least, in the past, where fuller political languages flowered; and Rancière's formulations do seem to have a sheen of longing about them.

What might encourage such a more responsive linguistic malleability? Yet behind this intractable if natural question, we can also hear the murmur of settled identities both swelling and falling day by day, and sense them chattering away within us. This might serve to reduce our anxieties to a tolerantly resigned fellow-feeling with Wordsworth, as change and decay in all around we see.[91] Both the melancholic's and the realist's attitude to that question (which we may sense to be misguided yet cannot quite suppress) as to the engine of improvement, would be a fatalistic pragmatism—that the language will continue to evolve, or to conserve, just as it will. But some interpellative emergency—for example, to be pinioned by name on the streets of Kigali—would be well beyond the slower reaches of this linguistic amelioration.[92] A less leisurely placed observer, at the sharp end of altering political languages, will not escape the speculation that the less massively singular a category of identification is and the more components it has, the more remote its risk of petrification into a nationalism which may take cruel turns; and for someone so placed, the question of linguistic categorical intervention may urgently reassert itself. That by no means innocent installation of a supposed religious ethnicity in those aggressively amassed as 'muslims' is a case in point.[93] Ivan Lovrenovic evokes a fight against the restrictive naming of ethnicisations: 'The first step in the reconstitution of Bosnian culture must be a relativization of political-national identity'.[94] But perhaps we could also distinguish another stance, which would not exactly hope to intervene in the political language by directly 'inciting' anything, beyond those great powers to incite that naming its hopes enacts—for the linguistic event is as profoundly historical an event as any other. Instead, this particular response to the question of change would draw some consolation from what it sees as the inherently ironic capacities of language to become sick of the repetitions of identities.

If our present rush to self-description as identification must cause hesitancy, and if few can confidently live in any identity for long—while the results of punitively doing so are distressing—there's also tireless life in the workings of language, whose self-curing possibilities eat into its own perpetuation of the damage that elsewhere it pronounces. This is not to forget that innovations in deathly speech are also always at hand. Yet if, as my earlier chapters here proposed, interpellation's syntax lies uncomfortably close to guilt, if identification runs towards accusation, and if the whole affair of self-description is a vast if productive trouble, then this aspect of irony supplies some optimism to my short roster of somewhat overcast linguistic affect. 'Irony, however, has no past', says Kierkegaard,[95] for it isolates, in order to interrogate a category. It rises above the solemn chronology of descriptions, always poised to wrench a phrase out of its context. It commits this linguistic violence of dismembering, not gratuitously but as it exposes the contingent formation of that very context—and so, ultimately, restores its history to it. That salutary deflation of some excessively vaunted category, so that it suddenly seems bizarre to itself and from then onward cannot endure its own repetitions, *just is* irony at work. Here irony's political astringency, ruthlessly democratic, acts on the side of the angels. Insofar as the corrosion of the monuments of selves can sensibly be described as 'ethical' at all, that is where the ethical aspect to irony lies. And this springs up immediately within it, is heard first by its utterers, and is not conveyed from some resolutely willed ethical terrain lying elsewhere. It's just one instance of a linguistic affect at work in the commonest mechanisms of spoken and written reiteration. This essay has ventured an idea of a powerful linguistic-emotive effectivity which also operates at the level of language's formal structures, and which is by no means unsociable or estranging, since the greater the graspable reach and flexibility of language in all its aspects, the more the possibilities for understanding both presence and change. But don't these suggestions evacuate the effectiveness of human speakers in all this? They do and they don't. They do, because my rather hopeful account of irony's self-reflexive interventions may boil down to this suggestion: that there may, also, be a productive dialogue between language and its own unconscious.[96] They don't, because the work of critical reflection subsequent to this dialogue is done by voices which are neither the exertion of pure will nor are being straightforwardly spoken. Here they have a claim to principled ambiguity. This need not, and indeed cannot, rest on any claim to individual uniqueness. That someone is speaking also means that it is being spoken, and 'I' vanish into my long home as a faint rustle within a broad murmur among anonymous voices.[97] For 'There is always another breath in my breath, another thought in my thought, another possession in what I possess, a thousand things and a thousand beings implicated in my complications [. . .]'.[98] Just as the 'subject founded in division' finds the very ground for its empathetic solidarities not despite but *within* its loneliness, so, too, is there nothing remotely inhuman about this generous dispossession. It can be taken in good heart. That is again made clear in a fine passage by Deleuze, which itself, with Klossowski's counterpoint, performs the polyphony that it values: 'That everything is so "complicated", that *I* may be an other, that something else thinks in us in an aggression which is the aggression of thought, in a multiplication which is the multiplication of the body, or in a violence which is the violence of language—this is the joyful message. For we are so sure of living again (without resurrection) only because so many beings and things think in us: because "we still do not know exactly if it is not others who continue to think within us (but who are these others who form the outside in relation to this inside which we believe ourselves to be?)—everything is brought back to a single discourse, to fluctuations of intensity, for instance, which correspond to the thought of everyone and no one."'[99]

Reference Matter

Notes

Introduction

1. Wallace Stevens, 'Adagia', in *Opus Posthumous* (London: Faber and Faber, 1959).

2. Theodor Adorno has a likeable discussion of the physiognomy of punctuation 'which cannot be separated from its syntactic function but is by no means exhausted by it', a point on which he refers to Karl Kraus. See Adorno's 'Punctuation Marks' in his *Notes to Literature*, vol. 1, ed. Rolf Tiedemann, trans. Shierry Weber Nicholsen (New York: Columbia University Press, 1991), 91.

3. That is, the concept of ideology sketched in Marx's 1859 *Preface to the Critique of Political Economy*, rather than, for instance, *The Communist Manifesto* of 1847. Etienne Balibar's discussion is very helpful here; see 'The Vacillations of Ideology in Marxism' in *Masses, Classes, Ideas*, trans. James Swenson (New York: Routledge, 1994), 87–123.

4. Friedrich Nietzsche, *Beyond Good and Evil* (1886), trans. R. J. Hollingdale (Harmondsworth: Penguin Books, 1981), 37, 47–48.

5. Nietzsche, *Beyond Good and Evil*, as discussed in Michel Foucault, 'Nietzsche, Genealogy, History', in *Language, Counter-Memory, Practice: Selected Essays and Interviews*, ed. Donald F. Bouchard, trans. Donald F. Bouchard and Sherry Simon (Ithaca, N.Y.: Cornell University Press, 1977), 149.

6. See also William E. Connolly, 'Democracy and Distance', chap. 6 in *Identity/Difference* (Ithaca, N.Y.: Cornell University Press, 1991), 158–97.

7. And, to add a footnote in 1999, some previously reluctant conviction of myself as 'Serbian' might be decisively hardened under bombardment.

8. 'Transcendent critique sympathises with authority in its very form, even before expressing any content: there is a moment of content to the form itself. The expression "as a . . . , I . . . ", in which one can insert any orientation, from dialectical materialism to Protestantism, is symptomatic of that'. Theodor Adorno, in *Hegel: Three Studies*, trans. Shierry Weber Nicholsen (Cambridge, Mass.: MIT Press, 1993), 194.

9. The murders of James Byrd and of Stephen Lawrence by white supremacists in 1998 and in 1993.

10. 'What I have in my consciousness, that is for me. *I* is this void, this receptacle for anything and everything, that for which everything is and which preserves everything within itself. Everyone is a whole world of representations, which are buried in the night of the *I*. Thus, *I* is the universal, in which abstraction is made from everything particular, but in which at the same time everything is present, though veiled'. 'Preliminary Conceptions', in G. W. F. Hegel, *The Encyclopaedia Logic*, Part 1 of the *Encyclopaedia of Philosophical Sciences*, trans. T. F. Geraets, W. A. Suchting, and H. S. Harris (Indianapolis, Ind.: Hackett, 1991), 57.

11. I have drawn the initial implication that there is an unconscious of language from Jean-Jacques Lecercle, *The Violence of Language* (New York: Routledge, 1990), 33–52.

12. There is a large body of analytical literature on the question of naming as description, such as Saul Kripke's *Naming and Necessity* (Oxford: Blackwell, 1980), which harks back to the work of Bertrand Russell and Gottlob Frege on proper names; but the concerns of these pages here are tangential to that.

13. For a detailed exposition of this critical possibility of 'an unconscious of language' and how far this includes but goes beyond slips of the tongue towards something substantially different, see Jean-Jacques Lecercle, 'A Theory of the Remainder', chap. 3 in *Violence of Language*, 103–43.

14. C. S. Peirce, 'What Pragmatism Is' (1905), *Collected Papers 1931–1958*, vol. 5, paragraph 417 (Bloomington: Indiana University Press, 1982–86).

15. Louis Althusser, 'Freud and Lacan', in *Lenin and Philosophy* (London: NLB, 1971), 192.

16. Moustapha Safouan, *L'inconscient et son scribe*, chap. 5 (Paris: Editions du Seuil, 1982), 106–30.

17. *Jacques Lacan and the Question of Analytic Training*, introduced and trans. Jacqueline Rose (London: Macmillan, 2000), in press.

18. See Lecercle's discussions of intentionality in *Interpretation as Pragmatics* (London: Macmillan, 1999), 118–51.

19. Jean-Claude Milner, *L'amour de la langue* (Paris: Editions du Seuil, 1978), trans. Ann Banfield as *For the Love of Language* (London: Macmillan, 1990), 64.

20. Jacques Lacan, *Ecrits* (Paris: Editions du Seuil, 1966), 469.

21. Again, for example, 'it is always from the outside that what one calls the internal process comes. It is first by the intermediary of the outside that it is recognised'. *Le Séminaire, Livre 1 (1953–1954): Les écrits techniques de Freud* (Paris: Editions du Seuil, 1975), 177.

22. This remark is a shorthand only. One could begin an argument either by asking what else a psychotherapeutics of the subject is supposed to do, or else by asking

if it can be right to maintain the position that the subject is being reformulated, in the teeth of passages such as this? Lacan says in Seminar VII, 'The Circuit', that 'This discourse of the other is not the discourse of the abstract other, of the other in the dyad, of my correspondent, nor even of my slave. It is the discourse of the circuit in which I am integrated. I am one of its links. It is the discourse of my father for instance, in so far as my father made mistakes which I am absolutely condemned to reproduce—that's what we call *the super-ego*. I am condemned to reproduce them because I am obliged to pick up again the discourse he bequeathed to me, not simply because I am his son, but because one can't stop the chain of discourse, and it is precisely my duty to transmit it in its aberrant form to someone else. I have to put to someone else the problem of a situation of life or death in which the chances are that it is just as likely that he will falter, in such a way that this discourse reproduces a small circuit in which an entire family, an entire coterie, an entire camp, an entire nation or half the world will be caught. The circular form of a speech which is just at the limit between sense and non-sense, which is problematic' (*The Seminar of Jacques Lacan*, ed. Jacques-Alain Miller, trans. Sylvana Tomaselli [Cambridge: Cambridge University Press, 1988], Book II, 89–90). On a related note in the same volume, Seminar V, 'Homeostasis and Insistence' proposes 'The subject is no-one. It is decomposed, in pieces. And it is jammed, sucked in by the image, the deceiving and realised image of the other, or equally by its own specular image. That is where it finds its unity. [. . .] Someone here, whose identity I have no need to disclose, said to me after my last lecture—*This consciousness, it seems to me that after having badly mistreated it you bring it back in with this voice which reintroduces order, and which regulates the ballet of the machines.* Our deduction of the subject however demands that we locate this voice somewhere in the interhuman game' (54–55). This is where Lacan settles, after musing aloud as to whether Valéry's phrase 'the voice of no one' could be more apposite. And in Seminar XXII, 'Where is Speech? Where is Language?' Lacan reminds his hearers that while 'The world of language is possible in so far as we have our place in it anywhere', not all ways of being within language will work with equal efficacy and that 'not every random bit of language has the same value for the subject' (278). The present writer will always demand more cruelty.

23. Slavoj Žižek, *The Sublime Object of Ideology* (London: Verso, 1989), 110–14.

24. Denise Riley, *'Am I That Name?' Feminism and the Category of 'Women' in History* (London: Macmillan, 1988).

Chapter 1

1. Frank O'Hara, 'In Memory of My Feelings' (1956), in *Collected Poems of Frank O'Hara*, ed. Donald Allen (New York: Knopf, 1979), 257.

2. Lynne Tillman, 'Madame Realism Faces It', *Art in America* 87, no. 2 (1999).

3. See Judith Butler's discussion about when being a self-declared homosexual may, in military regulations, constitute entrapment, in *Excitable Speech: A Politics of the Performative* (New York: Routledge, 1997), 106–26.

4. G. W. F. Hegel, *Phenomenology of Spirit*, trans. A. V. Miller (Oxford: Oxford University Press, 1977), 308.

5. The intentions of a speaker are discussed by Freud in 'Mourning and Melancholia' (1917), in *The Standard Edition of the Complete Psychological Works of Sigmund Freud*, vol. 14, ed. and trans. James Strachey (London: Hogarth Press, 1964), 256.

6. Maurice Merleau-Ponty, *Phenomenology of Perception*, trans. Colin Smith (London: Routledge and Kegan Paul, 1962), 434.

7. Phil Cohen, *Rethinking the Youth Question* (London: Macmillan, 1997), 7.

8. In Book 2 of his *Ethics*, Aristotle argues that dispositions are anchored through habitual actions: 'Anything that we have to learn to do, we learn by the actual doing of it: people become builders by building and instrumentalists by playing instruments. Similarly we become just by performing just acts, temperate by performing temperate ones, brave by performing brave ones'. *The Ethics of Aristotle*, trans. J. A. K. Thomson (Harmondsworth: Penguin Books, 1976), 91–92.

9. O'Hara, 'Mayakovsky', in *Collected Poems*, 202.

10. Karl Marx, *Grundrisse, Foundations for the Critique of Political Economy* (Harmondsworth: Penguin Books, 1973), 197, 496. See also Charles Taylor, *Sources of the Self: The Making of the Modern Identity* (Cambridge: Cambridge University Press, 1989).

11. Max Weber, *The Protestant Ethic and the Spirit of Capitalism* (1904–5), trans. Talcott Parsons (London: Allen and Unwin, 1976).

12. *The Social Psychology of George Herbert Mead*, ed. and introduced by Anselm Strauss (Chicago: Chicago University Press, 1965).

13. Mauss's 1938 lecture is, he insists, a preliminary attempt: 'A category of the human mind: the notion of person; the notion of self'. *The Category of the Person: Anthropology Philosophy History*, ed. Michael Carrithers, Steven Collins, and Steven Lukes, trans. W. D. Halls (Cambridge: Cambridge University Press, 1985), 1.

14. From the Zuni whose clan forenames determined their forms of social being and from the Kwakiutl of the American Northwest, for whom 'every stage of life is named, personified by a fresh name, a fresh title' (ibid., 9), and from Australian masquerades of 'the enraptured representation of the ancestor' (12).

15. The Latin *persona* derived from far older 'mask' civilisations, but its highly artificial character was transformed within Roman law (ibid., 17).

16. Mauss notes that this was the Roman notion of *persona*, and under law, 'the right to the *persona* had been established. Only the slave is excluded from it' (ibid., 17).

17. Ibid., 20.

18. 'The ideas of the Moravian Brothers, the Puritans, the Wesleyans, and the Pietists are those which form the basis on which is established the notion: the "person" (*personne*) equals the self; the self (*moi*) equals consciousness, and is its primordial category' (ibid., 21).

19. Ibid., 22.

20. Mauss cites Fichte's *Die Tatsachen des Bewusstseins*, 1810–11, recommending its summary in Xavier Leon, *Fichte et son temps*, vol. III (Paris, 1927), 161–69.

21. Peter Handke, *A Sorrow beyond Dreams*, trans. Ralph Manheim (London: Souvenir Press, 1976), 65.

22. Robert Musil, *The Man without Qualities*, trans. Eithne Wilkins and Ernst Kaiser (London: Secker and Warburg, 1953).

23. Miss Daisy Mowcher, observed by David Copperfield, has a keen sense of her capacities: '"Ain't I volatile?" she added, as a commentary on this offer, and, with her finger on her nose, departed'. Charles Dickens, *David Copperfield*, edited by Nina Burgis (Oxford: Clarendon Press, 1981), 285–86.

24. From my 'Disintegrate me', from 'Seven Strangely Exciting Lies', in *Penguin Modern Poets*, vol. 10, Douglas Oliver, Denise Riley, and Iain Sinclair (London: Penguin Books, 1996), 92.

25. Wolfgang Schadewaldt, *Von Homers Welt und Werk* (Stuttgart, 1951), 83–84.

26. Veronica Forrest-Thomson, 'Pastoral', in *On the Periphery* (Cambridge: Street Editions, 1976).

27. The solitary self isn't to be understood as prior to society; Marx mentions that 'the individual and isolated hunter and fisherman, with whom Smith and Ricardo begin, belongs among the unimaginative conceits of the eighteenth-century Robinsonades'. See his *Grundrisse*, 83.

28. Samuel Beckett, 'Not-I', *Collected Shorter Plays* (London: Faber and Faber, 1984), 213–23.

29. See Slavoj Žižek, 'The Supposed Subjects of Ideology', *Critical Quarterly* 39, no. 2 (summer 1997), on substitution as things being done for one, in one's name.

30. The question of submission and disobedience here is helpfully discussed throughout Butler's *Excitable Speech*.

31. William Wordsworth's sonnet on 'Mutability' (1822), in *The Oxford Authors: William Wordsworth* (Oxford: Oxford University Press, 1984), 353.

32. Gilles Deleuze ventures a psychic grammar, resting on an intermediary concept of the 'phantasm': 'It is therefore inevitable that phantasms have only an indirect and tardive relation to language and that, when they are verbalised afterwards, the verbalisation occurs in accordance with ready-made grammatical forms'. He continues, 'It seems to us, precisely, that the phantasm, properly speaking, finds its origin only in the ego of the secondary narcissism, along with the narcissistic wound,

the neutralisation, the symbolisation and the sublimation which ensue. In this sense, it is inseparable not only from grammatical transformations but also from the neutral infinitive as the ideational material of these transformations'. 'Thirtieth Series of the Phantasm' (1969), in *The Logic of Sense*, trans. Mark Lester from *Logique du sens* (London: The Athlone Press, 1990), 216.

33. This phrase is Jacques Rancière's book title, *La chair des mots: Politiques de l'écriture* (Paris: Galilee, 1998).

34. Or that with this claim, you must buy into a tarnished version of dialectical materialism, one belonging to the Engels of the *Anti-Dühring* rather than to Marx.

35. William Shakespeare, *King Lear*, 4.2.18 (Norton).

36. It's argued that the Saussurean *langue–parole* distinction must be explained within the fractious history of linguistics as an attempt to preserve and defend a particular 'autonomy' of linguistics; to keep it clear of sliding into other fields, it had to be construed as 'antimaterialist'.

37. See Joseph R. Roach, *The Player's Passion: Studies in the Science of Acting* (Newark: University of Delaware Press, 1985), 23–26.

38. In that evocative formula, 'a disputed author of uncertain date', proposed now as the second century B.C.

39. Demetrius, 'On Style', par. 192–95, *Aristotle, 'The Poetics'*, ed. and trans. Stephen Halliwell; *Longinus, 'On the Sublime'*, trans. W. H. Fyfe; *Demetrius, 'On Style'*, ed. and trans. Doreen C. Innes, in one volume (Cambridge, Mass.: Harvard University Press, 1995), 465.

40. His authorship, long disputed, was probably of the first century A.D. Longinus, 'On the Sublime', chaps. 1 and 2, 165.

41. Ibid., chaps. 21 and 22, 239.

42. 'On the Sublime' analyses the emotional effects of various rhetorical and prosody devices. By visualisation (*phantasia*), Longinus says he means what others call 'image-production', so he departs from the Stoic definition in which the term is used for anything which suggests a thought productive of speech. Longinus, 'On the Sublime', chap. 15, 215.

43. Ibid., 13.

44. Ludwig Wittgenstein, *Philosophical Investigations*, trans. G. E. M. Anscombe (Oxford: Blackwell, 1963), par. 93, 44e. Wittgenstein's own reading of Nietzsche is mentioned briefly in Ray Monk's biography *Ludwig Wittgenstein: The Duty of Genius* (London: Vintage, 1991), 121–23.

45. Ibid., par. 109, 47e.

46. Ibid., par. 257, 92e.

47. Friedrich Nietzsche, *Beyond Good and Evil* (1886), trans. R. J. Hollingdale (Harmondsworth: Penguin Books, 1981), 37.

48. Ibid., 46.

49. 'The singular family resemblance between all Indian, Greek and German philosophising is easy enough to explain. Where there exists a language affinity it is quite impossible, thanks to the common philosophy of grammar—I mean thanks to unconscious dominating and directing by similar grammatical functions—to avoid everything being prepared in advance for a similar evolution and succession of philosophical systems: just as the road seems barred to certain other possibilities of world interpretation'. Nietzsche extends this reflection to argue that 'the spell of definite grammatical functions is in the last resort the spell of *physiological* value judgments and racial conditions' (*Beyond Good and Evil*, 32).

50. Friedrich Nietzsche, *Twilight of the Idols* (1888), trans. R. J. Hollingdale (London: Penguin Books, 1968), 38. Also see Nietzsche's *Ecce Homo* (1888), trans. A. Ludovici (Edinburgh: T. N. Foulis, 1911), *A Genealogy of Morals* (1887), trans. William A. Haussman and John Gray (London: Unwin, 1899), and his *Beyond Good and Evil*.

51. Nietzsche, *Beyond Good and Evil*, 47–48.

52. Nietzsche, *Genealogy of Morals*. Butler's full exposition of these passages analyses this search for someone to blame as the retrospective installation of the grammatical subject; see her *Excitable Speech*, 45–46.

53. Nietzsche, *Beyond Good and Evil*, 29.

54. Wendy Brown, 'Wounded Attachments', in *The Identity in Question*, ed. John Rajchman (New York: Routledge, 1995), 199–225.

55. Nietzsche, *Beyond Good and Evil*, 27.

56. Jacques Derrida emphasises Nietzsche's notion of seduction as enacted specifically by Woman in *Spurs: Nietzsche's Styles*, trans. Barbara Harlow (Chicago: University of Chicago Press, 1979).

57. Jean Baudrillard holds that the seducer's forte is to simply 'to hang out signs'. In *Seduction*, trans. Brian Singer from *De la séduction* (London: Macmillan, 1990).

58. Nietzsche, *Beyond Good and Evil*, 28–29.

59. 'Nothing determines me from outside, not because nothing acts upon me, but, on the contrary, because I am from the start outside myself and open to the world'. Merleau-Ponty, *Phenomenology of Perception*, 456.

60. Ibid., 183.

61. 'What misleads us in this connection, and causes us to believe in a thought which exists for itself prior to expression, is thought already constituted and expressed, which we can silently recall to ourselves, and through which we acquire the illusion of an inner life. But in reality this supposed silence is alive with words, this inner life is an inner language'. Ibid., 183.

62. Wyndham Lewis, *Time and Western Man* (London: Chatto and Windus, 1937).

63. Wyndham Lewis, *The Art of Being Ruled* (London: Chatto and Windus, 1926), 403.

64. 'I can only talk literally. Metaphor, litotes, and hyperbole call for a considered effort which has the effect of emphasising everything that is unreal and conventional in those figures of speech. I can imagine that this mental travail would be of extreme interest to a grammarian or a philologist; but to me it is a luxury which is both useless and destructive. For example, the notion of *depth* which I never troubled to scrutinise when using it in such expressions as "a deep thinker" or "a deep love."' From Michel Tournier's novel *Friday, or the Other Island*, trans. Norman Denny (London: Collins, 1969), 62.

65. 'What if that outer shell were solid, filled with sameness like a doll stuffed with bran? [. . .] I think the soul only acquires any notable content from beyond that barrier of skin which separates the inner from the outer world, and that it enriches itself only inasmuch as it flows out in widening circles from that central point which is me' (ibid.). Deleuze discusses Tournier here in *Logic of Sense*, 301–21.

66. Gilles Deleuze, 'Phantasm and Modern Literature', appendix II of *Logic of Sense*, 315. He takes the internal quotation from Tournier's *Friday* in its original publication as *Vendredi* in the *nrf* edition (Paris: Gallimard, 1967), 58. The translation here is by Denny from *Friday*, 62.

67. Wittgenstein, *Philosophical Investigations*, par. III, 47e.

68. Nietzsche, *Genealogy of Morals*, 104.

69. Hegel, *Encyclopaedia Logic*, 209.

70. Hegel quotes Goethe's 'Indignant Outcry' in the latter's *Zur Morphologie*, vol. I:3, in *Encyclopaedia Logic*, 210.

71. Deleuze, *Logic of Sense*, 260.

72. Ibid., 128–33.

73. Ibid., 'Second Series of Paradoxes of Surface Effects'; 'Valéry had a profound idea; what is most deep is the skin. This is a Stoic discovery, which presupposes a great deal of wisdom and entails an entire ethic' (10).

74. Ibid., 'The Simulacrum and Ancient Philosophy', appendix I: 'The heterogeneity of the diverse forms a sort of vitalism of seeds, but the resemblance of the diverse forms a sort of pantheism of mothers' (272).

75. William Blake, letter to George Cumberland, 12 October 1827, in *The Poetry and Prose of William Blake*, ed. David V. Erdman (Garden City, N.Y.: Doubleday, 1970), 707.

76. O'Hara, 'In Memory of My Feelings' (1956), in *Collected Poems*, 257.

77. From my 'Rayon', in *Penguin Modern Poets*, vol. 10, 79.

78. Zygmunt Bauman, *Life in Fragments: Essays in Postmodern Morality* (Oxford: Blackwell, 1995), 48.

79. This theme runs through Martin Heidegger's essays 'Poetically Man Dwells' and 'Building Dwelling Thinking' in *Poetry Language Thought*, trans. and introduced Albert Hofstadter (New York: Harper and Row, 1975), 213–29, 145–61.

80. Philippe-Auguste Villiers de l'Isle-Adam's drama, *Axel* (1890), 4.2, trans. Marilyn Gaddis Rose (Dublin: Dolmen Press, 1970).

81. Whitman is a loving ironist of self-description, but it's an irony of the utmost delicacy in his 1855 'Song of Myself', in *Collected Writings of Walt Whitman*, ed. H. W. Blodgett and S. Bradley (London: University of London Press, 1965), 28.

82. Simone de Beauvoir has an undeveloped sketch of a 'Social Other' in her 1947 essay on 'The Ethics of Ambiguity', trans. Bernard Frechtman (New York: Citadel Press, 1970).

83. Hegel, *Encyclopaedia Logic*, par. 140, 'Second Subdivision of the Logic', 211.

84. This is a version of the sixth of Marx's *Theses on Feuerbach* (1845): 'Feuerbach resolves the essence of religion into the essence of man. But the essence of man is no abstraction inherent in each single individual. In its reality, it is the ensemble of the social relations'. *Karl Marx and Frederick Engels, Collected Works*, vol. 5 (London: Lawrence and Wishart, 1976), 7.

85. 'This moreover is the Nietzschean discovery of the individual as the *fortuitous case*. Witness "the vehement oscillations which upset the individual as long as he seeks only his own centre and does not see the circle of which he himself is a part; for if these oscillations upset him, it is because each corresponds to an individuality other than that which he takes as his own from the point of view of the undiscoverable centre. Hence an identity is essentially fortuitous and a series of individualities must be traversed by each, in order that the fortuity make them completely necessary."' Deleuze, 'Twenty-fifth series of Univocity', in *Logic of Sense*, 178. He has taken the internal quotation from Pierre Klossowski's 'La période turinoise de Nietzsche', *l'Éphémère* 5 (spring 1968).

86. Nietzsche, *Beyond Good and Evil*, 31.

87. Ibid., 146.

88. See Charles Taylor, *The Ethics of Authenticity* (Cambridge, Mass.: Harvard University Press, 1991).

89. 'The actualisation of rational self-consciousness through its own activity', in Hegel, *Phenomenology of Spirit*, 217.

90. Hegel: 'too little, because in speech and action the inner turns itself into something else, into an other, thus putting itself at the mercy of the element of change, which twists the spoken word and the accomplished act into meaning something else than they are in and for themselves, as actions of this particular individual' (ibid., 187).

91. 'The first [principle] of each being is that it wills itself [. . .] But to will one-

self and to negate one's self as being are one and the same thing'. F. W. J. von Schelling, *Die Weltalter* (1811), trans. F. de Wolfe Bolman as *The Ages of the World* (New York: Columbia University Press, 1942), 110–11.

Chapter 2

1. Marianne Moore, 'Black Earth', *Selected Poems* (London: Faber and Faber, 1935), 59.

2. 'If psycho-analysis is to be constituted as the science of the unconscious, one must set out from the notion that the unconscious is structured like a language'. Jacques Lacan, 'The Field of the Other and Back to the Transference', in *The Four Fundamental Concepts of Psycho-analysis* (1973), ed. Jacques-Alain Miller, trans. Alan Sheridan (Harmondsworth: Penguin Books, 1977), 203.

3. Fran Lebowitz, *Social Studies* (New York: Random House, 1981), 6.

4. G. W. F. Hegel, *The Encyclopaedia Logic*, Part 1 of the *Encyclopaedia of Philosophical Sciences*, trans. T. F. Geraets, W. A. Suchting, and H. S. Harris (Indianapolis, Ind.: Hackett, 1991), 57.

5. Herman Parret, '"Ma vie" comme effet de discours', *La Licorne* 14 (1988): 161–77. I owe this reference to Robert Smith's *Derrida and Autobiography* (Cambridge: Cambridge University Press, 1995), which persuasively lays out the deathliness of that genre.

6. Jacques Derrida, 'La parole soufflée', trans. Alan Bass, in *Writing and Difference* (London: RKP, 1978), 178.

7. Antonin Artaud, letter to Jacques Rivière, 29 January 1924, in *Antonin Artaud: Collected Works*, vol. 1, trans. Victor Corti (London: John Calder, London 1968), 31.

8. Ibid., 214–15.

9. Michel Foucault, *The Archaeology of Knowledge* (1969), trans. Alan Sheridan Smith (London: Tavistock Books, 1972), 17.

10. 'Ce moi incertain et flottant dont j'ai contesté moi-même l'existence, et que je ne sens vraiment délimité que par les quelques ouvrages qu'il m'est arrivé d'écrire'. Marguerite Yourcenar, cited in Parret, '"Ma vie" comme effet de discours', 161.

11. Mikhail Bakhtin, 'Discourse in the Novel', in *The Dialogic Imagination: Four Essays*, trans. Caryl Emerson and Michael Holquist (Austin: University of Texas Press, 1981), 293.

12. *Letters of Emily Dickinson*, ed. Thomas H. Johnson (Cambridge, Mass.: Harvard University Press, 1958), L38.

13. Maurice Merleau-Ponty, *The Phenomenology of Perception*, trans. Colin Smith (London: Routledge and Kegan Paul, 1962), 456.

14. Jacques Derrida, *Mémoires, for Paul de Man*, trans. Cecile Lindsay, Jonathan Culler, and Eduardo Cadava (New York: Columbia University Press, 1986).

15. 'Tout discours de "ma vie" est un discours sur la Mort'. Parret, '"Ma vie" comme effet de discours', 177.

16. Martin Heidegger, 'Poetically Man Dwells', in Heidegger's *Poetry Language Thought*, trans. and introduced by Albert Hofstadter (New York: Harper and Row, 1975), 215–16.

17. Heidegger, 'A Meditation on Trakl', in *Poetry Language Thought*, 198.

18. Ibid., 207.

19. Roman Jakobson, 'Quest for the Essence of Language', in *Language in Literature*, ed. Krystyna Pomorska and Stephen Rudy (Cambridge, Mass.: Belknap Press of Harvard University Press, 1987), 423.

20. Heidegger, 'Poetically Man Dwells', in *Poetry Language Thought*, 216.

21. Tristan Tzara, *Dada Manifesto on Weak Love and Bitter Love* (1924), one of the *Sept Manifestes Dada*, in *Tristan Tzara, Oeuvres Complètes*, vol. 1 (Paris: Flammarion, 1975), 389.

22. Stephane Mallarmé, *Divagations* (Paris, 1879).

23. Wallace Stevens, 'Adagia', in *Opus Posthumous* (London: Faber and Faber, 1959).

24. W. S. Graham, 'What is the Language Using Us For?', in *Collected Poems 1942–1977* (London: Faber and Faber, 1979), 195–96.

25. Jean-Claude Milner, *L'Amour de la langue*, trans. Ann Banfield as *For the Love of Language* (London: Macmillan, 1990), 64.

26. Graham, 'What is the Language Using Us For?', 194.

27. 'Que le critique d'une part, et que le versificateur d'autre part, le veuille ou non' is Jakobson's mention of Saussure here. Jakobson, 'Subliminal Verbal Patterning in Poetry', *Language in Literature*, 250–61, 250.

28. Ibid., 251.   29. Ibid.

30. Ibid., 252.   31. Ibid., 253.

32. Jakobson, 'Language in Operation', *Language in Literature*, 54. Jakobson has borrowed his example from R. G. Kent, 'Assimilation and Dissimilation', in *Language* 12 (1936).

33. Sebastiano Timpanaro, *The Freudian Slip*, trans. Kate Soper from *Il Lapsus Freudiano* (London: New Left Books, 1976), 224.

34. Jean-Jacques Lecercle, in *The Violence of Language* (New York: Routledge, 1990), discusses Brisset (1837–1923) on 61–62 and elsewhere.

35. Sigmund Freud, 'The Work of Condensation in the Dream-Work', in *The Interpretation of Dreams*, vol. 4, ed. James Strachey (Harmondsworth: Penguin Freud Library, 1991), 383, 387.

36. Timpanaro, *Freudian Slip*, 141.

37. Ibid., 224.

38. R. D. Laing, *The Divided Self* (London: Tavistock, 1960), 203-4.

39. Wallace Stevens paraphrases Bateson like this in an essay written in 1942: 'The Noble Rider and the Sound of Words'. *The Necessary Angel* (London: Faber and Faber, 1960), 13.

40. Heidegger, 'Language', in *Poetry Language Thought*, 195.

41. Louis Althusser, 'Ideology and Ideological State Apparatuses', in *Lenin and Philosophy and Other Essays*, trans. Ben Brewster (London: NLB, 1971), 163.

42. Jean-Jacques Lecercle, 'The Reader, or: Imposture', chap. 4 in *Interpretation as Pragmatics* (London: Macmillan, 1999), 97; Judith Butler, *The Psychic Life of Power: Theories in Subjection* (Stanford, Calif.: Stanford University Press, 1997); Mladen Dolar, 'Beyond Interpellation', in *The Subject in Democracy* 1 (1988). Slavoj Žižek's discussion links it to Lacan's letter which always finds its addressee; in *Metastases of Enjoyment: Six Essays on Woman and Causality* (London: Verso, 1994), 60.

43. Althusser, 'Ideology', 163.

44. Ibid., 169.

45. Althusser, *L'Avenir dure longtemps* (1992), trans. Richard Veasey as *The Future Lasts a Long Time* (London: Chatto and Windus, 1993), 46.

46. G. W. F. Hegel, 'Independence and Dependence of Self-Consciousness: Lordship and Bondage', in *Phenomenology of Spirit*, trans. A. V. Miller (Oxford: Oxford University Press, 1977), 116. This interpretation is that of Alexandre Kojève, *Introduction to the Reading of Hegel*, ed. Allen Bloom, trans. James H. Nichols, Jr. (New York: Basic Books, 1969), 40.

47. Althusser, *Future Lasts a Long Time*, 46.

48. Ibid., 277.

49. Lecercle, 'The Reader, or: Imposture', 97.

50. Friedrich Nietzsche, 'On the Pale Criminal', in *Thus Spake Zarathustra: A Book for All and None*, trans. Alexander Tille (London: Unwin, 1899), 45; and noted by Sigmund Freud in his own paper, 'Criminals from a Sense of Guilt', in *The Standard Edition of the Complete Psychological Works of Sigmund Freud*, vol. 14, ed. and trans. James Strachey (London: Hogarth Press, 1964), 332-33. See also Karl Jaspers, *Die Schuldfrage* (1946), trans. E. B. Ashton as *The Question of German Guilt* (New York: Dial Press, 1947).

51. Strachey notes the case studies of 'Little Hans' and the 'Wolf Man' here. Freud's 'Those Wrecked by Success' is in Freud's 'Some Character-Types Met with in Psycho-Analytic Work' (1916), vol. 14, *Standard Edition*, 316-31.

52. Freud, 'Criminals from a Sense of Guilt', 332.

53. Butler, *Psychic Life of Power*, 109.

54. Ibid., 113.

55. Gen. 2 and 3, Authorised King James version.

56. John 1.1 King James.

57. Althusser, 'Ideology', 165.

58. Mt. 16.18 King James.

59. Merleau-Ponty, *Phenomenology of Perception*, 410.

60. Theodor Adorno, 'On Lyric Poetry and Society', in *Notes to Literature*, vol. 1, ed. Rolf Tiedemann, trans. Shierry Weber Nicholsen (New York: Columbia University Press, 1991), 43.

61. Doris Lessing, *The Golden Notebook* (1962; reprint, St Albans, UK: Panther Books, 1973), 638.

Chapter 3

1. Longinus, *On Sublimity*, no certain date but assumed to be the first century A.D., trans. D. A. Russell (Oxford: Clarendon Press, 1965), 7.

2. See, for instance, *The Poet's I in Archaic Greek Lyric*, ed. S. R. Sling (Amsterdam: UU University Press, 1990).

3. Friedrich Schlegel, *Critical Fragments*, §39 in *Friedrich Schlegel's 'Lucinde' and the Fragments*, trans. Peter Firchow (Minneapolis: University of Minnesota Press, 1971), 147.

4. Remark attributed in 1997 to the late Harold Brodkey.

5. Robert Graves, *The Greek Myths*, vol. 1 (Harmondsworth: Penguin Books, 1960), 286–88.

6. Friedrich Nietzsche, *Beyond Good and Evil* (1886), trans. R. J. Hollingdale (Harmondsworth: Penguin Books, 1981), 74.

7. Friedrich Nietzsche, *The Gay Science*, §335, trans. Walter Kaufmann (New York: Vintage Books, 1974) 263.

8. Lucian, *Dialogues of the Dead* II, *Lucian's Dialogues*, trans. with notes by Howard Williams (London: George Bell and Sons, 1888), 91. Williams comments here that 'Menander, the first of the New Comedy dramatists, parodies this well-worn adage and holds that "Know Others" might be more useful' (91).

9. G. W. F. Hegel, *The Encyclopaedia Logic*, Part 1 of the *Encyclopaedia of Philosophical Sciences*, trans. T. F. Geraets, W. A. Suchting, and H. S. Harris (Indianapolis, Ind.: Hackett, 1991), 212.

10. Søren Kierkegaard, *The Concept of Irony; with Constant Reference to Socrates*, trans. and historical introduction by Lee M. Capel (London: Collins, 1966), 202.

11. Dore Ashton recalls the painter's assertions that to aim at self-expression is erroneous in art, since the point is to be drawn well outside oneself. She discusses his

enthusiasm for Nietzsche here in her *About Rothko* (New York: Oxford University Press, 1983), 120.

12. Jacques Lacan, 'From Love to the Libido', in *The Four Fundamental Concepts of Psycho-analysis*, ed. Jacques-Alain Miller, trans. Alan Sheridan (Harmondsworth: Penguin Books, 1977), 195.

Chapter 4

1. Lucian, *Dialogues of the Dead*, in *The Works of Lucian of Samosata*, vol. 1, book 20, trans. H. W. Fowler and F. G. Fowler (Oxford: Clarendon Press, 1905), 141.

2. Plato, *The Republic*, book 10, trans. Robin Waterfield (Oxford: Oxford University Press, 1993).

3. 'We should always keep to the upward path, and we should use every means at our disposal to act morally and with intelligence, so that we may gain our own and the gods' approval, not only during our stay here on earth, but also when we collect the prizes our morality has earned us, which will be just as extensive as the rewards victorious athletes receive from all quarters' (ibid., 379).

4. Lucian, *Dialogues*, book 4, 112.

5. Ibid., book 10, 119–23.

6. Klossowki's gloss has little to do with Plato and much more with a wish to build a bridge to Nietzsche's understanding of *amor fati*. See Pierre Klossowski, *Un si funeste désir* (Paris: Gallimard, 1963), 23–24, 31.

7. Friedrich Nietzsche, *The Gay Science*, trans. Walter Kaufmann (New York: Vintage Books, 1974), par. 341, book 4, 273.

8. Nietzsche continues, 'Or how well disposed would you have to become to yourself and to life to crave nothing more fervently than this ultimate eternal confirmation and zeal?' (ibid., 274).

9. From my 'Laibach Lyrik', in *Penguin Modern Poets*, vol. 10, Douglas Oliver, Denise Riley, and Iain Sinclair (London: Penguin Books, 1996), 60.

10. William Shakespeare, *Othello*, 1.111.329 (Oxford).

11. Jean-Paul Sartre, *Being and Nothingness* (1943), trans. Hazel E. Barnes (New York: Washington Square Press, 1966), 100. This figure recalls Nietzsche's objections to slavish promise-keeping in *Genealogy of Morals*, second essay, 'Guilt, Bad Conscience and the Like', trans. William A. Haussman and John Gray (London: Unwin, 1899), 71. To retain intransigence in the face of change, is, as many would rejoin, the whole point of promising.

12. Sartre, *Being and Nothingness*, 98.

13. Ibid., 101.   14. Ibid., 107.

15. Ibid., 107.   16. Ibid., 108.

17. Ibid., 109.

18. Ibid., 116.

19. Jean-Paul Sartre, *Anti-Semite and Jew* (1948), trans. George J. Becker (New York: Schocken Books, 1995), 69.

20. Ibid., 58.

21. Ibid., 146–47.

22. G. W. F. Hegel, *Phenomenology of Spirit*, trans. A. V. Miller (Oxford: Oxford University Press, 1977), 400.

23. Slavoj Žižek, *The Sublime Object of Ideology* (London: Verso, 1989), 216–17.

24. Gilbert Sorrentino, *Selected Poems, 1958–80* (Santa Barbara, Calif.: Black Sparrow Press, 1981).

25. Lucretius, *De Rerum Natura (On the Nature of the Universe)*, book 4, trans. R. E. Latham (New York: London, 1979), 162–63.

26. Lucretius continues his advice to those frustrated in love thus: 'Your only remedy is to lance the first wound with new incisions, to salve it, while it is still fresh, with promiscuous attachments; to guide the motion of your mind into some other channel' (ibid., 163).

27. Judith Butler, *The Psychic Life of Power: Theories in Subjection* (Stanford, Calif.: Stanford University Press, 1997), 104.

28. Judith Butler, *Excitable Speech: A Politics of the Performative* (New York: Routledge, 1997), 99.

29. Flora Tristan is the author of *Promenades dans Londres* (1840), trans. Dennis Palmer and Guiselle Pincetl as *Flora Tristan's London Journal* (London: George Prior, 1981).

30. 'The spoken word is a gesture and its meaning, a world'. Maurice Merleau-Ponty, *Phenomenology of Perception*, trans. Colin Smith (London: Routledge and Kegan Paul, 1962), 184.

31. From *True Stories: Fetishes*, directed by Nick Broomfield (London, UK: Channel 4 Television), 10 September 1998, 50 minutes.

32. Gilles Deleuze, *Sacher-Masoch, an Interpretation*, trans. Jean McNeil (London: Faber and Faber, 1971), 76–77.

33. Merleau-Ponty, *Phenomenology of Perception*, 456.

34. Merleau-Ponty's reading of the trio's dilemma (in Simone de Beauvoir's novel *L'Invitée*), trans. Hubert Dreyfus and Patricia Dreyfus from *Sens et non-sens* as *Sense and Non-Sense* (Evanston, Ill.: Northwestern University Press, 1964), 40.

35. Søren Kierkegaard, *The Concept of Irony; with Constant Reference to Socrates*, trans. and historical introduction by Lee M. Capel (London: Collins, 1966), 339.

36. Deleuze respects Lucretius' naturalism as deeply 'demystifying': 'From Lucretius to Nietzsche, the same end is pursued and attained'. 'The Simulacrum and

202 NOTES TO PAGES 129−35

Ancient Philosophy', appendix 1 of *The Logic of Sense*, trans. Mark Lester from *Logique du sens* (London: The Athlone Press, 1990), 279.

37. Deleuze, 'Twenty-First Series of the Event', in *Logic of Sense*, 149.

38. Srebrenica was the site of the so-called United Nations' 'safe area' in Bosnia-Herzegovina, where more than seven thousand men were massacred by Serbian nationalists, apparently with the passive connivance of Dutch UN soldiers, July 1995.

39. Deleuze, *Logic of Sense*, 3.

40. Wendy Brown, *States of Injury* (Princeton, N.J.: Princeton University Press, 1995), 74.

41. Judith Butler, *The Identity in Question*, ed. John Rajchman (New York: Routledge, 1995), 135.

42. Virtually anything can tip you into a new self-categorisation, claim Gilles Deleuze and Félix Guattari in *A Thousand Plateaus: Capitalism and Schizophrenia*, trans. Brian Massumi (London: The Athlone Press, 1988): 'You don't deviate from the majority unless there is a little detail that starts to swell and carry you off. [. . .] Anything at all can do the job, but it always turns out to be a political affair. Becoming-minoritarian is a political affair and necessitates a labour of power, an active micropolitics' (292).

43. Michel Foucault, 'Nietzsche, Genealogy, History', in *Language, Counter-Memory, Practice: Selected Essays and Interviews*, ed. Donald F. Bouchard, trans. Donald F. Bouchard and Sherry Simon (Ithaca, N.Y.: Cornell University Press, 1977), 150.

44. Zygmunt Bauman, *Life in Fragments: Essays in Postmodern Morality* (Oxford: Blackwell, 1995), 82.

45. Brown, *States of Injury*, 55.

46. Alain de Benoist, *Dix ans de combat culturel pour une renaissance* (Paris: GRECE, 1977), 19, quoted in Zygmunt Bauman's 'The Making and Unmaking of Strangers', in *Debating Cultural Hybridity*, ed. Pnina Werbner and Tariq Modood (London: Zed Books, 1997), 55.

47. Julius Evola, *Eléments pour éducation raciale* (Paris: Puiseaux, 1985), 29, quoted in Bauman, 'Making and Unmaking', in *Debating Cultural Hybridity*, 55.

48. As Zygmunt Bauman writes presciently, 'I propose that the racist fellows in the bed of communitarianism are perhaps a nuisance for its new occupants, but by no means a surprise. They were there first, and it is their birthright to be there. Both occupants, the old ones and the new, have been lured into that bed by the same promise and the same desire—of "re-embedding" what has been "disembedded", of release from the formidable task of individual self-reconstruction, and from even more awesome and burdensome individual responsibility for its results'. Bauman, 'Making and Unmaking', in *Debating Cultural Hybridity*, 56.

49. The history of English legislation is relevant here: the 1975 Children's Act al-

lowed illegitimate adults first access, if only after mandatory 'counselling', to information about their backgrounds.

50. Very few states, as I write in the autumn of 1998, have so far unsealed their records, even to adopted enquirers over the age of eighteen.

51. Ian Hacking, 'The Making and Moulding of Child Abuse', *Critical Inquiry* 17 (1991): 253–88. See also his *Rewriting the Soul: Multiple Personality and the Sciences of Memory* (Princeton, N.J.: Princeton University Press, 1995).

52. For many years, we have endured radio and newspaper reiterations about the ill effects of 'broken homes'. But this barrage has not resulted in what one would have predicted, an uncritical public support for proposed reductions in the welfare benefits paid to single parents, if only because the condition it targets is now so widespread.

53. Appeal in the May 1932 issue of *The Negro Worker*, quoted by James A. Miller and Susan Pennybacker in 'Images of Scottsboro'.

54. See James A. Miller and Susan Pennybacker, 'Images of Scottsboro: Racial Politics and Internationalism in the 1930s', paper given at 'Racialising Class, Classifying Race—A Conference on Labour and Difference in Africa, USA and Britain', 11–13 July 1997, at St Antony's College, Oxford University, 18.

55. Violette Leduc, *La Bâtarde, an Autobiography* (1964), trans. Derek Coltman (London: Virago, 1985), and Jean Genet, *A Thief's Journal*, trans. Bernard Frechtman (Harmondsworth: Penguin Books, 1967).

56. This is, I think, consonant with Butler's different conclusion for her study of 'hate speech' in her chapter on 'Sovereign Performatives': 'The public display of injury is also a repetition, but it is not simply that, for what is displayed is never quite the same as what is meant, and in that lucky incommensurability resides the linguistic occasion for change' (*Excitable Speech*, 102).

Chapter 5

1. 'They certainly don't make love like this in Italy'. 'They definitely don't make love like this in Turkey'. From Felice Romani's libretto for Gioachino Rossini's opera, *The Turk in Italy* (1814).

2. Frank O'Hara, 'Ode to Michael Goldberg', in *Collected Poems of Frank O'Hara*, ed. Donald Allen (New York: Knopf, 1979), 297.

3. A full history of irony has not yet been produced, to the best of my knowledge. In English, see D. C. Muecke, *The Compass of Irony* (London: Methuen, 1969), and Wayne Booth, *A Rhetoric of Irony* (Chicago: University of Chicago Press, 1975).

4. The high speed of this superficial 'irony' ensured that shortly after this was written (in 1997), this garb had slipped into fashion's unironic mainstream.

5. Plato's *Meno*, ed. and trans. R. W. Sharples (Warminster, UK: Arris and Phillips, 1985).

6. For Aristotle, comedy is tolerable since it is not wholly vicious. Free of real pain, 'the laughable is one category of the shameful'. *The Rhetoric*, trans. J. E. C. Welldon (London: Macmillan, 1886), 301.

7. Aristotle, *Rhetoric*, xi.

8. In Shakespeare's *A Winter's Tale*. In Sophocles' play *Electra*, the tyrant Aegisthus believes that he's about to unveil the covered corpse of Orestes. Anticipating the pleasure of looking on that dead face in the company of his love, Clytemnestra, he instructs her daughter Electra to call to her if she's in the house. Electra (who, like the audience, already knows the truth) replies, 'She is near you now, not far to see'. The stage direction is 'Aegisthus uncovers the body'—Clytemnestra's.

9. So the moral irony of Jonathan Swift's 1729 'A Modest Proposal' suggests a rational way of mitigating the famine in Ireland: that children, being tasty, nutritious, and in all too adequate a supply, should be killed for eating.

10. Samuel Beckett, *Worstward Ho* (London: John Calder, 1983).

11. Friedrich Schlegel, 'Mit der Ironie ist durchaus nicht zu scherzen' in *Über die Unverständlichkeit (On Incomprehensibility)* (ca. 1798), reprinted in *Friedrich Schlegel's 'Lucinde' and the Fragments*, trans. Peter Firchow (Minneapolis: University of Minnesota Press, 1971).

12. In Gary Handwerk's account, 'Ironic conscience is the displacement of the dependence of the subject on an ineffable Absolute into the realm of intersubjectivity, the conversion of a negative epistemological dilemma into a positive socialising one'. *Irony and Ethics in Narrative: From Schlegel to Lacan* (New Haven, Conn.: Yale University Press, 1985), 53.

13. Schlegel, *On Incomprehensibility*, 267.

14. Søren Kierkegaard, *The Concept of Irony; with Constant Reference to Socrates*, trans. and historical introduction by Lee M. Capel (New York: Collins, 1966), 265.

15. Ibid., 269.

16. Hegel, *The Introduction to Hegel's Philosophy of Fine Art*, trans. Bernard Bosanquet (London: Kegan Paul, Trench, Trubner, 1905), chap. 4, 160–61. Here, Hegel is carping at both the Schlegels and at Fichte.

17. Schlegel, 'Critical Fragments', §108 in *Friedrich Schlegel's 'Lucinde'*, 156.

18. Kierkegaard, *Concept of Irony*, 282.

19. Ibid., 338–39.

20. For example, see Stephen Willats's pieces from 1991 and 1992, such as 'Multiple Clothing, Personality Display' (rubber cloth, text cards, and mixed media; edition of ten). For details of Willats's works, see the exhibition catalogue, *Addressing the Century: 100 years of Art as Fashion* (London: Hayward Gallery, 1998).

21. Swatch waterproof watches, London, late 1998.

22. Kierkegaard, *Concept of Irony*, 298–99.

23. Ibid., 299.

24. Ibid., 297.

25. Lucian, 'Menippus, a Necromantic Experiment', in *The Works of Lucian of Samosata*, vol. 1, book 20, trans. H. W. Fowler and F. G. Fowler (Oxford: Clarendon Press, 1905), 164.

26. Schlegel, 'Critical Fragments' §42 in *Friedrich Schlegel's 'Lucinde'*, 148.

27. Foucault continues his exposition of Nietzsche: 'The second use of history is the systematic dissociation of identity. This is necessary because this rather weak identity, which we attempt to support and unify under a mask, is in itself only a parody: it is plural; countless spirits dispute its possession; numerous systems intersect and compete. [. . .] The purpose of history, guided by genealogy, is not to discover the roots of our identity but to commit itself to its dissipation. It does not seek to define our unique threshold of emergence, the homeland to which all metaphysicians promise a return: it seeks to make visible all those discontinuities that cross us'. Foucalt, 'Nietzsche, Genealogy, History', *Language, Counter-Memory, Practice: Selected Essays and Interviews*, ed. Donald F. Bouchard, trans. Donald F. Bouchard and Sherry Simon (Ithaca, N.Y.: Cornell University Press, 1977), 161–62.

28. George Orwell's essay 'Politics and the English Language' (1946), in *The Collected Essays, Journalism and Letters of George Orwell*, vol. 4, ed. Sonia Orwell and Ian Angus (Harmondsworth: Penguin Books, 1978), 156–70.

29. Claire Nouvet, 'An Impossible Response: The Disaster of Narcissus', *Yale French Studies* 79 (1991): 103–34.

30. Khlebnikov's writing and Russian futurism are documented and traced in Christopher Pike, ed., *The Futurists, the Formalists, and the Marxist Critique*, trans. Christopher Pike and J. Andrew (London: Inklinks, 1980).

31. Gilles Deleuze, 'The Simulacrum and Ancient Philosophy', appendix 1 of *The Logic of Sense*, trans. Mark Lester from *Logique du sens* (London: The Athlone Press, 1990), 253.

32. Compare Deleuze's 'Language is itself the ultimate double which expresses all doubles—the highest of simulacra'. In 'The Phantasm and Modern Literature', appendix 11 of *Logic of Sense*, 284.

33. Demetrius, *On Style*, par. 140, in *Aristotle, 'The Poetics'*, ed. and trans. Stephen Halliwell; *Longinus, 'On the Sublime'*, trans. W. H. Fyfe; *Demetrius, 'On Style'*, ed. and trans. Doreen C. Innes, in one volume (Cambridge, Mass.: Harvard University Press, 1995), 437.

34. Henri Bergson, *Le Rire* (1900), trans. Cloudesley Brereton and Fred Rothwell as *Laughter* (London: Macmillan, 1911), 66–67.

35. Papirer III B2, cited in the translator's historical introduction, by Lee M. Capel, to Kierkegaard, *Concept of Irony*, 23.

36. Kierkegaard, *Concept of Irony*, 14.

37. Friedrich Schlegel, *Lucinde, a Novel* (1799), in *Friedrich Schlegel's 'Lucinde'*, 132.

38. Kierkegaard, *Concept of Irony*, 340.

39. For one conception of 'practical identity', see Christine Korsgaard, *The Sources of Normativity* (Cambridge: Cambridge University Press, 1996).

40. Kierkegaard, *Concept of Irony*, 340.

41. 'Thus if philosophy mediates all opposites, then it is essential that this abundant actuality in truth become visible' (ibid., 340).

42. Roman Jakobson, 'What is Poetry?', in *Language in Literature*, ed. Krystyna Pomorska and Stephen Rudy (Cambridge, Mass.: Belknap Press of Harvard University Press, 1987), 378.

43. Hanif Kureishi, *'My Beautiful Laundrette' and 'The Rainbow Sign'* (London: Faber and Faber, 1986), 17.

44. Eleven, including Slansky, were executed in November 1952, as a result of Klement Gottwald's Stalinist purges of the party.

45. There are recorded examples of the humour that circulated among camp internees. I am grateful to Dror Wahrman for these references: Roy Kift, 'Comedy in the Holocaust: the Theresienstadt Cabaret', *New Theatre Quarterly* 48 (1996): 299–308; Richard Raskin, 'Far from Where? On the History and Meanings of the Classic Jewish Refugee Joke', *American Jewish History* 85, no. 2 (1997): 143–50; Uli Linke and Alan Dundes, 'More on Auschwitz Jokes', *Folklore* 99, no. 1 (1988): 3–10.

46. See Handwerk, *Irony and Ethics*, 16.

47. 'Satire is a prodigious art of regression. Height, however, prepares new values for language and affirms in it its independence and its radical difference from depth. Irony appears each time language deploys itself in accordance with relations of eminence, equivocity, or analogy' (Deleuze, 'Thirty-Fourth Series of Primary Order and Secondary Organisation', in *Logic of Sense*, 246).

48. Paul de Man, *Blindness and Insight: Essays in the Rhetoric of Contemporary Criticism* (Minneapolis: University of Minnesota Press, 1983), 226; discussed in Handwerk, *Irony and Ethics*.

49. Denise Riley, *'Am I That Name?' Feminism and the Category of 'Women' in History* (London: Macmillan, 1988), 70–95.

50. An arch Spoonerism was used by the London-based women's theatre and performance group which in the 1980s christened itself 'The Cunning Stunts'.

51. 'If one black boy calls another a "jungle bunny" it will be read as a term of friendship not abuse, a mark that they are "best mates" by virtue of the fact that they can share its use against its racist connotation'. Phil Cohen, 'The Perversions

of Inheritance', in *Multiracist Britain*, ed. P. Cohen and H. Bains (London: Macmillan, 1988), 83.

52. The implications of Richard Delgado's phrase 'words that wound' in the context of jurisprudence and critical race studies are analysed as cited in Judith Butler, *Excitable Speech: A Politics of the Performative* (New York: Routledge, 1997), 100.

53. As Wayne Booth inquires of literary criticism, in his *A Rhetoric of Irony* (Chicago: University of Chicago Press, 1975), 193.

54. Adorno continues immediately: 'Which is why total decay has absorbed the forces of satire'. But Adorno's objection is, again, to the person of the ironist. From *Minima Moralia: Reflections from Damaged Life*, trans. E. F. N. Jephcott (London: Verso, 1978), 211.

55. I'm embroidering an observation made by Lecercle; see his *Interpretation as Pragmatics* (London: Macmillan, 1999), 176.

56. For ancient Greek, see Harry and Agathe Thornton, *Time and Style: A Psycho-Linguistic Essay in Classical Literature* (London: Methuen, 1962).

57. See, analytically, Lecercle, *Interpretation as Pragmatics*, 183–85. Or, psycho-analytically, Butler, *Excitable Speech*, 106–9, 129.

58. Edmond Jabès, *A Foreigner Carrying in the Crook of His Arm a Tiny Book*, trans. Rosmarie Waldrop (Middletown: Wesleyan University Press, 1993), 15.

59. Friedrich Nietzsche, *Beyond Good and Evil*, trans. R. J. Hollingdale (Harmondsworth: Penguin Books, 1981), 186.

60. Jean-Jacques Lecercle, *The Violence of Language* (London: Routledge, 1990).

61. J. A. Cuddon, 'Slogan', in *The Penguin Dictionary of Literary Terms and Literary Theory* (London: Penguin Books, 1991), 887.

62. Hope for the slogan need not be extinguished, for its double-barrelled form, capable of bringing down several targets at once, lives on: In the spring of 1998 the Countryside Alliance's march in London, organised largely by the nation's fox hunting enthusiasts, sported placards enjoining the meat-fearing townie onlookers to 'Eat British Lamb! Fifty Thousand Foxes Can't Be Wrong'.

63. Jacques Rancière, 'Politics, Identification, and Subjectivisation', in *The Identity in Question*, ed. John Rajchman (New York: Routledge, 1995), 87–88.

64. Ibid., 69–70.

65. Russell Jacoby's indicative title is *Social Amnesia: A Critique of Conformist Psychologies from Adler to Laing* (Boston: Beacon Press, 1975).

66. Ryszard Kapuscinski, *Imperium*, trans. Klara Glowczewska (New York: Vintage, 1995), 283.

67. Rancière, 'Politics', 65–67.

68. In the documentary film *UUU: Usines Universités Union*, assembled from footage shot by French students in 1968. This amateur documentary recording stu-

dent militance was made collectively and anonymously. It was shown in May 1998 by the Ciné Lumière at the French Institute in London; its running time is about forty minutes.

69. See Nikos Papastergiadis, 'Tracing Hybridity in Theory', in *Debating Cultural Hybridity*, ed. Pnina Werbner and Tariq Modood (London: Zed Books, 1997). Stuart Hall, 'The Local and the Global: Globalisation and Ethnicity', in A. King, ed., *Culture, Globalisation, and the World-System* (London: Macmillan, 1991). Homi Bhabha, *The Location of Culture* (London: Routledge, 1994). Zygmunt Bauman, *Life in Fragments: Essays in Postmodern Morality* (Oxford: Blackwell, 1995).

70. Rancière, 'Politics', 70.

71. Phil Cohen, *Rethinking the Youth Question* (London: Macmillan, 1997), 14–15. He comments, 'Whether this was done out of a refusal to take responsibility for any damage done to others' property by his own, or from some high-minded concern with animal rights, is not recorded, though we may have our suspicions'.

72. Deleuze mentions this possibility in his lucid study of Foucault's work, *Michel Foucault* (London: The Athlone Press, 1988).

73. Hegel avows the intimacy of identity and distinctiveness; *The Encyclopaedia Logic*, Part 1 of the *Encyclopaedia of Philosophical Sciences*, trans. T. F. Geraets, W. A. Suchting, and H. S. Harris (Indianapolis, Ind.: Hackett, 1991), par. 116, p. 181.

74. Marx writes, 'The decomposition of man into Jew and citizen, Protestant and citizen, religious man and citizen is neither a deception practised against citizenhood, nor is it a circumvention of political emancipation, it is *political emancipation itself, the political* method of emancipating oneself from religion' (Marx, 'On The Jewish Question', in *Karl Marx and Friedrich Engels, Collected Works*, vol. 3, 1843–1844 (London: Lawrence and Wishart, 1975), 155. Wendy Brown's *States of Injury* (Princeton, N.J.: Princeton University Press, 1995), 100–114, offers an enlightening commentary on this.

75. William Carlos Williams, 'A Sort of Song', from 'The Wedge', in *William Carlos Williams: Selected Poems*, ed. Charles Tomlinson (Harmondsworth: Penguin, 1976), 133.

76. See, for example, C. Eric Lincoln, *The Black Muslims in America* (Boston: Beacon Press, 1973); Clifton E. Marsh, *From Black Muslims to Muslims: The Transition from Separatism to Islam 1930–1980* (Metuchen, N.J.: Scarecrow Press, 1984); and Martha F. Lee, *The Nation of Islam: An American Millenarian Movement* (Lewiston, N.Y.: Edwin Mellen Press, 1988).

77. Evelyn Brooks Higginbotham adds that 'Although racialised cultural identity has served blacks in the struggle against discrimination, it has not sufficiently addressed the empirical reality of gender conflict within the black community or class differences among women themselves'. 'African-American Women's History

and the Metalanguage of Race', *Feminism and History*, ed. Joan Scott (Oxford: Oxford University Press, 1996), 184. See Paul Gilroy's discussion of a 'vision of the world in which "race" will no longer be a meaningful device for the categorisation of human beings'. *The Black Atlantic: Modernity and Double Consciousness* (Cambridge, Mass.: Harvard University Press, 1993), 218. For differing retrievals of 'race', however, see Lucius T. Outlaw, *On Race and Philosophy* (London: Routledge, 1996), and John P. Pittman, ed., *African-American Perspectives and Philosophical Traditions* (London: Routledge, 1997).

78. Paul Gilroy, *Small Acts: Thoughts on the Politics of Black Cultures* (London: Serpent's Tail, 1993), 14.

79. Cuddon, 'Meiosis', in *Penguin Dictionary*, 536.

80. A governmental apology based on a country's 'collective guilt' for atrocities enacted by earlier generations is apt to lack conviction and falter because it will be rhetorically unworkable; a supposedly culpable-by-association 'we' of the present may feel itself to be empty.

81. A Scots Orangeman, moreover, who had travelled there for the marching season all the way from Glasgow, as an anonymous interviewee, on the 'Broadcasting House' programme, BBC Radio 4, 12 July 1998.

82. Wyndham Lewis, chap. 7, 'People's Happiness Found in Type-Life', in *The Art of Being Ruled* (London: Chatto, 1926), 167.

83. It then becomes, for instance, the pseudocurrency of 'warring factions'. That vacuous term, beloved of the British Foreign Office and the BBC in the early 1990s and deployed by them throughout the disintegration of the former Yugoslavia, is an instance of a false equivalence held between badly misconceived categories.

84. The rector of the University of Sarajevo, Professor Nedzad Mulabegovic, speaking with the prorector of the University of Tuzla, Professor Enver Mandzic, under the auspices of the Academic Lifeline for Bosnia, at the London School of Economics, November 1995.

85. Jacques Rancière, 'Post-Democracy, Politics and Philosophy, an interview', by Jelica Sumic and Rado Riha, *Angelaki* 1, no. 3 (1994): 174.

86. Ibid., 177.

87. Rancière adds, 'Racism [. . .] appears when there is a striving to remove from the people its character of *appearance*, either in the name of an organicism of the community, or of a realistic calculation of the parties involved and their social interests. When the "appearance" collapses, what's left is the naked reality of identities and their alterities. [. . .] The ideal of so-called "realist" politics is to identify subjects with real groups. In this way, the "realist" wisdom prepares the ground for an identitary ethnic and racist madness. Subjects, different from themselves, which characterise democracy, are not wanted. Its people are dismissed as a phantom. As a

consequence, we see the return of the "real" people: that which is defined by race, blood and so forth' (ibid., 177–78).

88. Brown, *States of Injury*, 75–76.

89. Ibid., 75.

90. Rancière, 'Politics', 67.

91. As Brown describes it, 'Even as the margins assert themselves as margins, the denaturalising assault they perform on coherent collective identity in the centre turns back on them to trouble their own identities. Even as it is being articulated, circulated, and lately institutionalised in a host of legal, political and cultural practices, identity is unravelling—metaphysically, culturally, geographically, and historically—as rapidly as it is being produced. The same vacillation can be seen in the naturalistic legitimating narratives of collective identity known as nationalism' (*States of Injury*, 55).

92. The capital of Rwanda; the scene in 1994 of many deaths of Tutsis at the hands of Hutu groups and of fighting between Tutsi-dominated rebel forces and the Rwandan army.

93. Those Bosnians undiscriminatingly massed under the heading of 'muslim', whatever their religious observance or its lack, came to be redesignated by the revived description of 'Bosniak' in Bosnia-Herzegovina during the course of the war. (The government of Yugoslavia had in its 1974 constitution formally recognized the designation of Muslim Slav, although not to signify a religious group but as what it termed a particular 'nation' for electoral purposes. This designation had been used earlier in the 1971 elections. It saved those it named as Muslim from being forcibly absorbed into either Croatian or Serbian electoral interests in Bosnia.)

94. Ivan Lovrenovic continues, 'If you want Bosnia, you must be Bosnian; which means you cannot be only a Bosniak, a Croat or a Serb. I keep repeating: I am no less a Croat because I am not only a Croat. And if each Bosnian can admit that to himself, then we are on the way to rebuilding Bosnia-Herzegovina. But I must remind you that the cultural ambiance of Bosnia today—of Sarajevo in particular and especially, if I may say so, of the Bosniaks—is far from that. I know what I am saying, I know that in a way it has to be like this, and I can even appreciate it, since I am well aware of the Bosniaks' political and historical suffering in the modern period of our history'. *Bosnia Report*, new series no. 2 (January–February 1998), 13.

95. Kierkegaard, *Concept of Irony*, 274.

96. See Lecercle, 'A Theory of the Remainder', chap. 3 in *Violence of Language*, 103–43.

97. 'But all these positions [for the speaking subject] are not the various forms of a primordial "I" from which a statement stems: on the contrary, these positions stem from the statement itself and consequently become the categories of "non-

person", "he", "one", "he speaks", or "One speaks", which are defined by the family of statements. Here Foucault echoes Blanchot in denouncing all linguistic person-ology and seeing the different positions for the speaking subject as located within a deep anonymous murmur. It is within this murmur without beginning or end that Foucault would like to be situated, in the place assigned to him by statements. And perhaps these are Foucault's most moving statements' (Deleuze, *Michel Foucault*, 7).

98. Deleuze, *Logic of Sense*, 298.

99. Ibid., 298–99. Deleuze has fleshed out his thought with apt remarks by Pierre Klossowski; the internal quotation here is from the latter's 'Oubli et anam-nèse dans l'expérience vécue de l'éternel retour du Même' in his *Nietzsche* (Paris: Cahiers de Royaumont, éditions de Minuit, 1967), 233.

Index

In this index an "f" after a number indicates a separate reference on the next page, and an "ff" indicates separate references on the next two pages. A continuous discussion over two or more pages is indicated by a span of page numbers, e.g., "57–59." *Passim* is used for a cluster of references in close but not consecutive sequence.

Atopia: Philosophy, Political theory, Aesthetics

Denise Riley, *The Words of Selves: Identification, Solidarity, Irony*

James Swenson, *On Jean-Jacques Rousseau: Considered as One of the First Authors of the Revolution*